Death Rituals Among
the Karanga of Zimbabwe

Death Rituals Among the Karanga of Zimbabwe

Praxis, Significance, and Changes

JOHN CHITAKURE

RESOURCE *Publications* • Eugene, Oregon

DEATH RITUALS AMONG THE KARANGA OF ZIMBABWE
Praxis, Significance, and Changes

Copyright © 2021 John Chitakure. All rights reserved. Except for brief quotations in critical publications or reviews, no part of this book may be reproduced in any manner without prior written permission from the publisher. Write: Permissions, Wipf and Stock Publishers, 199 W. 8th Ave., Suite 3, Eugene, OR 97401.

Resource Publications
An Imprint of Wipf and Stock Publishers
199 W. 8th Ave., Suite 3
Eugene, OR 97401

www.wipfandstock.com

PAPERBACK ISBN: 978-1-6667-3075-3
HARDCOVER ISBN: 978-1-6667-2264-2
EBOOK ISBN: 978-1-6667-2265-9

SEPTEMBER 15, 2021

To my brother and mentor, Arturo Chavez, PhD,
who taught me that one's cultural identity and integrity are
indispensable, and that all cultures are equal although different.

Since all cultures are equal, but different, there should not be any cultures that claim to be either superior or inferior because all serve their purpose, and should be treated with equal dignity. The people who claim to belong to superior or inferior cultures are ignorant of this noble truth, and are also unaware of the fact that there is always a lot to learn from, or teach to people of other cultures. However, despite this resultant, inevitable cultural dynamism, every culture should maintain some cultural constants that continue to give its people their cultural identity and integrity.

Contents

Preface | ix

Acknowledgements | xi

Abbreviations | xiii

INTRODUCTION | 1

Chapter 1
TERMINOLOGICAL CLARIFICATION | 11

Chapter 2
METHODOLOGICAL AND PHILOSOPHICAL FRAMEWORKS | 31

Chapter 3
SHONA CAUSES OF SICKNESS AND DEATH | 58

Chapter 4
KARANGA PRE-BURIAL RITUALS | 87

Chapter 5
KARANGA BURIAL RITUALS | 101

Chapter 6
KARANGA POST-BURIAL RITUALS | 160

Chapter 7
KARANGA TRADITIONAL DEATH RITUALS MANUAL | 216

Chapter 8
THE WAY FORWARD | 239

Glossary of Foreign Words | 257

Bibliography | 265

Index | 273

Preface

THIS BOOK IS A result of the research that I pursued under the academic supervision of the University of South Africa in fulfilment of the requirements for the degree of Doctor of Philosophy in Religious Studies, which was done from 2017 to 2020. The fieldwork for this study was carried out in Nyajena, Masvingo, Zimbabwe, and the literature used was sourced and consulted in the United States. Although most of the original thesis chapters have been edited and reworked to make them suitable for a monograph, a few chapters have, to a larger extent, maintained their originality.

As I was busy reshaping my thesis into a monograph, I realized that chapter 1, though dealing mostly with methodological issues as dictated by doctoral thesis writing requirements, had to be revised and included in this monograph, for a couple of reasons. First, the qualitative research methodology, which I used in this study is relevant to many postgraduate student researchers who may want to use it in their studies, and may not be able to lay their hands on other relevant or classic sources. This chapter offers such postgraduate student researchers an introductory survey of the qualitative research designs, particularly ethnography. Second, as I explored and employed postcolonial theory as a philosophical framework for my study, I found it very useful and relevant to the understanding of the changes in, and at times, the demonization of African cultures, and I felt that I needed to share it with my readers. Hence, the information, which was under chapter 1 in the thesis, has now been shifted to chapter 2, and even though a bit technical in nature, lays the foundation for understanding the subsequent chapters of this work and the conclusion drawn from the study.

It should be noted that even though the study was done among the Karanga of Nyajena, in the Province of Masvingo, in Zimbabwe, most of the findings are equally true about all other Shona peoples of Zimbabwe, and to a larger extent, other African peoples of Bantu origins. The rituals explored in this book are by and large, carried out by most Shona ethnical groups. In this book, where certain rituals are only performed by a particular Shona ethnic group, it is specified.

The primary aim of the research that gave birth to this book was to compose a Karanga death ritual manual so that Shona people can consult it if they decide to bury their beloved ones according to Shona traditional burial rituals. This manual is provided in chapter 7 of this book.

I should hasten to mention that since I am a Karanga myself, I am considered an insider concerning the issues that I investigated. Even though being an insider has its fair share of advantages when carrying out a study of this nature, it also has its setbacks, which I clearly declare in chapter 2. Hence, I do not deny that my preconceived ideas and understanding of the issues under investigation have played a significant role in the gathering and analysis of the data. Furthermore, I am a practical theologian, and I must admit that Christian theology has had its fair share of influence on me too. Be that as it may, I must emphasize that professionalism, as dictated by qualitative ethnography, was maintained at all the time. Although I could not stay with the people I studied for a longer period of time, I have lived in Nyajena most of my life, and I have participated in most of the rituals, which are explored in this book.

John Chitakure, 2021

Acknowledgements

I would like to thank a number of people for their assistance with this book. First of all, it would not have been possible to produce the thesis that culminated in this book had it not been for the timeous, insightful, and encouraging feedback, and guidance from my PhD thesis supervisor, Rev. Dr. Elijah Elijah Ngoweni Dube of UNISA.

I am immensely grateful to the research participants, whom I observed and interviewed in Nyajena, Masvingo, Zimbabwe. Their trust and respect for me and their traditions encouraged them to unreservedly share their knowledge of Karanga death rituals.

Also, I wholeheartedly thank Jacob Maburuse, an all-weather family friend, Lovemore Manaka, a talented man who respects and performs Karanga death rituals, and Nichodimus Magwati, a man who teaches people about how to fruitfully work the soil. All the three men generously helped me to gather and understand some of the data that I used for this book. Their knowledge of the issues under study made it easier for me to analyze some of the research data for this book.

On a personal level, I am exceedingly indebted to my brother and mentor, Dr. Arturo Chavez, PhD, for inviting me to learn intercultural competencies from him, for entrusting me with the task of training others, and generously assisting my family when we first arrived in San Antonio, Texas.

My wife, Blessing, and our sons, Nyasha, and Mufaro, also played an important part as they have always done, and I would like to thank them wholeheartedly for their unwavering support.

Lastly, I am tremendously grateful to Juanita G. Vicente, a librarian at the Elizondo Library of the Mexican American Catholic College, and the librarians at J. E and L. E. Mabee Library of the University of the

Incarnate Word, San Antonio, Texas, for providing some of the research materials used to compose this book.

ABBREVIATIONS

AIDS	Acquired Immunodeficiency Syndrome
ER	Emergency Room
GPS	Global Positioning System
HIV	Human Immunodeficiency Virus
IV	Intravenous
PhD	Doctor of Philosophy
UNISA	University of South Africa
USCCB	United States Catholic Church Bishops

Introduction

I BEGIN THIS EXPLORATION of Karanga death rituals by sharing an experience that I had several years ago. I attended a funeral of a relative who had died in a traffic accident, at one of the villages in my rural home of Nyajena, in Masvingo, Zimbabwe. As the dying man laid on his deathbed, begging his ancestors for longevity in futile, he was said to have instructed his family that he wished to be buried according to Karanga death rituals. Since the Karanga of Nyajena have only two sets of burial rituals—Karanga and Christian, it seems that the dying man was against being buried according to Christian burial rituals. Of course, there was a reason for this afterlife advance directive. It was reported that the dying man had witnessed some of his non-Christian relatives and friends being buried according to the Christian rituals against their wishes, and in violation of their traditional ways. Some of the close family members of those deceased persons were reported to have violated the explicit or implicit wishes of their departed relatives in order to appease their Christian dictates at the expense of the deathbed wishes of the departed. So, the deceased in my experience, is said to have decided to unambiguously communicate his wishes to his family. He was said to have threatened them with some calamity if they refused to follow his burial wishes meticulously. When that instruction was given, it seemed that none of the deceased's family members who were in the room, disputed the dying man's end of life directives because they thought that they were reasonable and doable.

Even though all the relatives of the deceased who were present at the funeral wanted to fulfil the deathbed wishes of their departed family member, a hurdle that made the deceased's wishes difficult to fulfil became apparent. As the relatives were preparing the corpse for burial, the dead man's nuclear family members and other mourners realized that the elders who were expected to preside at his burial as ritual practitioners had failed to turn up for the burial. It was not clear whether the elders' absence was by design or accident. Of course, the absence could not have been significant if any of the elders who were present had a sufficient expertise of how to perform all the required Karanga death rituals. However, I doubt if all the elders who were present did not remember the praxis of a Karanga traditional burial. Perhaps, they were reluctant to preside over the rituals because of the fear of making mistakes, which would negatively impact the welfare of the spirit of the deceased, and of the living family members.

Initially, elderly relatives were asked to step forward and act as ritual practitioners, and when no one volunteered to lead the proceedings, the family members of the deceased asked the local Church of Christ pastor, who was among the mourners, to preside over the burial rituals. Since the deceased was not a member of the Church of Christ (although his wife was), and the deceased was reported to have categorically opted for an exclusively Karanga traditional burial, the pastor reluctantly agreed to preside over the burial rituals, but on one condition—that he would perform the funeral rites his own way—the Christian way. Fearing to offend the spirit of the deceased, the family of the deceased declined the pastor's offer, and withdrew the request.

The burial had to go on. In fits and starts, one of the available elders officiated over the traditional death rituals as per the request of the departed and his family. He started well, but as the performance of the rituals progressed, it increasingly became apparent that, apart from having no adequate know-how of the death rituals to be carried out, the presider did not understand why some rituals had to be performed. For instance, as the body was being transported from the hut to the grave, numerous disagreements occurred, and the sacred practitioner could not resolve them satisfactorily. First, the mourners disagreed on the number of times the corpse was supposed to be rested before reaching the burial place. Some said three times, and others argued that it was not necessary to rest the body since the day was almost gone. Second, when the rocks were being brought to the grave, one of the young men was reprimanded for carrying two stones to the grave at the same time, and the young man wanted to know why it was tabooed, since carrying more than one rock would facilitate a quick completion of the burial. The issue was brought to the attention of the ritual practitioner, and to my greatest embarrassment, he did not know why it was tabooed to carry to the grave, two or more stones at once. He only said that it was the way of the elders, and it had to be followed strictly, which I thought was a wise but unhelpful answer to the young man's question. When other mourners were consulted about the same issue, there was no agreement concerning the sanction. Third, as the body was being lowered into the grave, there was a heated debate concerning the direction to which the deceased was supposed to face. Again, the ritual leader could not competently and satisfactorily resolve the bone of contention.

Eventually, the burial was completed, and I left the funeral very sad. Perhaps, other mourners felt the same too. It seemed that our people had forgotten their traditional ways of sending off the dead. Logically, a people that does not remember how to perform its rituals, and has forgotten its rituals' significance, is likely to lose its cultural identity and integrity. This incident generated in me the assumption on which the investigation that resulted in the writing of this book was built. The incident confirmed that human minds have a proclivity to forget, or change procedures unless there exists a written manual that they can use as a reference source. The above-mentioned disagreements could have been avoided or minimized if a written document of the Karanga death rituals existed. I realized that the absence of a Karanga burial rites manual or any other written document that could be consulted as a reference source, worsened the situation. Since the Karanga people contend that the dead must be rendered befitting burial rituals, and unwaveringly believe that, failure to do so has adverse consequences for the spirit of the dead and his surviving relatives, a written document of these rituals can boost their confidence and refresh their memories. In addition to that, a Shona death rituals manual can reduce the number of mistakes that may be committed during traditional burials.

This book is about Karanga death rituals as they were and are practiced by the Karanga of Zimbabwe, with special reference to the Karanga of Nyajena. The book explores Karanga death rituals by doing four primary things. First, it describes the causes of death, and the praxis of death rituals among the Shona people, as they were understood and practiced then and now. Second, the book explores and examines the past and present significance of the explored death rituals. Third, the book traces and identifies any cultural changes that may have happened to the praxis and significance of some selected Karanga death rituals, due to various transformational compulsions such as colonialism and the passage of time. Finally, the book provides a brief manual for the performance of

Karanga death rituals as they are practiced by the Karanga of Nyajena, and as recorded by some earlier researchers. The data used in the writing of this book were collected and analyzed using the qualitative research tradition of ethnography.

It should be noted right from the onset that death rituals are important to people of every culture because one of the fundamental existential truths with which humans must grapple, which is the fact that no one lives forever. Everyone dies. Kübler-Ross aptly observes that "Dying is an integral part of life, as natural and predictable as being born."[1] Despite the inevitability and naturality of death, some, if not most people fear it. Choron postulates that there are about three varieties of the fear of death, namely, the fear of what happens after death, the fear of the event of dying itself, and the fear of ceasing to be.[2] Although all the three fears are valid, for me, and perhaps for many other people, it seems that the greatest impediment to embracing the reality of dying is the unavailability of scientifically verifiable knowledge of what happens beyond death. Of course, dying people know that they will be buried, but then what next? If people knew exactly what would happen after they are dead, they would better prepare for it. Undoubtedly, no one can adequately prepare for an event that no one has ever experienced before and come back. Of course, unverifiable claims have been peddled about what happens in the hereafter, but since death is a subjective experience, such claims cannot be relied on to give us scientific knowledge of what happens after death.

Despite the uncertainties and mysteries surrounding what happens in the hereafter, many religious and secular traditions of the world believe that the deceased acquire some kind of supernatural life and powers that may be either beneficial or hazardous to their living relatives, depending on the appropriateness of the death rituals carried out for them, and the deceased's individual pre-death compliance with other social and moral qualifications, as determined by each people's cultural heritage. Hence, in every culture, death rituals must be performed meticulously to avoid infuriating the dead, whose displeasure may bring serious retribution upon their living family members and the communities to which they belong. For the Karanga of Zimbabwe, perhaps just like many other Shona and African ethnicities, these death rituals are not tabulated, and consequently, some of them, and their significance might have been lost, or are at the

---

1. Kübler-Ross, *Death: The Final Stage of Growth*, 5.
2. Choron, *Death and Modern Man*, 73–79.

verge of extinction due to the passage of time and other irresistible forces of social and cultural change such as colonialism. Colonialism and its effects on African people will be explored in detail in chapter 2.

Before I delve into the crux of the matter, it should be noted that the study that gave birth to this book focused on the Karanga of Nyajena, popularly known as Vajena, a name which can be understood in two different ways. First, the term Vajena refers to the people of Nyajena in general, popularly known as *vanhu vekwaNyajena* (people of Nyajena). Second, Vajena refers to a specific group of people who live in Nyajena, who belong to the totem of Moyo, Mirambwi of Vajena. The latter meaning is the most conventional among the people of Nyajena. Hence, a distinction should be made between the people of Nyajena, which refers to everybody who lives in Nyajena irrespective of his or her totem, and the term, Vajena, which refers to the people who live in Nyajena and belong to the totem, Moyo of the Vajena, whose sub totem is Mirambwi.

The Vajena belong to the aristocracy, and Nyajena is their clan. Their cultural identity is explored in detail in chapter 1. All other people who live in Nyajena might have come there because of intermarriages or migrations, consequently most of them are related to the Vajena in one way or the other. Although oral tradition has it that some non-Vajena people in Nyajena may have been the indigenous inhabitants of Nyajena, it is not clear as to who was already in Nyajena when Vajena arrived.

I should mention that this study focused on all people living in Nyajena (*vanhu vekwaNyajena*), irrespective of their totems. Hence, throughout this book, the terms Karanga of Nyajena, Shona, or even Africans, are used instead of Vajena, to avoid confusion. Since the Karanga are a sub-group of the Shona people, wherever applicable, the name Shona will be used instead of Karanga. Because the people of Nyajena are Karanga, and the Karanga are Shona, and the Shona are Africans, it should be noted that the term Africans is also employed where the phenomena that can safely be applied to most Africans are being discussed. However, the terms Karanga and Shona will be used the most, except in chapter 7, which provides a manual for death rituals as they are specifically performed by the Karanga of Nyajena. Most of the explored rituals are almost similar in outlook, to the same rituals as performed by other Shona ethnicities. However, despite such concurrences, the details and significance of most rituals may vary from one Shona ethnical group to another.

I am aware that the question concerning whether or not a book of this caliber is needed is likely to arise, and such a question requires some sort of justification for this book. First, the fact that culture is dynamic is incontestable. No ethnic group escapes the cultural transformations brought about by acculturation and the passage of time. Even though cultural dynamism is inevitable, each ethnic group should maintain some cultural constants to retain its cultural identity and integrity. Among the Shona of Zimbabwe, cultural dynamism has been exacerbated by several factors. The Shona's forced encounter with Europeans as a result of colonialism brought about acculturation, which can be defined as a cultural give-and-take that takes place whenever two or more cultures meet. Gittins has accurately noted that "Virtually no culture today exists in complete isolation, so culture-contact is a universal social fact, accelerated by the internet and associated technologies."[3]

According to Kim, this inevitable cultural dynamism can be either positive or negative.[4] If cultural encounters had mutual benefits and effects, the process would be more or less acceptable, but they do not offer mutual benefits. Some cultures are more powerful or are imposed more forcefully than others. Any cultural encounter becomes counterproductive if one culture is completely overpowered by the other to the extent of having its adherents beginning to lose their cultural identity and integrity. However, the same cultural dynamism can be beneficial to the receiving culture, particularly when a people borrow some positive cultural practices from another people to produce something new; maybe a hybrid culture. Seemingly, some of the cultural changes that took place among Karanga death rituals undermined the Karanga traditional rituals in favor of Western ones. If the Karanga are to reclaim their cultural identity and integrity, they should rediscover and tabulate their own cultural practices such as death rituals. This book attempts to do that.

Second, most Africans have no written documents and rubrics of their death rituals, for they rely on oral tradition. Even though oral tradition is recognized as an important source of history, people tend to forget or even exaggerate certain aspects of their traditions if they are not written. Hence, there is a need to compile and preserve the Karanga death rituals for posterity by providing a written document to those who would want a source of reference. In addition to that, it is important for

---

3. Gittins, *Living Mission Interculturally*, 59.
4. Kim, *Multicultural Theology and New Evangelization*, 11.

people to know the reasons for performing the rituals that society deems obligatory and pertinent. Since burial rituals are mandatory, and should be "performed appropriately and efficiently," as Shoko has observed, a written record of the rituals will aid the memories of those who would have forgotten how to perform them.[5] In every culture, the surest method of protecting the traditions of a people is to write them down before they are lost, changed, or distorted. This book intends to do just that.

Third, some of the young Karanga people have converted to other religious traditions, such as Christianity, which forbids them to participate in traditional death rituals actively and publicly. For instance, some Christian denominations demonize some Shona rituals and compel their adherents to discard them. The most significant challenge that some of these Christianized Shona people encounter is the expectation by some of the communities that they should sometimes, if not most times, bury their departed relatives according to traditional rituals, and therefore, should know the process and significance of performing such rituals. A written document may be of great help to those reluctant adherents of African Traditional Religion if they find themselves in a situation where they are required to perform such traditional death rituals.

Fourth, in most cases, Africans learn the praxis and significance of traditional rituals through participant observation. Hence, attending traditional rituals is crucial for the acquisition of the knowledge of the praxis of such rituals. Although, among the Karanga, every relative who can, should attend the funeral of a deceased family member, this required attendance may not be long or frequent enough to convince some people of the value of the death rituals that they participate in. The infrequent occurrences of such rituals may make it difficult for the youth to acquire the knowledge of performing them. In addition to that, some Karanga youths have been influenced by the forces of modernity, which were brought to Africa by colonialists, to despise and forgo their cultural practices. Consequently, some of the cultural practices are criticized for being archaic and uncivilized since they do not conform to forces of modernity. For a person to learn how to do something, one must appreciate the value of that which must be mastered. Hence, it is difficult to learn something by heart if you do not give any importance to it. Indeed, the youth may attend funerals, but if they do not appreciate the value of the traditional rituals that are performed, they may never learn how to perform them.

---

5. Shoko, *Karanga Indigenous Religion in Zimbabwe*, 86.

If a written document is available, it would give such reluctant learners some knowledge of their traditional death rituals even if they opt not to practice them. They would use the manual as a reference source whenever they find themselves in a situation where they should perform such rituals.

Fifth, death comes whenever it wants, for it does not have a schedule. This sporadic occurrence of death makes death rituals mere crisis ceremonies, which are performed infrequently. This irregular happening of death makes it difficult even for those who attend funerals regularly to learn the appropriate ritual procedures and the significance of ritual praxis. More so, when death strikes, some family members, may not be able to attend the funeral, so they are excluded in the process of learning through praxis. Both the infrequent occurrence of death and the failure to attend some death rituals when death occurs by some family members, may prevent those members from acquiring the knowledge of performing the rituals, and of their significance. Hence, they need a manual to refresh their minds whenever necessary.

Finally, although some studies of death rituals have been carried out among other Shona ethnic groups, such as the Budya, Korekore, and Manyika, not much research has been done on death rituals among the Karanga of Nyajena. Michael Gelfand, one of the few and earliest researchers to study the Karanga of Nyajena (1962), only dealt with death rites in passing, for his main objective was to explore the general culture and traditional religion of Nyajena. To complement his efforts, this book is a result of the survey of the praxis, significance, and possible changes in the death rituals as they are performed and understood by the Karanga people, in order to record them for future generations. The availability of a written document of the Karanga of Nyajena's death rituals would give mourners and the bereaved a source of reference. Since the people of Nyajena share many rituals with other Shona ethnic groups, this book is likely to benefit most Shona ethnic groups.

This book is divided into eight chapters. Chapter 1 deals with the clarification of key terms and concepts that are used in this book. This clarification serves to conscientize the reader about the meanings that I assign to such terms and concepts to avoid ambiguity or confusion. The chapter explores key terms such as Shona, rituals, death, cultural change, and the Karanga of Nyajena.

Chapter 2 deals with two issues. First, it explores the methodological issues particularly the qualitative research methodology in general, and ethnography, in particular, which were used in the collection and analysis of the data for this book. It describes qualitative data collection methods such as interviews and participant observation, sampling, data analysis, data verification, and ethical considerations. Second, it explores and evaluates the philosophical or theoretical framework through which the topics and concepts dealt with are understood.

Chapter 3 explores the causes of sickness and death among the Karanga of Nyajena in particular, and the Shona and other African peoples, in general. In most normal cases, sickness precedes death, and consequently, to understand Karanga death rituals, one needs to delve into its causes. The causes of sickness and death that this chapters explores are witchcraft, evil spirits, familiars (*zvidhoma*), ancestors, avenging spirits (*ngozi*), alien spirits, and God. The chapter ends by describing the Karanga healing methods, which in most sicknesses, are relied on to restore the sick person's health.

Chapter 4 deals with pre-burial rituals, which refer to the rites that are performed before death. I will restrict myself to the rites, which are performed from the time a person is grievously or terminally ill until he dies. These rituals include but are not limited to veiled threats to name the witch (*bembera*), divination to find out the identity of the witch (*gumbwa*), relocation of the terminally ill person to some other place outside the home (*kusengudza*), accompaniment or watching of the ill person (*kurindira*), visitation of the ill person (*kuvona mugwere*), among others. This chapter builds on the process that began in chapter 3 by navigating the pre-burial rituals as they are performed, not only by the Karanga of Zimbabwe, but also by a few other African peoples.

Chapter 5 deals with burial rituals, which are performed from the time the ill person breathes his last, until soon after the burial when mourners go back to their homes. These rituals, by far, outnumber the pre-burial and post-burial rituals. They include the folding of hands and legs, closing of eyes and mouth, wailing, announcing death, payment of the death token, washing and dressing of the corpse, body viewing, resting the body on the way to the grave, the forbidden time of burial, farewell speeches, lowering the body into the grave, the people who are not allowed to attend the burial, the direction to be faced by the corpse, putting soil and stones onto the grave, the sweeping of the grave area after burial, and placing *mutarara* branch on the grave. In addition to general burial rites, the chapter also deals with special burial rituals such as those performed during the burial of a fetus or a pregnant woman, an unmarried woman or man, and the burial by proxy.

Chapter 6 explores the post-burial rituals as they are understood and practiced by the Karanga people. The Karanga, just like other Shona ethnical groups, believe that death is a process—the beginning of a new life, and not an end to life. Hence, post-burial rituals continue for several years after death. The following post-burial rituals are explored in this chapter as being performed by the Karanga of Nyajena: consulting a diviner about the cause of death, cleansing of undertakers, placing the stones on the grave, resting days, commiserating with the bereaved, distribution of personal belongings, distribution of estate, cleansing of tools, and the cleansing of weapons.

Chapter 7 provides a brief, pocketable, and intelligible manual of selected pre-burial, burial, and post-burial rituals. The manual contains clear instructions for a quick perusal by those who would want to follow the Karanga traditional burial procedures.

Finally, chapter 8 has three sections. The first section gives a synopsis of the preceding chapters, and the findings of the inquiry. The second section offers recommendations concerning how and why the Karanga of Nyajena, Shona peoples, and Africans should reclaim and affirm their cultural identity, particularly their traditional death rituals. The third section proposes a philosophical framework called radical ethnification, which encourages Africans to extricate themselves from Western cultural imperialism, relearn and preserve their cultures, and write down their rituals. Radical ethnification should be understood as a form of postcolonial theory performed from a cultural point of view. It should be noted that these recommendations come as suggestions, and not as catechetical prescriptions. Each ethnic group should assess its cultural situation and come up with recommendations that are relevant to its context using these suggestions as a framework.

Chapter 1

Terminological Clarification

INTRODUCTION

This book is about death rituals among the Karanga of Zimbabwe with special reference to the Karanga of Nyajena. Although this topic is commonplace, there are some terms and phrases, which are used in this exploration that need to be clarified. This clarification gives the reader an understanding of how the terms are employed and understood in this book, since scholars of religion and culture do not define them in a homogenous manner. This chapter, in an endeavor to prepare the reader for a deeper comprehension of the subsequent chapters, explores five terms, namely, rituals, death, the Karanga/Shona of Nyajena, Karanga/Shona Religion and worldview, and cultural change.

RITUALS

This book is about Karanga death rituals, and it is important to give an outline of the study's understanding of the meaning and significance of rituals from a general point of view. Cunningham and others have defined a ritual as "a ceremonial act or repeated stylized gesture used for specific occasions."[1] From this definition's point of view, there are many ordinary rituals in life, such as the way we greet people, the manner in which we wake up every morning, eat and drink, rejoice, build our homes, grieve, die, and honor deceased members of our families. Some rituals have become part of our everyday lives that we do not even notice them. However, other rituals are so special and infrequent that we have to learn how to perform them, lest we get chastised or sanctioned by family or communal leaders if we do not perform them appropriately. Religious rituals have actions that "connect the individual and the community to the sacred reality.[2] Sometimes, the ritual actions and words should be performed synchronistically, avoiding making mistakes. Hence, most ritual practitioners receive specialized training, which impart on them the expertise of ritual praxis of their respective traditions. Some have to read the sacred words or prayers during the performance of rituals to avoid making mistakes, and if mistakes are committed, such rituals are sometimes rendered invalid and inefficacious.

Rituals have certain characteristics that make them recognizable when they occur. All rituals have a history of their inception and transmission, as Brodd and others have noted.[3] Adherents can go back to their historical archives or oral traditions to find out the approximate date on which certain rituals started, and how or why they were incepted. Also, rituals have a tradition, which means the transmission of culture and religious beliefs and practices from one generation to the next. According to Esposito and others, the traditions include actions that try to reenact the stories that are passed on from generation to the next.[4] Hence, Esposito and others claim that the religious stories (myths) and the symbolic reenactment of the stories (rituals) are closely connected. Some rituals dramatize the myths, which sometimes are the foundations on which the rituals are built. Most of the times, that which was passed on from one generation to the next changes because of acculturation, which Gittins defines as the encounter between two or more cultures, whose outcome could be a mutual or unequal give and take of cultural practices and values.[5]

1. Cunningham, *et al.*, *The Sacred Quest*, 2nd Edition, 79.
2. Esposito et al., *World Religions*, 7.
3. Brodd, *et al*, *Invitation to World Religions*, 2nd Edition, 20.
4. Esposito, 7.
5. Gittins, *Living Mission Interculturally*, 59.

Most rituals are accompanied by symbolic actions such as kneeling, standing, singing, crying, sitting, prostrating, clapping of hands, and genuflecting, and so on, which the adherents can interpret in more or less the same way. There are also symbolic food and drink. These ritual symbols are attempts to visualize, interpret, and understand the rituals' significance. Although, the symbolic gestures may slightly differ as per the demands of each faith community, the similarities between similar rituals far outweigh the differences. Consequently, the significance of ritual actions such as the sign of the cross or kneeling are universally recognized. The use of symbols is important because there are certain religious beliefs and practices that cannot be explained intelligibly by the use of words alone.

Repetition is another key feature of rituals. The sacred gestures, words, or actions should be repeated accurately and uniformly in every similar ritual to foster uniformity. The repetition may be in the form of the same ritual being performed in the same way on different subjects or occasions, and at different times. For example, Catholics teach that baptism cannot be repeated on the same recipient, but the same ritual is performed on different recipients as needed. However, the repetition can be in the form of the same ritual being repeated by the same recipients. For instance, the Christian ritual of Holy Communion can be repeated on a daily basis. The repetitive nature of rituals fosters uniformity and predictability in their performance. Hence, some religious traditions have written documents that contain prayers and hymns to foster uniformity and integrity in ritual celebration. Repetition enables adherents to memorize and internalize the rituals, and that repetition gives the ritual its form and identity. The memorization of rituals prevents any unwarranted mistakes in their performance, and discourages unauthorized changes to the rituals. Although African Traditional Religions are not too rigid concerning the wording of the rituals, it is insisted that the meaning and spirit of the rituals be maintained.

Every ritual calls for the active participation of the participants and their ritual leaders. The active participation can be in the form of drama, dance, song, prostrating on the ground, among others. Most religious traditions believe that such actions are didactic in nature. Sometimes, the active participation may be in the form of eating sacred food and uttering uniform responses. Cunningham and others assert that this dramatization of rituals may be an attempt to reenact the original activity of the event such as the Christian Last Supper, or the creation of the world.⁶ Once a ritual is performed, there should be some mystical edification in the participants. If the participants do not get anything out of rituals, they would be discouraged from performing them again. Moreover, the consuming of the sacred food is believed to transform the lives of the adherents. However, sometimes both profane and sacred food is shared during rituals as a sign of hospitality. For instance, there is both profane and sacred food at weddings, and at other rites of passage such as the Apache's Sunrise Dance and the Navajo's Kinaalda Ceremony. Although the ritual food is consumed by the adherence, it is believed that the invisible members of the communities—ancestors, also partake in the consummation of the food.

In addition to that, some rituals demand some form of abstinence from food or sexual intercourse before they are performed. For instance, the *mutoro* ritual beer of the Karanga people, which is performed to ask for rain from God via the ancestors, is brewed by women who have gone past child-bearing ages. It is generally believed that menstrual blood may defile the ritual, and render it ineffective. Likewise, sometimes, sexual activities are believed to drive ancestors away. Fasting from food is a universally recognized spiritual exercise that can be performed during rituals. For example, Muslims fast during the month of Ramadan. Catholics fast on Ash Wednesday and Good Friday. Most religions believe that fasting can draw people closer to the sacred reality.

Kesler contends that "sacrifice plays such a central role in so many different rituals," and is a theme that permeates most religious teachings and practices.⁷ Kesler lists many examples of sacrifices that accompany rituals such as slaying of animals for their blood or meat, and the offering of vegetables or cultural products to the gods. In some religions, fruits, cloths, blankets, weapons, and so on are also sacrificed in rituals. For Kessler, every sacrifice has four elements, namely, the participants, the sacrificial animal, vegetable, artefact, object, "the mode of sacrifice, and those who receive the sacrifice."⁸ In African Traditional Religion, goats, chickens, and cattle are sacrificed to the ancestors.

Rituals serve significant purposes in people's lives. Some rituals, such as weddings, ordinations, and circumcision give individuals the

---

6. Cunningham et al., 80.
7. Kessler, *Studying Religion*, 114.
8. Ibid., 114.

courage and authority to face new social roles that accompany the different stages of physical and intellectual development at which they are. Mbiti contends that one of the great significances of the rites of passage is to introduce the candidates to adult life, which allows them "to share in the full privileges and duties of the community."[9] The initiated also acquire new responsibilities, education, and rights, which befit adult members of the community. If the ritual in question is that of marriage, the couple is assured of becoming ancestors if they die after begetting children.

Some rituals, such as *magadziro*, assist the spirit of the deceased in entering the realm of spirits by purifying them after burial. Most mourning rituals help the bereaved to cope with their loss as they experience life without the deceased member of the family. Death brings with it much grief, and the bereaved family members are assisted by the community to go through that grief by the use of rituals. The community gives the bereaved the needed accompaniment and emotional support. In some communities, mourners assist the bereaved financially or by offering them food handouts during the funeral. Most post-burial rituals bring closure concerning the finality of physical death, and ushers the prospect of the attainment of a spiritual life by the deceased. Therefore, among the Karanga of Nyajena, as soon as the deceased is buried, his family hopes that he will come back home as an ancestor at the appropriate time.

Some rituals foster a spirit of fraternity among the people who perform them together. Participants share food and drink, and that hospitality unites them. Such rituals give the participants a common identity. For example, the people who were baptized into a particular Christian denomination acquire a common religious identity by virtue of the same baptism they would have received. Hence, the baptized of a particular denomination believe that they are related in one way or the other. The same applies to ethnicities, which initiates their boys and girls into adulthood. Those that are initiated together assume a certain relationship and cultural identity.

Some rituals also entertain because of dance, song, and food that in most cases, accompany them. As Brodd and others have observed, "The rituals surrounding death are not always sad, and they may even be joyful."[10] Some candidates take part in certain rituals because of the enter-

---

9. Mbiti, *African Religions, and Philosophy*, 2nd Edition, 118.
10. Brodd et al., 82.

tainment involved. Also, such rituals may attract spectators from other communities if there are no taboos concerning who can attend. Some rituals are a means of communication, which allows the living members of a family to communicate with supper sensible realities, or the other way around. Other rituals are used to consecrate people or places for sacred offices or usage respectively.

There are several types of rituals, but the majority of scholars concur that about three of them are fundamental, namely, crisis, calendrical, and rites of passage. Crisis rituals are also known as rites of affliction because they focus on misfortunes and calamities in the community, such as illness, barrenness, drought, war, bad luck, death, failure, and many others. Their celebration is decided by the challenges that the society is facing at a particular time. They are not on the calendar. Examples of such rituals are death rituals because death comes when it wants to come. These rituals can be preventive if the misfortune has not yet happened, or propitiatory, if the misfortune has taken place. The rationale of performing preventive crisis rituals is to persuade the invisible members of the family to be vigilant, or to appease some angry spirits. They can also be used to appease the disgruntled spiritual members of the community, who may have allowed the misfortune to happen.

Calendrical rituals occur at set times according to the seasonal calendar of the believers. Usually, believers know when such rituals would be celebrated, and they thoroughly, prepare for them. Examples of calendrical rituals can be drawn from New Year celebrations, Christmas, Thanksgiving celebrations, Passover feast, Ramadan fasting, and so on. Most of these rituals occur annually, on the same date, unless the believers follow the lunar calendar. Most of these rituals are joyful celebrations, and many people and communities look forward to celebrating them. Some are accompanied by the sharing of sacred food and drink. For instance, the Jews eat seder food during the Passover celebrations.

Life cycle rituals are also known as rites of passage, a term that is believed to have been coined by Arnold van Gennep. Gennep defines them as "ceremonies whose essential purpose is to enable the individual to pass from one defined position to another which is equally well defined."[11] In support of that, Ludwig says that there are four critical passages of life, which are birth, puberty, marriage, and death, and these should be ritualized to indicate "the separation from the previous state,

---

11. Gennep, *The Rites of Passage*, 3.

the encounter with sacred power in the transitional liminal period, and the reincorporation into the community at the next level of human life."[12] Rites of passage are also performed to mark different stages in human physical, spiritual, and mental development. In his list of life cycle rites, Gennep includes "birth, childhood, social puberty, betrothal, marriage, pregnancy, fatherhood, initiation into religious societies, and funerals."[13] They are intended to celebrate the developmental milestone reached by the participant, and also to enlist the help of the good spirits to inspire, protect, and guide the initiated. In addition, they make the age or maturity milestone reached by the initiated public. For instance, in the past, if a girl were initiated into adulthood, it was a public sign that she was ready for marriage. Nowadays, things have changed because of the legal ages of adulthood, which differ from place to place.

It should be noted that the study that resulted in this book dealt with death rituals, most of which are performed to assist the bereaved to transition to a new life without the deceased member of the family, and also to "incorporate the deceased into the world of the dead," and such rituals "are elaborate and assigned the greatest importance in many religious traditions.[14]

DEATH

Although there is no conclusive definition of death, most medical practitioners agree that, "a person is dead when he has irreversibly lost all capacity to integrate and coordinate the physical and mental functions of the body."[15] O'Rooke, quoting the Pontifical Council *Cor Unum of Ethics Regarding the Fatally Ill and Nurses* (1981: 20–23), contends that the immediate signs of death are the spontaneous cessation of cardiac and respiratory functions, and the verification of "an irreversible cessation of every brain function."[16] Sankar has given a list of signs of the approaching of death, namely, the loss of sensation, motion, and reflexes, the becoming cold of arms and legs, more sleep, confusion, sight failure, loss of

---

12. Ludwig, *Sacred Paths*, 51.
13. Gennep, 3.
14. Ibid., 146.
15. O'Rourke, *Medical Ethics*, 3rd Edition, 78.
16. Ibid., 78.

bowel and urine control, increase in oral secretions, restlessness, appetite decrease, and irregular breathing.[17]

According to Imasogie, "Death is a very solemn event fraught with danger for both the deceased and the living; hence, precaution must be taken to ensure that everything is done properly."[18] Most people fear death because it reminds them of their physical limitedness and finitude. Hence, every ethnicity has euphemisms that it uses for death such as passing away, kicking the bucket, buying a farm, being called home, running a good race, resting, going before us, is no more, is gone, and so on. According to Corr and others, the euphemisms used for death are intended to prettify death.[19]

Apart from the fear, it is deeply ingrained in human nature that the dead have to be reverenced, as Mayer has rightly stated.[20] Many rituals are performed for the dead, and these have two major functions. First, they help the bereaved to progressively cope with grief of losing a family member. Scholars, such as Pine affirm that there are about five stages of grief that the bereaved should be helped to go through.[21] These are: disbelief when the message of death is communicated, anger that a beloved has died, desperation, and eventually resolution. For Praagh, there are seven grief stages, namely, shock, denial, bargaining, anger, guilt, sadness or depression, and acceptance.[22] Death rituals help the bereaved to move from one stage of grief to the other. However, the movement is not necessarily linear, because there is no formula of dealing with grief. Second, death rituals prepare the dead to enter the realm of the ancestors, and at times and in some cultures, enabling their spirits to come back into their families as ancestors.

In most societies, death rituals should be performed meticulously to avoid upsetting the deceased and the ancestors. This book explores how these death rituals were and are performed by the Karanga of Nyajena, Masvingo, Zimbabwe.

---

17. Sankar, *Dying at Home*, 150–151.
18. Imasogie, *African Traditional Religion*, 60.
19. Corr, et al, *Death and Dying, Life and Living*, 87.
20. Mayer, *Embalming, 4th Edition*, 4.
21. See Pine, "Dying, Death, and Social Behavior," 37–38.
22. Praagh, *Healing Grief*, 13–15.

THE KARANGA OF NYAJENA

Since the fieldwork for this study was done among the Karanga of Nyajena, it becomes imperative to explore their identity among Shona ethnic groups. The Karanga of Nyajena are a segment of the Shona people who live in the province of Masvingo, Zimbabwe. Zimbabwe is a landlocked country in southern Africa. Its population is approximately 15 million. It borders Zambia in the north, South Africa in the south, Mozambique in the east, and Botswana in the west. There are several ethnical groups in Zimbabwe, and each has its own cultural practices and beliefs, which to a large extent are similar to those of other Shona ethnicities. In other words, the cultural differences among Shona ethnicities are negligible. Despite those minute dissimilarities, most of Zimbabwe's ethnicities linguistically fit into two principal groups—the Ndebele and the Shona. The Ndebele are said to have migrated from South Africa around 1840 under the leadership of King Mzilikazi, and are mainly found in the Matabeleland Provinces whose capital city is Bulawayo, which is Zimbabwe's second-largest city. They constitute about a quarter of Zimbabwe's 15 million population, according to some informal estimations.

The Shona, who constitute about three-quarters of Zimbabwe's population, comprise groups such as the Karanga in the south, Zezuru in central Zimbabwe, Korekore in the north, and Ndau and Manyika in the east. Rayner asserts that the Shona are Bantu people who came from the North a long time ago in a wave of migrations, which historians call, "Bantu migrations."[23] However, he claims that the Shona have forgotten the circumstances surrounding their arrival in Zimbabwe because nothing was recorded. All the information that is available concerning the Shona's occupation of Zimbabwe is sourced from oral traditions.

There is no consensus among historians concerning how the people of Zimbabwe came to be known as "Shona people." Rayner claims that the name Shona is likely to have been derived from the Ndebele word, *Amasvina*, meaning the "unwashed ones," which the Ndebele derogatorily used for the people they found in Zimbabwe upon their arrival from South Africa, in the nineteenth century.[24] Bourdillon, supporting the same theory, postulates that the word *Shona* "appears to have been used first by the Ndebele as a defamatory name for the people they had

---

23 Rayner, *The Tribe and Its Successors*, 20.
24 Ibid., 41.

defeated, particularly the Rozvi."²⁵ It should be noted that the Rozvi are Karanga people. Just like Rayner's theory, Bourdillon's theory is based on the word *Masvina*. Both Rayner and Bourdillon concur that the name Shona was an imposition by the Ndebele, which was resented in the past, until it was popularized, and perhaps, sanitized by the British in their endeavor to find a unifying name for the indigenous people of Zimbabwe.

Mlambo suggests a different derivation of the word, Shona. He alleges that it was a creation by the colonial rulers of Zimbabwe, the British, who occupied it in 1890.²⁶ Eventually, the term was used to classify all the people of Zimbabwe who had a "similar linguistic, cultural, and political past."²⁷ This classification was enforced by the colonial education system that standardized Karanga, Zezuru, Makorekore, Ndau, and Manyika to produce standard Shona, which is primarily based on Zezuru. The standardized Shona is still being studied in Zimbabwean schools, although more and more people now advocate for the study of other ethnic languages in their own right. Even though Mlambo's theory sounds plausible, it can only make sense if used in collaboration with Bourdillon and Rayner's theories. The colonial administrators might not have created the term, Shona, from a vacuum. It must have come from somewhere. It is likely that the name, Shona, was invented by the Ndebele, and formalized and popularized by the colonial administrators, and reluctantly embraced by the named people.

Some people have argued that the people who came to be known as Shona, were indeed, Karanga people. So, before they were nicknamed, Shona, they were known as Karanga people, a name, which was maintained by one of the ethnicities. Consequently, some Shona people, particularly of Karanga ethnicity, denounce the name, Shona, as derogatory, and an imposition by the British colonial administration.

Even though the derivation of the word Shona may be controversial, and some people unhappy because of its use, the ethnicities that belong to the Shona ethnical group are known. As has been already mentioned, one of the major ethnical groups, which constitute the Shona peoples are the Karanga, whose current habitat, Masvingo, the then Fort Victoria, is in the southern part of the country. Hence, the derogatory name, "Mavhitori," (people from Fort Victoria) is sometimes applied to people who

---

25. Bourdillon, *The Shona Peoples, Revised Edition*, 17.
26. Mlambo, *A History of Zimbabwe*, 10.
27. Ibid., 10.

come from that province. Mlambo asserts that the Karanga's presence in Masvingo goes back to the Great Zimbabwe civilization of about the thirteenth to the sixteenth centuries.[28] The Karanga have several clans, each with its own principal identity that is derived from its totem. Some of the clans are Bikita, Chivi, Gutu, Mwenezi, Nyajena, Zaka, Masvingo, and Chiredzi.

This study was done in Nyajena, the then Nyajena Tribal Trust Land, which is found in the southern part of Masvingo. According to Gelfand, Nyajena lies 60 miles southeast of Masvingo, and its area originally covered about 136 000 acres.[29] However, it should be noted that more land was added to Nyajena starting in 1980, at Zimbabwe's independence, with the introduction of the government's "willing seller and willing buyer" Land Resettlement Scheme, which saw thousands of black people being resettled in the land that was originally owned by white farmers. People from Nyajena acquired land in the former Makosi River Ranch, which was owned by the Anglo-American Corporation. More so, the compulsory land acquisition led by the late president of Zimbabwe, Mr. Robert Mugabe, which started in 2000, also witnessed more land being acquired for the Nyajena people at Mavhumatema or Nuanetsi, near Triangle.

Nyajena borders Zaka in the east, Chiredzi in the south, Chivi in the west, and Mushawasha Native Purchase Land in the north. The paramount chief of Nyajena is called Nyajena, a name that goes back to one of the progenitors of the clan. In the past, Chief Nyajena was assisted by three headmen (*sadunhu*) namely, Maregere, Marebe, and Magudu. Currently, it seems that only Maregere and Magudu have remained influential. The people of Nyajena identify with Moyo (cow heart) totem. According to Freud, "As a rule it (a totem) is an animal, either edible and harmless, or dangerous and feared; more rarely the totem is a plant or a force of nature (rain, water), which stands in a peculiar relation to the whole clan. The totem is first of all the tribal ancestor of the clan, as well as its tutelary spirit and protector; . . .."[30] Among the Shona, totems are hereditary through the paternal line. Every totem has a prayer or poem of praises, which is used for the people who belong to that totem.

28. Ibid., 10.
29. Gelfand, *An African's Religion, The Spirit of Nyajena the case of the Karanga*, 2.
30. Freud, *Totem and Taboo*, 2.

Gelfand states that the founder of Nyajena was Nyanga, who migrated from Mazungunye.[31] Originally, he belonged to the Moyo of the Rozvi totem. Gavhure, his eldest son, succeeded him as the chief after his death. Gelfand claims that Gavhure had three sons: Muchibwa, Marivadze (Nyajena), and Mupfurashanga.[32] Mupfurashanga had four sons, namely, Gwaendepi (Mukarudzi), Mapfekera, Muvango, and Murinini.

Tichagwa, quoting the *Delineation Report for Nyajena Tribal Trust Land* of 1965, claims that the Vajena trace their kinship to the Jiri of Bikita, and Chief Bota of Zaka.[33] Tichagwa states that the Vajena's principal families are Nyajena, Mudarikwa (son of Nyajena), and Maregere. She claims that the house of Mudarikwa, which consists of the families of Mavuku, Chikwadze, Maramwidze, Muganyi, Makumbe, and Mundingi has the primary religious task of rainmaking.[34] So, during years of drought, they used to send emissaries to Matonjeni to ask for rain. Matonjeni was the national shrine of the Shona God (Mwari), located near Bulawayo, Zimbabwe's second-largest city. According to Tichagwa, Maregere, who is considered a son by Nyajena, is the headman of the area called Nyamande, and it is said that he has, in the past, clashed with Chief Nyajena regarding jurisdictional issues.

Other oral traditions, support Gelfand's claim that the Vajena came from the Duma of Mazungunye. Such oral traditions claim that Gavhure was excommunicated by Mazungunye after he had committed the abominable and pernicious offence of incest with his sister. Tichagwa, quoting Bogomas (1970), alleges that Gavhure, indeed married his sister and fled home, and resettled on the Chitakai Mountain, in the area later to be called Nyajena, where he established a dynasty.[35] The *chidavo* (sub-totem) Mirambwi, which can be translated as "the Rejected One" is claimed to have originated from Gavhure's incest that led to his expulsion by Mazungunye. It is believed that upon his arrival in the new land, Gavhure conquered the people who already lived in the Nyajena area. However, there is no agreement as to the identity of the people who were vanquished by Gavhure. It is likely that the Vajena people co-existed with the indigenous people of Nyajena since they were not powerful and

---

31. Gelfand, *An African's Religion, The Spirit of Nyajena the case of the Karanga*, 5.
32. Ibid., 5.
33. Tichagwa, "Local histories and present realities," 24.
34. Ibid., 20.
35. Ibid., 26.

numerous enough to be able to completely subdue the original inhabitants of the area, which they later renamed, Nyajena.

Even though Vajena are the dynastic rulers of Nyajena, there are many other Karanga groups, which live among them. These other inhabitants of Nyajena can only be identified and differentiated from the Vajena by their totems. Some of them belong to the following totems: Shoko (monkey/baboon), Shumba (Lion), Dube (Zebra), Nungu (Porcupine) Shava (Eland), and many others. There are also the non-Shona ethnicities such as VaRemba, who are scattered in Nyajena and other areas of Zimbabwe. In addition, there are Hlengwe people of Magudu who are likely to be descendants of the Tsonga people.

There is no clear answer concerning the origin of these non-Vajena people in Nyajena. Some of these people may have been found living in the area that became Nyajena. Others may have migrated to Nyajena later after the dynasty had been founded. Hence, it is important to emphasize that while this book is about the people of Nyajena, it is not only about the Vajena people who are technically the only members of the Nyajena aristocracy, but it is about the people of different totemic groups that consider Nyajena as their ancestral home. Most of these people, except VaRemba, who claim to be one of the black Judaic tribes, share the same cultural, religious, and social aspects of their lives with the Vajena. They perform and celebrate death rituals together.

THE KARANGA/SHONA RELIGION AND WORLDVIEW

The Karanga of Nyajena subscribe to the Shona version of African Traditional Religion, which is the indigenous faith of most indigenous people of sub-Saharan Africa. Scholars of religion do not have a consensus as to the appropriate nomenclature that should be given to this religious tradition. Some scholars claim that the name of the religion of Africans is too contentious in the sense that it includes three terms whose definitions are controversial, and can be understood subjectively. For instance, there is no scholarly agreement concerning the meaning of the word African. Some scholars have tried to use skin color in defining Africans, but this perspective has been challenged by the fact that some Africans such as Egyptians, Libyans, and a few others may be considered to be white. More so, most of them have become predominantly Muslims. In countries such as the United States, some white people have claimed to be black, while some black people or Africans have also claimed to be white. This phenomenon complicates the definition of the adjective, African.

Furthermore, the adjective 'traditional,' which is part of the nomenclature of the religion, can be understood both negatively and positively. On the one hand, it can mean something old-fashioned and less desirable. On the other hand, it may refer to something primary, very important, and cherished. Therefore, some scholars are not comfortable with the use of the word, "traditional" as part of the name of the religion of Africans. As if that is not contentious enough, some scholars such as Hall, Pilgrim, and Cavanagh have found the word "religion" very difficult to define conclusively and clearly.[36] The trio explored several definitions of religion that were propounded by other scholars and concluded that most of them were wanting due to their vagueness, narrowness, compartmentalization, or prejudice. In other words, the explored definitions either do not sufficiently capture the essence of religion as understood by the adherents of diverse religious traditions, or are too focused on an aspect of religion to the exclusion of many other significant attributes of religion. Smith insists that the plurality of religious traditions makes it difficult to find a conclusive and definitive definition of religion.[37] In support of the arguments concerning the difficulties of attaining a definition of religion that satisfies everybody, Idowu predicts that scholars of religion are at the verge of giving up the pursuit.[38]

As if the challenges concerning the definitions of the constituent words used in the name of this religion are not complicated enough, there is another controversy, which concerns whether Africans have a homogenous or heterogenous religion. On the one hand, scholars such as Mbiti, Taylor, Idowu, Magesa, and several others contend that African Traditional Religion is homogenous. Magesa holds that although there are varieties of the expression of African Traditional Religion, the basic beliefs are similar.[39] According to Mbiti, there are many commonalities in African belief. For instance, they have a common conception of God, morality, rituals, cosmology, and so on.[40] While these scholars acknowl-

---

36. Hall, et al, *Religion*, 5–9.
37. Smith, *The Meaning and The End of Religion*, 17.
38. Idowu, *African Traditional Religion*, 69–70.
39. Magesa, *African Religion*, 16, 170.
40. Mbiti, *African Religions and Philosophy*, 2nd Edition, 2.

edge the existence of differences, they maintain that these should be downplayed, as they are in other world faiths. Hence, African Traditional Religion is one faith, that has several variations as dictated by the contextual and cultural needs of a given people.

On the other hand, there are scholars who insist that Africans do not have a homogenous religion. Each ethnical group has its own version of religious beliefs and practices. Even within one ethnic group, their religious practices and beliefs vary according to clans and families. Therefore, the name of the religion should be African Traditional Religions, in the plural.

The failure to reach a scholarly consensus on the nomenclature of this religion has led some scholars to advocate for a new name for the religion of Africans that would avoid the word "traditional." Scholars such as Bourdillon, Shoko, and many others have derived the name of the religion from some specific ethnicities such as Shona, Karanga, Igbo, Zulu, Ndau, and so on. Some of the suggested names are African Religion, African Indigenous Religion, African Traditions, Karanga Traditional Religion, Zulu Indigenous Religion, Igbo Traditional Religion, and many others. It should be noted that there is no consensus concerning the nomenclature of the religions of Africans. Be that as it may, whatever name is used for this religion, captures a part of its essence.

Some of these disagreements stem from the demonization that African Traditional Religion has suffered at the hands of Western scholarship. P'Bitek accuses the Western scholarship of African Religion as being influenced by the Westerners' dichotomized worldview, which professed their own as "civilized, great, developed," and the non-Westerners' worldviews, as "uncivilized, simple, and undeveloped."[41] Hence, many derogatory and prejudicial terms were used by early Western scholars for Africans and their religion. Quarcoopome explains how biased and prejudicial, terms such as paganism, heathenism, fetishism, idolatry, animism, and polytheism are.[42] He takes time to explain why Western scholars were wrong in their perception of the religion of Africans. The religion was also termed, ancestor worship, a term which is said to be the brainchild of Hebert Spencer. Mbiti vehemently disagrees with its usage to refer to the Traditional Religion of Africa.[43] Mbiti calls its use,

41. P'Bitek, *Decolonizing African Religions*, 15.
42. Quarcoopome, *West African Traditional Religion*, 46, 51.
43. Mbiti, *African Religions, and Philosophy, Second Edition*, 9.

"blasphemous" because Africans do not worship ancestors, but only offer them hospitality, respect, and honor.[44] This denunciation can be interpreted as an endeavor to portray African Traditional Religion as a monotheistic religious tradition to enable it to earn some respect from Abrahamic religions, which are sometimes at the forefront in belittling polytheistic religions.

Despite all the controversies concerning African Traditional Religion, many scholars concur concerning the nature and essence of African spirituality, its practices, and beliefs. It has been asserted that Africans are irredeemably and even dangerously religious. Africans have their religion as an integral aspect of their daily lives. It is almost impossible to separate them from their religion because it is intricately woven into their very cultural identity. Their births, names, stories, celebrations, food, songs, clothes, and houses are part of their religion. Consequently, it is difficult to separate adherents of African Traditional religion from non-adherents because even non-adherents practice the religion, either willingly or unconsciously. Mbiti postulates that Africans are deeply prayerful people, and they pray for wealth and prosperity.[45] For Africans, wealth includes, cattle, sheep, and goats, for they provide milk, meat, sacrifices, and payment of bridewealth. That is why Africans believe that bridewealth, wives, and children, as Kuper observes, come from their ancestors.[46]

In agreement with Mbiti, Chitakure contends that the spirituality of Africans in general, and the Shona, in particular, focuses on three pillars, which are prosperity, good health, and longevity.[47] Prosperity is important because it promotes good health, and good health leads to a long life. Wealthy people can appease the good spirits, in exchange for protection. They can also exorcise bad spirits if need be. More so, the Shona do everything in their power to promote good health. They work hard in their fields to produce enough food for their families' nourishment. They also solicit for the help of good spirits to protect their families from the never-ending onslaught by evil spirits.

Of course, the good spirits do not give this protection for nothing; they offer it in exchange for recognition, appeasement, and honor. It is believed that if the benevolent spirits withdraw their protection, their

---

44. Ibid., 9.
45. Mbiti, *Introduction to African Religion*, 53.
46. Kuper, *Wives for Cattle*, 16, 26.
47. Chitakure, *African Traditional Religion Encounters Christianity*, 2–3.

family members become vulnerable to all kinds of misfortunes, including death. The Shona understand death as "simply a transition like any other, and the dead man is not one who has been struck off the roll, nor even one who has been reincarnated but at most one who has returned and, as a rule, who is still present," as Van der Leeuw has aptly put it.[48] Although death is understood as a continuation of this physical life, albeit in the spiritual form, the Shona try to prevent it from happening because of the uncertainties it brings about.

Since the Karanga of Nyajena are a branch of the Shona people, and the Shona being Africans, their cosmologies and worldviews are strikingly similar. The African cosmology is inhabited by both spirits and human beings. The invisible spiritual and the visible physical members constitute the African community. Since the spiritual members of the African communities are not limited by space and time, they are necessarily omnipresent. Some of these spirits are benevolent, while others are malevolent, unpredictable, and malicious. Included among the good spirits are God, ancestors, and some alien spirits. The evil spirits include some alien spirits and *zvidhoma*. Kalu postulates that the African cosmology is replete with both good and evil spirits, and human beings must maneuver them to "tap the resources of the benevolent spirits to ward off the machinations of the devouring spirits."[49]

Likewise, human beings can be good or evil. In African cosmology, the evilest human beings are the witches who are people who possess mysterious powers, which they can use to harm others secretly. Most Africans believe that sickness and death can be caused by either good or evil spirits, and also by evil human beings, particularly, witches.

CULTURAL CHANGE

Etymologically, the word "culture" is derived from the Latin verb *colere*, which can mean to cultivate the ground, hence the phrase, *cultura animi*, meaning cultivation of the souls is believed to have its roots in *colere*.[50] So, culture means that which shapes the human being as specifically human.[51] Many cultural anthropologists agree that it is difficult to come

---

48. Leeuw, *Religion in Essence and Manifestation*, 213.
49. Kalu, "Ancestral Spirituality and Society in Africa," 56.
50. USCCB, *Building Intercultural Competence for Ministers Bilingual*, 8.
51. Ibid., 8.

up with an inclusive, definitive, and conclusive definition of culture. However, the failure to propound a universally acceptable definition of culture by scholars has not deterred them from putting forward functional definitions that help users to explore and comprehend the cultural topics under investigation. Driven by the same spirit, Law defines culture as the "the values, beliefs, arts, food, customs, clothing, family and social organizations, and government of a given people in a given period."[52] In support of Law's definition, Lustig and Koester describe culture as "a learned set of shared interpretations about beliefs, values, norms, and social practices, which affect the behaviors of a relatively large group of people."[53] Consequently, culture involves the total identity of a people: their values, food, songs, stories, dances, art, clothes, language, architecture, religion, politics, and their relationships with each other. Culture is who people are.

The USCCB note that culture has three distinct dimensions. First, cultures have ideas and ways of expressing them, and these include beliefs about God and people, values, language, feelings, way of living. Second, cultures have behaviors, which include rules about morality. Third, cultures have material dimensions, such as art, architecture, and other tangible symbols.[54]

All cultures are dynamic and imperfect, and this inevitable cultural dynamism can be either positive or negative as Kim has noted.[55] This cultural change is driven by several factors, one of which is acculturation. Shorter defines acculturation as "the encounter between one culture and another, or the encounter between cultures," which is "the principal cause of cultural change."[56] This encounter of members of different cultures has been exacerbated by globalization, which Schreiter has described as having something to do with "the increasingly interconnected character of the political, economic, and social life of the peoples of this planet."[57] Although no particular period can be identified as the starting point of the process of globalization in Africa, scholars agree that the colonization of African countries by Europeans brought African and European

---

52. Law, *The Wolf Shall Dwell with the Lamb*, 4.
53. Lustig and Koester, *Intercultural Competence*, 25.
54. USCCB, 6.
55. Kim, *Multicultural Theology and New Evangelization*, 11.
56. Shorter, *Toward A Theology of Inculturation*, 7.
57. Schreiter, *The New Catholicity*, 5.

cultures into an encounter where the African cultures were overpowered and condemned as inferior, primitive, and worthless. For instance, the British who colonized Zimbabwe in 1890, condemned most of the Zimbabwean cultures, including religious practices, and then imposed their own as a superior culture, a phenomenon, which Shorter calls "cultural imperialism or dominance."[58] Hence, the cultural change that happened among the Shona people because of their forced encounter with the Europeans was lopsided. In other words, the Shona or Karanga have been alienated from their own culture. The colonialists managed to do this by the continual demonization of the Shona cultures, and the promotion of their own through the educational systems that they introduced, and Christianity, which they portrayed as the only religion in which salvation was possible.

The study that produced this book was concerned about identifying the cultural changes in death rituals among the Karanga of Nyajena. It observed that although some Karanga death practices have remained constant, many have changed. It should be noted that, not all cultural change is toxic, for every culture is dynamic, therefore, change is inevitable. However, any cultural or religious change that is imperialistic in nature is destructive to a people's cultural identity. A healthy cultural change should not be the result of the trashing and demonization of other people's culture by the one who wants to impose his as a better culture. In fact, no culture is qualitatively better than the other. All cultures are equal but different, and that difference should not be taken as a sign of the inferiority or superiority of a particular culture.

It is important for the Karanga to identify some of these cultural changes, whether imposed or natural. The identification of some of these cultural changes may lead the Karanga people to a process of ethnification, which Schreiter defines as "the process of rediscovering a forgotten identity based on one's cultural ties," and is about "the assertion of a local identity, especially amid the experience of social change and cultural instability."[59] This study observed that the unearthing of the traditional death rituals among the Karanga of Nyajena is not an easy task because of the cultural hybridization caused by the encounter between Karanga culture and other cultures, and the lack of written documents of Karanga death rituals.

58. Shorter, *Toward A Theology of Inculturation*, 8.
59. Schreiter, *The New Catholicity*, 23.

As has been alluded to above, this book makes two significant assumptions about the meaning of culture, which are important to mention at this juncture. First, this writer understands religion as an aspect of culture. In other words, the religion of a people is a part of that people's culture. Second, among the Karanga, religion and other aspects of culture are inseparably intertwined. What is attributed to religion is also attributed to culture. Hence, Gittins, in addition to exploring religion as an aspect of culture, also explores other aspects of culture such as material culture, symbolic culture, moral culture, and institutional culture, which are connected to religion in one way or the other.[60] Religious beliefs can be expressed in all these other aspects of culture. This book does not make a distinction between culture and religion because it does not exist among the Karanga of Nyajena. The study that resulted in this book was about Karanga death rituals, which are both their religious and cultural practices.

CONCLUSION

It should be noted that, even though the above-explored terms can be understood in other different ways, in this book, they are conceived as explained above. This work is about death rituals as they are understood and performed by the Shona people of Zimbabwe, with special reference to the Karanga of Nyajena, which is located in the southern part of Zimbabwe's city of Masvingo. Since the explored death rituals are a part of the people's religion, which is an aspect of culture, Karanga/Shona Religion and its worldview have been explored briefly. This work also acknowledges that the Karanga/Shona Religion is related to the religious traditions of other African peoples. consequently, whenever necessary, examples or comparisons are drawn from other African ethnicities.

---

60. Gittins, *Living Mission Interculturally,* 35, 45.

Chapter 2

Methodological and Philosophical Frameworks

INTRODUCTION

EVERY RESEARCH NEEDS A research methodology, which gives the researcher guidelines on how to interact with, gather, and interpret the gathered data. A research methodology gives direction to a study as if it were a Global Positioning System (GPS), which is used to give travelers directions to their destinations. It gives the study boundary lines within which to explore the topic in question. The study for this book employed the qualitative research methodology, which Creswell has defined as, "involving fieldwork for prolonged periods, collecting words and pictures, analyzing this information inductively while focusing on participant views, and writing about the process using expressive and persuasive language."[1] In addition to that, the collection and analysis of the data, which was used for this book were done from a postcolonial theoretical framework. Although the book is more explorative than prescriptive, it gently reminds the Karanga people of the need to retrace their footsteps back to their cultural identity and integrity by valuing and practicing their traditional death rituals without the fear of being condemned by other people. The influence of postcolonial theory, though felt throughout this

---

1. Creswell, *Qualitative Inquiry and Research Design*, 24.

writing, is more vivid in the final chapter of this book, which suggests the possible way forward for the Shona people, and a brand of postcolonial theory, which I call radical ethnification.

QUALITATIVE RESEARCH METHODOLOGY

Generally, qualitative research methodology includes several research designs, such as phenomenology, narrative inquiry, grounded theory, ethnography, and qualitative case study. However, this study utilized ethnography. Merriam and Tisdell postulate that qualitative researchers, as "primary instruments of data collection," focus on the meaning and understanding of the issue under investigation to build "concepts, hypotheses, or theories," inductively and descriptively.[2] Hence, researchers should possess a particular level of competency, such as curiosity, tolerance for ambiguity, attentive observation and listening, asking right questions, reasoning inductively, and tolerance for writing.

The study for this book employed ethnography, which involves a "description, and interpretation, of a cultural or social group or system" to understand the meanings of behavior, language, or cultural interactions of its members, as noted by Creswell.[3] It also incorporated participant observation, which DeWalt and DeWalt define as "a method in which a researcher takes part in the daily activities, rituals, interactions, and events of a group of people as one of the means of learning the explicit and tacit aspects of their life routines and their culture."[4] Davies contends that "In its classic form participant observation consists of a single researcher spending an extended period of time (usually at least a year) living among the people he or she is studying, participating in their daily lives in order to gain as complete an understanding as possible of the cultural meanings and social structures of the group and how these are interrelated."[5] Be that as it may, cultural anthropologists concur that the immersion period can be significantly shortened if one studies his own culture, which was the case in this study. Although studying one's own culture has some disadvantages, in this study, these were outnumbered by the advantages of doing so. This takes us to the insider or outsider

---

2. Merriam and Tisdell, *Qualitative Research*, 15–18.
3. Creswell, *Qualitative Inquiry and Research Design*, 58.
4. DeWalt and DeWalt, *Participant Observation*, 1.
5. Davies, *A Reflexive Ethnography*, 67.

debate in the study of culture, which will not be explored in detail here. However, it suffices to mention that in cultural anthropology, "insiders" refer to researchers who belong to the culture or religion under investigation, and "outsiders" refer to researchers who do not belong to the culture, which they are studying. Both have advantages and disadvantages, and can fruitfully study culture provided they stick to professionalism. However, many scholars think that the best perspective for outsiders to take is that of the insiders.

According to Davies, participant observation as a research strategy became the hallmark or "rite of passage" for anthropologists, and can be traced back to Bronislaw Malinowski, a British anthropologist who found himself trapped on the Trobriand Islands during the First World War, where he discovered or developed the research strategy.[6] Its primary objective is to give the researcher an insider's perspective on the issues under investigation by taking part in and observing the cultural practices under investigation. Ethnography incorporates interviews, documents, observation, the use of key informants, and other qualitative research strategies.

As has been mentioned above, this study used qualitative research methodology for collecting and analyzing research data. One of the advantages of qualitative research is its holistic approach to issues under investigation. According to Janesick, "It looks at the large picture, the whole picture, and begins with a search for understanding of the whole."[7] So, what is observed of the particular, is applied to the general by looking at general patterns. The other strength of qualitative inquiry is its "richly descriptive nature," which makes the outcome easier to read and understand, even for non-academic audiences, as noted by Merriam and Associates.[8] The readability and intelligibility of any research outcome are important aspects because every research is done to benefit the readers from diverse backgrounds, and not necessarily academic audiences. The readers should learn something about the phenomena under investigation, and it would be a waste of time for any researcher to produce research results that no one understands. According to Corbin and Strauss,

---

6. Davies, *A Reflexive Ethnography*, 17.
7. Janesick, "The Dance of Qualitative Research Design," 42.
8. Merriam, "Introduction to Qualitative Research," 5.

many qualitative researchers hope that their works would be of relevance to non-academic audiences because of their clarity and intelligibility.[9]

In addition to that, Creswell and Poth assert that qualitative data are collected at the site "where participants experience the issue or problem under study."[10] Because of that interaction between researchers and the researched, Corbin and Strauss condend that qualitative research "allows researchers to get at the inner experience of participants, to determine how meanings are formed through and in culture, and to discover rather than test variables."[11] In support of that, Silverman contends that qualitative research encourages innovativeness by researchers because of its flexibility, for nothing is cast in iron.[12] Creswell and Poth aptly describes this flexibility as follows: "The questions may change, the forms of data collection may be altered, and the individuals studied, and sites visited may be modified during the process of conducting the study."[13] This flexibility makes the researcher the master of his research instead of being its servant. It makes the data gathering process more natural, which allows for more spontaneity.

Qualitative research also promotes objectivity, which encourages the qualitative researcher to suspend or set aside "his or her own beliefs, perspective, and presuppositions.[14] Other scholars, such as Snape and Spencer refer to this phenomenon as "empathic neutrality, whereby the researcher uses personal insight while taking a non-judgmental stance."[15] In research, there is nothing that beats objectivity. It is easier to read objective and non-judgmental research outcome that those that are subjective and prejudicial of other cultures. Objectivity should be the hallmark of any civilized and prolific academic discourse.

In addition to that, qualitative research allows for the use of small samples, which are manageable, and whose data can be representative of a larger population. This saves time and resources in gathering and analyzing data. Berg and Lune hold that "The logic behind this has to do with the fact that few human behaviors are entirely unique, idiosyncratic,

---

9. Corbin and Strauss, *Basics of Qualitative Research*, 14.
10. Creswell, and Poth, *Qualitative Inquiry and Research Design*, 43.
11. Corbin and Strauss, 12.
12. Silverman, *Doing Qualitative Research*, 2.
13. Creswell, and Poth, 44.
14. Taylor and Bogdan, *Introduction to Qualitative Research Methods*, 6.
15. Snape and Spencer, "The Foundations of Qualitative Research," 4.

and spontaneous."[16] Hence, the predictability and similarity in human behaviors allow for educated generalization of research findings. Smaller research samples that are professionally and thoroughly investigated can be more valuable than a sample of a thousand participants who are not given an opportunity to share thick descriptions of their cultures.

Furthermore, Taylor and Bogdan contend that qualitative inquiry is "naturalistic and unobtrusive" because the interviews are just like normal day to day conversations.[17] People tend to exaggerate and act out if they know that they are under study. They can easily forget that they are being observed or studied if the researcher tries to be as natural and unobtrusive as possible. Too structured interviews may produce artificial outcomes. Moreover, Creswell and Poth claim that qualitative research utilizes a variety of data forms such as "interviews, observations, and documents," that can be used independently or in liaison with each other.[18] On top of that, Janesick contends that "qualitative design requires the researcher to become the research instrument. As a research instrument, the researcher must have the ability to observe the behavior and must sharpen the skills necessary for observation and face-to-face interviews."[19] That is why Taylor and Bogdan insist that qualitative methods are intended to serve the researcher, rather than enslaving her or him to procedure and technique.[20] Flexibility and freedom are the mothers of creativity and innovativeness.

The other strength of qualitative research designs that I experienced in the study that produced this book involved the subject of this inquiry. Even though death is surrounded by mysteries, and perhaps fears and ignorance, its occurrence is commonplace. Kubler-Ross holds that because of society's youth-worshiping and progress-orientation, people try to evade, ignore, and deny the topic of death. For her, it is almost as if society has taken death as just another disease to be vanquished, which is erroneous because in a matter of time, everyone dies.[21] Death is inevitable and unconquerable. Of course, its occurrences can be delayed, but only delayed. In this study, most of the participants, in one way or the other,

---

16. Berg and Lune, *Qualitative Research Methods for Social Sciences*, 341.
17. Taylor and Bogdan, *Introduction to Qualitative Research Methods*, 6.
18. Creswell, and Poth, *Qualitative Inquiry and Research Design*, 43.
19. Janesick, 42.
20. Taylor and Bogdan, 8.
21. Kubler-Ross, x.

had a relative who had died, and they had participated in most of the death rituals explored in this work. These participants' experiences were valuable to this inquiry. Of course, in qualitative research, every participant's point of view matters, as affirmed by Merriam and Associates.[22]

Additionally, this topic generated a lot of interest among elderly informants since some of them were Karanga ritual practitioners by virtue of their age or position in the family or community. During the interviews, some of them felt that their expertise in death rituals was being affirmed, and their wisdom valued, and appreciated. Moreover, I have personally assisted in burying relatives, and I had observed several Karanga burial rituals before this study. Consequently, I was psychologically prepared for the emotional challenges that might be encountered in a study of this caliber, as noted by Chitakure.[23] Lastly, this topic was pertinent to future generations because death will continue to happen, and the Karanga people will almost always be called upon to bury their dead properly, according to their traditions.

I should also mention that my status as an insider among the Karanga of Nyajena contributed several advantages to this study. I was born and bred in Nyajena, and I am familiar with the topography, demography, context (social, political, and historical), and mentality of the people among whom I carried out my research, which is helpful in qualitative research. Moreover, the area of research was relatively manageable, and almost homogenous in terms of culture. I understood the verbal and signal languages of the Karanga of Nyajena, which Chitakure pronounces as one of the advantages in doing qualitative investigation.[24] I knew how to find gatekeepers to facilitate relatively easier entrance into sacred spaces. To a certain extent, I am an insider in Karanga religious or cultural traditions, and I possess most of the advantages that insiders are believed to have when studying their own communities, such as the knowledge of the language, how to establish relationships, and having the interests of the researched people at heart, as Bourdillon has encouraged.[25] Affirming the above claim, Jorgensen has insisted that the inside perspective is critical in participant observation.[26]

22. Merriam, "Introduction to Qualitative Research," 6.
23. Chitakure, *Shona Women in Zimbabwe—A Purchased People*, 43.
24. Ibid., 41.
25. Bourdillon, "Anthropological Approaches to The Study of African Religion," 143.
26. Jorgensen, *Participant Observation*, 60–65.

Although qualitative research was ideal for this study, Creswell and Poth warn researchers that collecting data, verifying, and writing descriptions is "time-consuming and a complex process."[27] They are right. In this study, the process of writing and analyzing data seemed to be never-ending. Also, while the use of small samples was helpful, I was on a constant check for haste and unhelpful generalizations. Furthermore, data analysis using any research methodology is always demanding, and if not done meticulously, it may distort the outcome of any inquiry. For instance, I discovered that data coding was more complicated than just taking note of the notions scribbled inside or on the margins of the field notes. Corbin and Strauss were right when they asserted that coding involves "interacting with data (analysis) using techniques such as asking questions about the data, making comparisons between data, and so on, and in doing so, deriving concepts to stand for those data, then developing those concepts in terms of their properties and dimensions."[28] This process was not easy at all. I also realized that Taylor and Bogdan were spot on when they warned that the recognition of patterns can be hard because of the unavailability of a one size fits all formula for selecting themes and developing concepts.[29]

Qualitative research requires sensitivity from the researcher. Corbin and Strauss define sensitivity as "having insight, being turned in to, being able to pick up on relevant issues, events, and happenings in data. It means being able to present the view of participants and taking the role of the others through immersion in data."[30] And, this is not always easy to achieve.

In addition to the above weaknesses, a qualitative researcher is warned that he may end up learning more than he had intended to know.[31] In support of this point, Rubin and Rubin offer the example of the participants who may be involved in ethically unacceptable or criminal ways.[32] That is the reason every ethnographer should warn or give informants an opportunity to retract what they would have said or quoting

---

27. Creswell and Poth, 47.
28. Corbin and Strauss, 66.
29. Taylor and Bogdan, 130.
30. Corbin and Strauss, 32.
31. Berg and Lune, *Qualitative Research Methods for Social Sciences*, 219.
32. Rubin and Rubin, *Qualitative Interviewing*, 100.

them anonymously if what they are saying may get them into trouble.[33] To counteract this challenge, I made it clear to the interviewees that they could withdraw from the interview at any moment if they felt that they no longer desired to share their experiences. I also warned them not to share anything that could get them into trouble by the law of the land.

More so, some of the qualitative research traditions, such as participant observation requires the physical participation and observation by the researcher, and my ability to do that was limited because of the infrequent nature and occurrences of death rituals. Death rituals are impromptu rituals, and as such, are not frequently performed. Consequently, I was able to attend only one funeral and *magadziro* (making of an ancestor ritual). In addition, Lee-Treweek and Linkogle allege that some researchers may be exposed to physical and emotional dangers if they are studying communities in high crime areas, war zones, and infectious diseases.[34] Fortunately, I was never exposed to any danger except the possibility of being bitten by snakes.

Moreover, death is an emotional topic whose discussion is likely to invoke emotions in the interviewees, and this could deter some of the informants from freely sharing their experiences. The discussion on death rituals, to a certain extent, could revive almost healed wounds caused by the loss of informants' beloved ones, since the length of the mourning period for each bereaved person is difficult to determine. Gennep has rightly observed that during the period of mourning, social activities are almost adjourned for the bereaved families, "and the length of the period increases with the closeness of the social ties to the deceased."[35] Hence, it is difficult to tell if someone is still mourning a deceased family member or not. Consequently, extreme caution should be taken to prevent the revival of emotional pain to participants. Be that as it may, to a certain extent, one of the ways to deal with grief caused by the loss of a beloved one is to share one's experiences and feelings openly. In a sense, interviewing such people can shorten their healing period. Hence, interviews about deceased family members can either be therapeutic or traumatic, or even both. The researcher should refer those interviewees still in grief to community counselors who can help them.

---

33. Berg and Lune, 219.
34. Lee-Treweek and Linkogle, "Putting Danger in the Frame," 11, 13.
35. Gennep, 148.

METHODOLOGICAL AND PHILOSOPHICAL FRAMEWORKS 39

Besides, participant observation is somewhat difficult to perform in certain rituals, particularly those that demand the involvement of close relatives or members of the group only. Some cultural practices are secretive, and might be dangerous for a researcher to experience or witness. For instance, witchcraft may be dangerous for outsiders to observe. Furthermore, the "status of insider is not often clear-cut," as Bourdillon has asserted.[36] In Karanga Traditional Religion, one is considered an insider in rituals, which are performed by his family only. Therefore, one is considered an outsider, even in the same village where he lives, as long as he is not related to the family performing the ritual. For Bourdillon, being an insider, has more other disadvantages such as taking things for granted, hinderance from personal views, observing what is supposed to happen rather than what does happen, lack of interest and objectivity, among other things.[37] In the research that produced this book, weaknesses of this nature were guarded against throughout the study.

Even though Nyajena is relatively a small area, still it was not easy for me to have all the villages evenly and fairly represented in this study. It is difficult to speak for all the Karanga of Nyajena since death rituals "vary widely among different peoples and that further variations depend on the sex, age, and social position of the deceased," as pointed out by Gennep.[38] Also, since most of the road networks have been neglected and rendered impassable, it was difficult to reach some parts of Nyajena. Hence, this study only probed the people who live in accessible areas. In addition to the above setbacks, the Karanga, like any other ethnic group in Zimbabwe, have been affected by acculturation, and some respondents could not remember how and why some rituals were performed in the past. Although the hunt for people with knowledge of Karanga death rituals was doable, it was not an easy task.

Despite the shortcomings of qualitative inquiry that are explained above, in general, and the particular challenges surrounding my study of death rituals in Nyajena, the use of qualitative research methodology remains critical to cultural investigations, and the outcome of such studies is usually fruitful and enlightening. In this case, the topic, of death rituals proved to be pertinent, and the area in which the study was carried out

---

36. Bourdillon,141.
37. Bourdillon,141.
38. Gennep,146.

was appropriate. This exploration was carried out objectively and professionally that the reliability and validity of its results are guaranteed.

POSTCOLONIAL THEORY

Postcolonial theory is something that I came across late in my academic life. Although I had read books by some postcolonial theorists before, it was my doctoral supervisor who introduced it to me as a helpful and enlightening theoretic framework. As I was doing research for this book, I decided to use postcolonial theory to provide the philosophical worldview or assumptions through which I would understand and analyze death rituals among the Karanga of Nyajena in particular, and the Shona in general. Creswell and Creswell have defined a theoretical framework as a "broad explanation for behavior and attitudes," which "provides an overall orienting lens" and a "transformative perspective that shapes the types of questions asked, informs how data are collected and analyzed, and provides a call for action or change."[39] It is the "underlying structure, the scaffolding," or the perspective that a researcher brings to the study, as Merriam and Tisdell have succinctly pointed out. It refers to the angle from which the investigator interprets and understands the topic.[40] Even though these definitions are intelligible and clearly expose the essence of a theoretical framework, they seem to negate the fact that every research tries to be as objective as possible. The above definitions seem to suggest that the investigator can be influenced by her presumptions about some phenomenon under study, and if that is the case, then the researcher's objectivity is rendered questionable.

Even though this is an important observation, objectivity is not as clear cut as we would want it to be. We are products of our environments, societies, cultures, education, beliefs, and convictions, which form our worldviews. These worldviews will always guide our different ways of understanding and interpreting reality. To a certain extent, it is possible for a researcher to be objective within a certain philosophical framework. It is important that every researcher should declare her theoretical framework right from the onset, so that readers of the outcome of the research may deduce why she uses a certain line of argument. Objectivity does not demand uniformity, but respectfully putting forward one's perspective,

---

39. Creswell and Creswell, *Research Design*, 5th Edition, 62.
40. Merriam and Tisdell, 85.

while acknowledging the existence of other equally important perspectives even though the researcher does not subscribe to them. That is why I would like to share the theoretical framework that shaped my desire to study the Karanga death rituals, my data analysis, and the conclusion I drew out of the study.

Postcolonial theory, which is the theoretical framework that I used in the study that produced this book, is intimately related to the process of colonialism by which Western countries went to Africa and other continents, conquering, subjugating, exploiting, and oppressing the indigenous people of such continents. This process was mainly championed by European countries, individuals, and companies. For instance, at the Berlin conference of 1884 at which no African representative was invited, Europeans partitioned Africa and shared it among themselves as if it had no inhabitants. Hence, for one to intelligibly and fruitfully explore and expound postcolonialism as a theory, the effects that colonialism had on both the colonized and the colonizers should also be examined because it was in the process of colonialism that the Westerners demeaned and condemned most of the cultures of the colonized, and unremorsefully exploited their natural resources. As if that was not disrespectful enough, they imposed their own culture on the colonized.

Osterhammel defines colonialism as "a relationship of domination between an indigenous (or forcibly imported) majority and a minority of foreign invaders."[41] Colonialism involved the military invasion, massacre of indigenous peoples, the dispossession of the indigenous people of their land, the exploitation of the natural resources of the colonized countries, and the imposition of the colonizer's culture upon the colonized. In some cases, treaties to occupy or takeover the countries earmarked for colonization were obtained through hook and crook, and in most cases, such apparently innocuous treaties were followed by lethal force against the indigenous people.[42] For instance, in Zimbabwe, the Rudd Concession was signed in 1888, by Cecil John Rhodes' representatives, Charles Rudd, Rochfort Maguire, and Francis Thompson, and Lobengula, the Ndebele King. Mlambo argues that King Lobengula of the Ndebele people was reluctant to sign the treaty until he was outwitted by Rhodes' representatives because of the misrepresentations made to him by the Reverend Helm, a member of the London Missionary Society,

---

41. Osterhammel, *Colonialism*, 16–17.
42. Osterhammel, 16–17.

stationed in Bulawayo, who King Lobengula considered a friend.[43] The unsuspecting king thought that he had a trustworthy friend in the man of the cloth, only to be betrayed.

The Rudd Concession was followed by the physical occupation of Mashonaland by the Pioneer Column, in 1890, and the subsequent vanquishing of the Ndebele people during the Anglo-Ndebele War of 1893. This War was followed by the Ndebele and Shona Uprisings, which historians call the First *Chimurenga/Umvukela* of 1896. In both revolts, both the Ndebele and the Shona were totally defeated and disarmed, and subsequently subjected to the brutal, oppressive, and exploitative British rule for almost a century. In Mashonaland, Charwe, the spirit medium of Mbuya Nehanda, and Sekuru Kaguvi, and many others were executed for leading the revolt.

The same sad story was repeated in other African countries. Between 1904 and 1908, the German's Lieutenant General Lothar von Trotha and his armies butchered thousands of the Herero and Namaqua of Namibia, before they were booted out after losing the First World War. In 1885, King Leopold II of Belgium colonized Congo and is believed to have massacred more than 10 million people, and treated the survivors in the unimaginable, worst cruel, and barbaric manner. The story was almost the same wherever colonialism took place.

Wherever the indigenous people were vanquished, the colonizers made it abundantly clear that everything about themselves was superior to that of the conquered people. It was impressed upon the minds of the indigenous people, that the colonizer's intellect, education, philosophy, psychology, language, food, songs, dances, religion, and so on, were superior to those of the colonized people. The normal way of life of the colonized was trampled upon. Quarcoopome brings this point home to Africa by stating that the colonized Africans were seen as "uncultured" and "primitive," and their religion was referred to as "paganism," "heathenism," "animism," and "ancestor worship."[44] Idowu and many other African scholars condemn the use of such misleading and derogatory terms about Africans and their religions.[45] Indeed, everything about Africans, such as food, songs, dances, names, rituals, and gods was denigrated.

---

43. Mlambo, *A History of Zimbabwe*, 38.
44. Quarcoopome, 15.
45. See Idowu, 109.

In Zimbabwe, just like what happened in other African States, Mwari, the Shona God was belittled, and his sacred shrines at Matonjeni, violated and desecrated by the missionaries. In reference to Mwari, Thomas Morgan Thomas, a member of the London Missionary Society, who worked in Matabeleland during that time wrote, "In reality, however, he (Mwari) is no other than one of the original aristocrats of the country, who being well versed in the traditions of his forefathers, the priestcraft and witchcraft of his tribe, manages to blind the people and hide his true character from them."[46] Thomas further argued that (Mwari) Ukwali's knowledge and wisdom was a result of the conniving between the high priest and the people who lived in the shrine village. For Thomas, Mwari was a fake god, and not worthy of praise and worship.[47] Surprisingly, Rev. Thomas believed his Christian God to be real, just because he was a European God.

Although colonialism refers to a specific era, which is supposed to have ended with the decolonization of the colonized countries, postcolonial theorists argue that its effects on both the colonizer and the colonized are ongoing. One of the postcolonial theorists who systematically expounded the process and effects of colonialism on both the colonizer and the colonized is Alberti Memmi, a Tunisian of Jewish origins. In his book, *The Colonizer and The Colonized*, published in 1965, he explores North Africa's attainment of independence from France in 1956. Even though he writes from that particular perspective, the theories he propounded are applicable to most colonized peoples. In this book, Memmi explores the powerful position the colonizer has at his disposal, which he uses to define and determine the fate of the colonized. Memmi alleges that the colonizer achieves that objective by doing two things. First, by constantly portraying the colonized by what he is not, and describing him as a good for nothing person—lazy, diseased, and uneducated.[48] Second, "The colonized is never characterized individually; he is entitled only to drown in an anonymous collectivity."[49] For instance, the sin that has been committed by one of the colonized is attributed to all of them, and may be used to stereotype and dehumanize all of their kind. Once one is found wanting, all are condemned.

46. Thomas, *Eleven Years in Central South Africa*, 17.
47. Thomas, 17.
48. Memmi, *The Colonizer and the Colonized*, 85.
49. Ibid., 85.

In the same spirit, Césaire explores the connection between the colonized and the colonizer as follows: "Between colonizer and colonized there is room only for forced labor, intimidation, pressure, the police, taxation, theft, rape, compulsory crops, contempt, mistrust, arrogance, self-complacence, swinishness, brainless elites, degraded masses."[50] Césaire further alleges that the physical condemnation of the colonized leads to psychological colonization, which compels the colonized to accept the inferiority he and his kind are accused of.[51] The myth of the colonized's inferiority is then accepted by the colonized. This acceptance of a distorted identity leads to the self-alienation and hate of the colonized. Memmi argues that the colonized and the colonizer are joined together as if by fate, and in this relationship, every act in the daily life of the colonizer "places him in a relationship with the colonized, and with each act, his fundamental advantage is demonstrated."[52]

In all this, the colonizer creates a system that gives him advantages, and enables him to exploit Africans easily. Memmi paradoxically describes the relationship between the colonizer and the colonized as both "destructive and creative," because it disfigures the oppressor into "a partial, unpatriotic and treacherous being, worrying only about his privileges and their defenses," and it turns the colonized into a dehumanized, violated, and "oppressed creature."[53]

Césaire pursues Memmi's line of argument, by accusing colonization of decivilizing, brutalizing, and degrading the colonizer, in order to "awaken him to buried instincts, to covetousness, violence, race hatred, and moral relativism . . .."[54] In the same spirit, Osterhammel defines colonialism as an affinity between the oppressors and the subjugated, "in which an entire society is robbed of its historical line of development, externally manipulated and transformed according to the needs and interests of the colonial rulers," which are to subjugate and pillage.[55] Césaire claims that colonizers demonized and stifled every aspect of the conquered societies and buried their potential of ever developing their own economy. In this criticism of the colonialists, Césaire ropes

50. Césaire, *Discourse on Colonialism*, 42.
51. Ibid., 42.
52. Memmi, 11–12.
53. Ibid., 89.
54. Césaire, 35.
55. Osterhammel, 15.

in Christianity by condemning missionaries as the chief culprits, who "laid down the dishonest equations Christianity = civilization, paganism = savagery."[56]

In support of Césaire's sentiments, Osterhammel postulates that colonization was preached as the fulfilment of the Whiteman's divine mandate to save and "civilize" the "savages."[57] Osterhammel, does not spare the missionaries. For him, even though, some missionaries criticized the oppression of the colonized indigenous peoples, others actively supported colonialism and the dispossession of the colonized. They converted them to Christianity, and established schools at which the Western cultural values were transmitted as the exclusive divinely prescribed truths, and the English language imposed as the most advanced language. By so doing, they suppressed indigenous religious beliefs and practices by encouraging the people to accept Western values such as individualism, which undermined the extended family model, and severely disrupted their cultures.[58]

The unequal relationship between the colonized and colonizer inevitably created poverty for the colonized, and tremendous benefits for the oppressors. Of course, the lopsided relationship was freely accepted by the colonizers because they stood to benefit from it, but the colonized were dragged into it, and most of them initially abhorred and resisted it, before they were brainwashed into blind assimilation. Memmi contends that the painful result of this relationship was that the colonized started emulating the master, although such efforts were received with contempt by the colonizer.[59] Fanon thinks that the black man accepted and acknowledged "the undeniable superiority of the white man," and endeavored to achieve a white existence."[60] Fanon further alleges that the black man so much wants and hopes to be like the white to the extent that his destiny is that of becoming a white man.[61] For Memmi, the black man is never successful in becoming White, for he suffers alienation from which he should be cured first.[62] This cure will lead to the cessation of his

---

56. Césaire, 33.
57. Osterhammel, 15.
58. Ibid., 15, 97, 102.
59. Memmi, 124.
60. Fanon, *Black Skin, White Masks*, 202.
61. Fanon, *The Wretched of the Earth*, 141.
62. Memmi, 124.

alienation from himself. Fanon prescribes a way to decolonize the mind, which begins with the colonized conquering himself, and redeeming himself from the religion of the colonizer, and ceasing to define himself through "the categories of the colonizer."

WHAT IS POSTCOLONIAL THEORY?

According to Mishra and Hodge, etymologically, the term postcolonialism is a compound word formed by two Latin words, *post* and *colonia* or *colonus* whose primary root meaning was an inhabitant farmer, before it drifted to refer to an invasive settler in a foreign place.[63] Mishra and Hodge, make a distinction between colonist and colonialist, whereby colonists created a colony by their actions, but colonialists instilled colonial qualities, attributes, and attitudes associated with associated with a colony[64] Therefore, colonists were responsible for the physical occupation of the colonies, and colonialists were responsible for the mental colonization of the colonized.

Essentially, postcolonialism is a contestable term, and as a result of that, it does not have a universally acceptable and conclusive definition. Be that as it may, scholars are not deterred in offering working definitions of the term. According to Hiddleston, postcolonialism refers to the "events that succeeded" the onset of the post-colonial period, and it "names the period of colonial rule, together with its gradual weakening and demise."[65] For Maldonado-Torres, coloniality refers to deep rooted systems of power that were created by colonialism, "but that define culture, labor, intersubjective relations, and knowledge production well beyond the strict limits of colonial administration."[66]

According to Hall, postcolonial refers to a descriptive and "not evaluative process," of detachment from the multi-faceted and inescapable "colonial syndrome," which affects all the people of the colonized countries.[67] It admits that the colonial created a culture that continues to live in its "aftereffects."[68] Lynes contends that "Postcolonialism is a field of

---

63. Mishra and Hodge, "What Was Postcolonialism?" 378.
64. Ibid., 378.
65. Hiddleston, *Understanding Postcolonialism*, 3
66. Maldonado-Torres, "On the Coloniality of Being," 243.
67. Hall, "When was 'the Post-Colonial'? Thinking at the Limit," 246.
68. Ibid., 248.

study primarily composed of the critique of a variety of different colonial endeavors undertaken by a range of different countries and political regimes."[69] Postcolonial theory evaluates the circumstances of colonized peoples both during and after colonialism.

Postcolonial theory evaluates the effects of colonial practices such as exploitation, oppression, dehumanization, and demonization of the cultural identity of the colonized, and admits that they cannot easily extricate themselves from its legacy because it has been internalized. Its legacy is still rife in the colonized. Although some people try to resist postcolonial slumber, the conscientious objectors are sometimes booed down by their own people, who so much strive to be white. The residue of colonialism continues to keep the former colonized people, captive, and suffering from an inferiority complex. This captivity is by and large mental colonialism, whereby the mind of the former colonized is still under the influence of the doctrines, beliefs, and mindset imposed by the colonizer. Postcolonial theory acknowledges that this grip must be dealt with if the former colonized are to be free, and reattain their cultural identity and integrity.

Young observes and acknowledges the inequalities and divisions between the people of the West (Europeans, Americans) and non-west (Asians, Latin Americans, and Africans), which he claims were caused by the colonization of the latter by the former, and the subsequent subordination and dehumanization of the colonized.[70] In this light, Young asserts that postcolonial theory is an ongoing, anti-colonial struggle, which names a "philosophy and politics" that can be used to eradicate the differences caused by colonialism.[71] In addition to that, postcolonial theory seeks to promote the "knowledge, as well as needs, developed outside the West," by promoting the articulation of the politics of the "subordinated classes and peoples."[72] For instance, African students who study abroad are subjected to intelligence and psychological tests that were composed and set by Western experts for Westerners, using their own contexts and knowledge, which are different from those of Africans. If the African students do not perform as well as their Western counterparts in those standardized tests, they are deemed less intelligent.

69. Lynes, "Postcolonialism," 688.
70. Young, *Postcolonialism*: 2–6.
71. Ibid., 4–6.
72. Young, 2–6.

For Ndlovu-Gatsheni, postcolonial theory explores and exposes the "coloniality of being," which he defines as "the social, ideological, and epistemological process of reproduction of black people as a different human species, which is not worthy of treatment in an ethical way."[73] Quoting Grosfoguel (2007), Ndlovu-Gatsheni asserts that "The black inferior other was reproduced ideologically and represented socially as lacking soul, history, writing, religion, culture, knowledge, development, human rights, and lacking democracy."[74] Looking at postcolonialism from this perspective, Ndlovu-Gatsheni advocates for the cultural transformation of Higher Education to promote and produce African graduates who utilize African perspectives, and are not "copycats" of Europeans and Americans.[75] In addition to that, Ndlovu-Gatsheni proposes a postcolonial theory that produces an "African renaissance," whose sole objective is to transcend the "vicissitudes of histories of Orientalizing, inferiorizing, and othering of African subjectivity," which is informed by a profound knowledge of both African and global history.[76] For Ndlovu-Gatsheni, this process will produce Africans who can rise above "discourses of equilibrium," and eradicate the alienation that Africans have suffered on the hands of Westerners, and this African reawakening will help Africans in "transcending the distractions cascading from colonialism."[77]

A quick glance at the university curricula of former colonized people confirms Ndlovu-Gatsheni's sentiments. To a certain extent, it can be argued that African universities are replete with intelligent professors who have never published a single book that is related to the subject matter of the courses that they teach. Some of them make it harder for students who want to be creative, and do not quite follow the Western prescribed rubrics of writing dissertations and essays. That is one of the reasons African university libraries are full of irrelevant and unpublishable dissertations because most of them would have been written just to fulfill a requirement for graduation rather than to benefit the community. Even those dissertations that are publishable are still not very useful because some of them do not focus on the subject matter of what is taught at universities. Consequently, topics such as HIV/AIDS, domestic violence,

---

73. Ndlovu-Gatsheni, *Empire, Global Coloniality and African Subjectivity*, 178.
74. Ibid., 178.
75. Ibid., 178.
76. Ibid., 130.
77. Ibid., 179.

and African Independent Churches are among the most popular topics for doctoral students in sub-Saharan Africa. This does not imply that African scholars are less intelligent than their Western counterparts, but it is part of the colonial residue that described them as not good enough. Some of those who dare challenge the system and transcend the colonial mentality, find themselves with no publishers willing to publish their works.

According to Göttsche, "The rise of postcolonial theory and research has been characterized by the deliberate blending of a historical, a political and a conceptual understanding of the postcolonial, understood as a socio-cultural condition as well as a critical and cultural discourse."[78] Göttsche claims that postcolonial theory is transformative in the sense that it "rereads and rewrites" "colonial history and culture, including their present-day extensions," with the intention of eradicating the resilient "legacies and recurring transformations of European colonialism and imperialism" in the formerly colonized world.[79] For Göttsche, postcolonialism is an ongoing process, which aspires to move beyond colonialism and its ongoing aftermath, by exorcizing the colonized of the colonizer's cultural residue by reeducating the colonized of the value of their demonized cultural heritage.[80]

For Hiddleston, postcolonial critique involves an examination of the consequences of colonialism during its zenith and aftermaths, by identifying, interrogating, and analyzing the mechanics of colonial power, and the economic exploitation it brought, by raising pertinent questions, condemning its politics and economics, and advocating a cultural uprising and renaissance.[81] Unfortunately, Hiddleston admits that postcolonial theory raises relevant questions about the past and present effects of colonization, but it does not have the answers to the pertinent questions that it asks.[82] Without the answers, it remains a mere sterile analytical tool.

---

78. Göttsche, "Post-imperialism, postcolonialism and beyond: Towards a periodization of cultural discourse about colonial legacies," 111–112.
79. Ibid., 112.
80. Ibid., 112.
81. Hiddleston, 4.
82. Ibid., 4.

MAJOR THEORISTS OF POSTCOLONIAL THEORY

Even though a myriad of theorists such as Homi Bhabha, Benedict Anderson, Kwaku Asante-Darko, William Boelhower, David Brooks, Partha Chatterjee, Hubert Harrison, Edward W. Said, Frantz Fanon, and Gayatri Chakravorty Spivak, among others, immensely contributed to postcolonial critique as an academic discipline, this section will briefly explore the thoughts of Frantz Fanon (1925-1961), Edward W. Said (1935-2003), and Gayatri Chakravorty Spivak (1942 – present). These scholars have been chosen not necessarily because their works are the most significant, intelligible, or cogent of all, but because their contexts and examples best serve the purpose of the study that produced this book.

Frantz Fanon (1925-1961)

According to Lynes, Frantz Fanon was born in Martinique, but his postcolonial theoretical contributions are principally based on his experiences of the Algerian war of independence (1958–1962). It is believed that his work as a psychiatrist in Algeria exposed him to the psychological challenges and effects of the war on both the colonized and the colonizers.[83]

In his book, *Black Skin, White Masks*, which was published in 1952, he deconstructs the experiences of the colonized black people, and explains how they dealt with the belittling and degrading mindsets and the oppression, which were imposed on them by the colonizers. Fanon argues that, although the black man can easily use the withdrawal strategy to defend himself against being dehumanized by Europeans, that mechanism is impotent because the black man desperately "needs white approval."[84] Because of the incessant demeaning and demonization of his culture, the black man hates himself and wants to be white.[85] For Fanon, although it is abundantly clear that the black man is dehumanized because of the color of his skin, some black men, because of their craving to assimilate into the white man's culture, deny that their black color is the cause of their dehumanization.[86]

---

83. Lynes, 691.
84. Fanon, *Black Skin, White Masks*, 34.
85. Ibid., 202.
86. Ibid., 202.

METHODOLOGICAL AND PHILOSOPHICAL FRAMEWORKS   51

Fanon observes that the black man suffers from dissociative identity disorder. He behaves like a black man when he is with his fellow Blacks, and like a white man, when he is with the Whites. The black man must master that split personality to appease his white doctors, and superiors. Furthermore, Fanon seems to praise the black man for rejecting or misunderstanding Christianity. He blames the lack of basic needs such as food for the Black's refusal to accept Christianity. He writes, "And if Blacks are impervious to the teachings of Christ, it's not because they are incapable of assimilating these teachings. Understanding something new requires us to be inclined, to be prepared, and demands a new state of mind." [87]

In his other book, *The Wretched of the Earth*, Fanon alleges that colonialism is "naked violence and only gives in when confronted with greater violence," and consequently calls for the use of greater violence to end it.[88] Fanon maintains that colonialism disfigures and distorts a people's history, and it alienates them from their culture by forcing them to confess to their inferiority.[89] This inferiority complex is repeatedly imposed upon the colonized until it is accepted and internalized. Fanon encourages decolonization—a creation of "new men," which seeks to dismantle the colonial order, and should be created by the men it liberates.[90] The colonized should use any means necessary to liberate themselves because their values are demonized, and "irreversibly poisoned and infected" by the colonizers. As if that is not evil enough, the values of the oppressors such as individualism, are imposed on the colonized. Fanon, claims that the liberation would make Blacks discover their dignified humanity.[91]

Fanon also revisits the evil contribution of Christianity to the oppression of Blacks by condemning the "colonial church," which he admonishes for not converting the colonized "to the ways of God, but the ways of the white man, to the ways of the master, the ways of the oppressor."[92] As he concludes his book, Fanon, encourages the colonized

---

87 Ibid., 75.
88. Fanon, *The Wretched of the Earth*, 23.
89. Ibid., 149, 171.
90. Ibid., 2.
91. Ibid., 8.
92. Ibid., 7.

who have attained liberation to find a new direction and to avoid imitating and competing with Europeans.[93]

Edward W. Said (1935-2003)

Edward W. Said was born in Jerusalem, in 1935, and was a professor of literature at Columbia University. His book, *Orientalism*, first published in 1978, is accepted as one of the significant works in postcolonial thought. Hence, he is respected as one of the founding fathers of postcolonial studies. In *Orientalism*, he deals with the manner in which the Westerners obtained and continue to acquire knowledge of the people of the Orient. Said argues that "The Orient was almost a European invention, and had been since antiquity a place of romance, exotic beings, hauntings memories and landscapes, remarkable experiences."[94] Furthermore, Said contends that "the cultural, temporal, and geographical" difference between the "West and the Orient was expressed in metaphors of depth, secrecy, and sexual promise," and consequently, phrases such as "the veils of an Eastern bride" or "the inscrutable Orient", were frequently used.[95]

Said defines Orientalism as "as a style of thought based upon an ontological and epistemological distinction made between "the Orient" and (most of the time) "the Occident."[96] In addition to that, he sees Orientalism "as a system of knowledge about the Orient, an accepted grid for filtering through the Orient into Western consciousness...."[97] It is "the discipline by which the Orient was (and is) approached systematically, as a topic of learning, discovery, and practice," and a brainchild of European imagination.[98]

Said condemns the relationship between the Orient and the West as one of power and domination by the Europeans. Reflecting on the domination of Egypt by the British, Said writes: "There are Westerners, and there are Orientals. The former dominates; the latter must be dominated, which usually means having their land occupied, their internal affairs rigidly controlled, their blood and treasure put at the disposal

---

93. Ibid., 238.
94. Said, *Orientalism*, 1.
95. Ibid., 222.
96. Ibid., 2.
97. Ibid., 6.
98. Ibid., 73, 3.

of one or another Western power."⁹⁹ For Said, the West uses degrading stereotypes about the East and find it extremely hard to overcome such negative generalizations. One of the peddled distorted information was that the people of the Middle East and Asia were so primitive that they were oblivious of their own history and culture, and therefore, in need of cultural salvation by the West.¹⁰⁰ This erroneous perspective served to justify the Western cultural imposition on the colonized people.

Gayatri Chakravorty Spivak (1942 – present)

Gayatri Chakravorty Spivak was born in 1942 in Calcutta, West Bengal. She is believed to have been popularized by her essay "Can the Subaltern Speak?" which is seen as one of the primary and classical conceptual writings in postcolonial studies. The essay was published in several journals, under different titles, starting in 1985. The essay's primary concern is how Western cultures study other cultures. She explores European writers such as Karl Marx, and expounds the ethical challenges scholars of his caliber encounter in relying on Western concepts and frameworks to investigate a different culture. Spivak offers an illustration of *Sati*, an Indian practice in which widows were expected or even encouraged to commit suicide.¹⁰¹ Spivak convincingly argues that the motives behind *Sati* may be difficult to "reclaim and rewrite" using Western historical frameworks.¹⁰² Spivak also accuses the West of trying to study third world subjects without cooperation from the colonized people, and she bemoans the challenges facing third world people, particularly if they are "poor, black, and female."¹⁰³ For her, the subaltern is those who belong to the third world.

She concludes her essay dramatically by saying, "The subaltern cannot speak. There is no virtue in global laundry lists with 'woman' as a pious item. Representation has not withered away. The female intellectual as intellectual has a circumscribed task which she must not disown with a flourish."¹⁰⁴ For Lynes, this does not imply that the third world women

---

99. Ibid., 36.
100. Ibid., 36.
101 Spivak, "Can the Subaltern Speak?: Speculations on Widow-Sacrifice," 96–98.
102. Ibid., 96–98.
103. Ibid., 96–98.
104. Ibid., 104.

cannot speak or write, but refers to the difficulty they have of "articulating deeply and creatively" any kind of knowledge.[105]

STRENGTHS AND WEAKNESSES OF POSTCOLONIAL THEORY

One of the strengths of postcolonial theory is its interdisciplinary approach. Kumar has asserted this point aptly as follows: "Perhaps, then, postcolonial theory is best suited to normative interdisciplinarity for its implied anti-disciplinary stance, that is, no single discipline better-equipped to articulate select social issues."[106] This embracing of a wide range of interdisciplinary methodologies brings it at home to a diverse audience. Any discipline can use it to articulate the issues of racial discrimination and oppression from that discipline's perspective.

In addition to that, postcolonial theory is to a certain extent, therapeutic because it acknowledges that the humiliation, dehumanization, subjugation, and oppression of the colonized by colonialists cannot be swept under the carpet. These evils need to be explored from a perspective that empowers and heals the battered cultural integrity of the colonized. Hence, the unhelpful revisitation of the trauma caused by colonialism on the colonized should be avoided. However, postcolonial theory may help people to explore their painful past and to reframe their present. It is also therapeutic to the colonizer, who was also affected by his abuse of power, exploitation, and dehumanization of the colonized and their resources. The colonizer needs to perform an introspection to discover where he went wrong so that he may repent and rediscover his humanity. Postcolonial theory provides such opportunities for both the wounded and the perpetrator.

However, postcolonial theory, like any other theory, has its weaknesses. It is a reactionary theory that responds to the injustices done, and the evil perpetrated upon the colonized by the colonizers. Some of the postcolonial theorists seem irreparably aggrieved because of the way the colonized were treated by the colonizers. Some of them, just like the rest of the colonized, seem to suffer from an injured conscience because of colonial past and its ongoing effects. Consequently, the blame they pile on colonizers, and sometimes, the language they use to describe the

---

105. Lynes, 694.

106. Kumar, "Postcolonialism: interdisciplinary or interdiscursive?" 666.

process of colonialism may be inflammatory, and may serve to harden the hearts of the colonizer.

In addition to the above, some postcolonial theorists write above their readers. They use technical jargon in a manner that impedes the understanding of what they are writing. Readability and intelligibility are important in scholarship because no one can apply knowledge that one does not understand. Since postcolonial theorists talk about effects of colonialism on the colonized, and prescribe some sort of therapy, that therapy can only be useful if the people understand how to use it to transform their lives and cultures. It seems that some postcolonial theorists' work is intended for readers in academic circles, hence it may have no relevance to the ordinary person on the street, who they intend to liberate. Therefore, unless such theorists find a vocabulary that is intelligible to the ordinary reader, their theories remain discourses of academics in universities and colleges.

According to Young, the term postcolonial is disliked by some people because of several reasons: First, it disturbs the world order. Second, it threatens the privileges and power of the former colonizer. Third, it does not recognize the superiority of Western cultures. Fourth, it demands equality and well-being of all people.[107] What Young articulates makes a lot of sense because often, we encounter people who think that the best solution to painful and traumatic experiences is to bury them under the carpet. Some postcolonial theorists encourage the offended to get over it and move on with life. For some people, this solution is preferable because it does not unsettle the waters. It does not interfere with the status quo created by cultural imperialism. It does not disarrange the peace. It does not incite the former colonized against the colonizers. Consequently, some postcolonial theorists are suspected of trying to gain political mileage out of their writings.

Mishra encourages postcolonial theory "to be forever vigilant," to avoid reducing "the lived experiences of people" to mere "abstractions or to some kind of absolute "gaze," the camera eye, fixed and unchanging, through which the other is given meaning and form."[108] But it is a fact that time changes things. Perceptions and feelings do not remain the same. Hence, culture is dynamic.

107. Young, 7.
108. Mishra, "Postcolonialism 2010–2014," 387.

In response to the interdisciplinarity of postcolonial theory, Kumar criticizes it as being "highly selective, tactful, contriving, and by no means uniform across the spectrum."[109] This multi-disciplinary character, makes the theory a bit complex to comprehend and prevents it from speaking with one voice, since the reader has to be acquainted with the concerned disciplines. While its interdisciplinary nature is positive, it may lead to confusion among its students. To a certain extent, the theory is too abstract, particularly for casual readers, and the fact that it derives its examples from unfamiliar territories and disciplines may be a challenge to some readers. One must be a scholar of world history, world geography, or philosophy, and so on, to fully comprehend the theory, and its main objectives and application.

At this juncture, the question to ask is how relevant postcolonial theory was to the study of death rituals among the Karanga of Nyajena and the Shona of Zimbabwe. Despite the weaknesses of postcolonial theory, it remained crucial and relevant to this study. Zimbabwe was a colony of Britain for almost a century (1890–1980). During that period, the indigenous people of Zimbabwe were demonized, dehumanized, exploited, oppressed, and segregated against because of their skin color. Every aspect of their culture was affected by the European culture that was sold to them as being superior to the black people's culture. Christianity was offered to the people, at times, forcefully. The indigenous people's religion was demonized, and their God and ancestors condemned and insulted. Indigenous death rituals were not spared in that condemnation.

The study that resulted in this book sought to retrace the African footsteps to the death rituals among the Karanga, as they were practiced in the past, establish their meanings then and now, and identify and describe how they have changed because of their encounter with other cultures. This exploration resulted in the composition of a death rituals manual recommended for the Karanga who still want to follow the Karanga traditional burial practices.

CONCLUSION

This chapter has explored the qualitative research methodology in general, and ethnography in particular. It has been shown that a general understanding of this research methodology was important in studying

---

109. Kumar, 668.

the death rituals of the Karanga of Nyajena. Its exploration was included here to help the reader understand how the data used to compose this book was collected and analyzed. Also, research data is not collected and analyzed in a vacuum, but within a certain philosophical framework. For this book, the postcolonial theory, understood as described above, played an important role, right from the choice of the topic, up to the analysis of the collected relevant data.

Chapter 3

Shona Causes of Sickness and Death

INTRODUCTION

THIS CHAPTER EXPLORES THE causes of sickness, which may ultimately lead to death among Africans in general, and the Shona peoples in particular. It also briefly explores healing among the Shona peoples. This chapter prepares the reader for chapter 4, which reviews Shona death rituals themselves. This chapter is important because, in most cases, death is preceded by sickness, and it is imperative that some of these causes be surveyed here. Chapter 3 is divided into five sections. The first section deals with the Godly causes of sickness and death. The second section explores human causes of sickness and death. The third section deals with spiritual causes of sickness and death, not only among the Karanga, but also other Shona peoples. The fourth section briefly explores healing among the Shona. The last section deals with the cultural changes that have taken place among the Karanga of Nyajena. The primary objective of this chapter is to give a prelude and foundation to the next chapter, which deals with death rituals. Death rituals can only be performed when death happens, and death can only occur if caused by something. Hence, this chapter seeks to present the findings of some of the scholars who have explored the causes of sickness and death among African peoples.

Although the study that resulted in the writing of this book was carried out among the Karanga of Nyajena, most of the beliefs that are explored in this chapter are shared by most Shona ethnic groups. Hence, the term Shona will be used mostly, and Karanga will be used when a cause under scrutiny is exclusively practiced by the Karanga, and when discussing the cultural changes. Occasionally, the two terms, Shona and Karanga will be used interchangeably.

Among most African people, sickness or death does not just happen—there should be a cause, which is usually understood and interpreted through the concerned people's worldview. In the case of sickness, the ill person or his family usually seeks medical attention as soon as possible to restore the patient's health. In addition to the medicines or therapy that the patient may receive from his family and healers, he or his family usually wants to know the cause of his ill-health, if it is not yet known. Ordinarily, some traditional medical practitioners provide their patients with such information voluntarily. Whatever the sickness is, knowing its cause is a part of the integral healthcare plan for the patient.

If the illness leads to the sick person's demise, it is natural for the deceased's relatives to consult a diviner to learn the cause of the death, if the information is not yet available at the time of death. The knowledge of the cause of illness by the patient, his relatives, and medical practitioners is crucial because it determines the kind of medical care that should be administered to him. If the sickness ends in the death of the ailing person, as sometimes happens, the awareness of its causes is important in avoiding deaths of the same nature in the future, if preventable. It is important to note that death is generally caused by sickness, unless it is accidental, suicidal, homicidal, or caused by war. In normal circumstances, the cause of death also refers to the cause of the sickness that would have consumed the deceased. However, for the Shona peoples, even accidental and homicidal deaths, whose causes might be apparent to people with different worldviews, there is always another cause, possibly spiritual, that might be revealed by a diviner. The Shona have a proverb, which affirms this point; *Chiripo chariuraya, zizi harifi nemhepo* (There is something that has killed it because wind cannot kill an owl), which means that in matters of death or serious issues, there is always a serious cause.

GODLY CAUSES OF SICKNESS AND DEATH

All the Shona ethnicities believe in Mwari (God), who they claim to be the final authority above the ancestors, as Daneel has observed.[1] Daneel also claims that in bygone times, Mwari was elaborately worshiped at the Matonjeni Shrine, near Bulawayo, and was largely consulted in times of drought or national crises.[2] This aloofness of the Shona God caused some researchers such as Gelfand to allege that God was remote and indifferent to the daily challenges faced by his adherents.[3] Bhebe claims that Mwari of Matonjeni opted to concentrate on national issues, and by so doing had little concern for the affairs of individuals.[4] It seems there is a general agreement as to who the Shona people worshiped before Christianity was introduced. They worshiped the God of Matonjeni, the provider of rain and abundant life.

However, there have been pockets of scholars who contested the claim that the Shona of Zimbabwe worshipped God. Kollbrunner presents Fr. Rubio as having written to Fr. Kumbirai, asserting that the Shona prayed to their ancestors, who they considered the "masters of death and life," not to God.[5] This assertion is not far-fetched because the Shona do not have many rituals, which are directed to God. In fact, God is seldomly mentioned in their ritual prayers, and this can lead a researcher to conclude that God is not worshiped. This observation has been rebutted by other scholars who argue that the seemingly distant relationship between Mwari and the Shona people was not a result of his indifference but a consequence of his ability to delegate his authority to the ancestors, who took care of the daily needs of the Shona. In support of that, Thorpe states that due to the Shona God's authority, he was approached indirectly through "mediums representing ancestral spirits."[6] To prove that Mwari was active and immanent among the Shona, the people used his praise names such as Nyadenga (owner of the skies), Musikavanhu (Creator of

---

1. Daneel, *The God of the Matopo Hills*, 15.

2. Ibid., 15.

3. Gelfand, *The African Witch with Particular Reference to Witchcraft Beliefs and Practice among the Shona of Rhodesia*, 20.

4. Bhebe, *Christianity and Traditional Religion in Western Zimbabwe 1859–1923*, 19.

5. Elsener and Kollbrunner, *Traditional and Christianized Rites of Accommodating the Spirit of the Dead*, 10.

6. Thorpe, *African Traditional Religions*, 54–55.

human beings), and Dzivaguru (The Great Pool), for him. These praise names reflected the work that God had already accomplished or was doing among his people. Even though his name was not always invoked in rituals, it was a household name for all Shona peoples.

The Shona, just like many other African ethnical groups, believe that some diseases and deaths come from God, although God is never seen as evil. Aschwanden claims that the death that comes from God is believed to be a consequence of humanity's misgivings.[7] Since God is the creator of all that exists, he has the responsibility to make wayward human beings accountable for their shortcomings. The diseases or deaths caused by God can be classified into three major categories: harmless, everyday illnesses, death caused by natural forces, and death of geriatrics.

Harmless, Everyday Illnesses

Starting with the small, everyday sicknesses, the Shona believe that these are harmless, and may not require serious medical attention. These include headaches, coughing, diarrhea, toothache, abscesses, small accidents, and many others. According to Aschwanden, since these ailments are usually harmless, they are considered to come from God.[8] Chavhunduka asserts that because of their regular occurrence and fleeting nature in the life of humans, these ailments are expected to resolve completely without the intervention by medical practitioners.[9]

The Shona understand that most of these seasonal diseases are bound to happen. They know that children will have diarrhea when they are cutting their teeth, or at the onset of Spring. They understand that colds are common in Winter. They are aware that kids will suffer from chickenpox or measles at some stage during their growth. They understand that kids will suffer bruises, will be pricked by thorns, and sometimes, sustain small fractures. It is understood that if no other evil forces get involved in such ailments, the sick person will recuperate without any serious medical attention being sought. They even guess the period a particular ailment is going to linger on. They know the signs when the sickness is about to appear or disappear. They are also aware of sicknesses

---

7. Aschwanden, *Symbols of Life*, 16.
8. Ibid., 16.
9. Chavhunduka, *Traditional Medicine in Modern Zimbabwe*, 68.

that can be spread to other people, and consequently, they take preventive measures.

Even though the Shona are aware of the Godly origin of such small diseases, most people know some herbs that may be used to alleviate the discomfort and pain that are caused by some of the small diseases. It goes without saying that *Zumbani* (*Lippia Javanica*), lemons, gumtree leaves, and numerous other herbs may be boiled and taken as a tea to alleviate the effects of common colds. In most cases, no one is expected to die from any of these diseases. It is only God who knows why such diseases must happen, and God cannot be brought to court for allowing these diseases to happen. In cases where such minor ailments seem to linger on more than expected, some Shona people may begin to suspect the involvement of witches or malicious spirits. Unless foul play is suspected, most people wait for God's healing, which always comes at the right time.

Old Age

Among the Shona, a long life is a sign of blessedness. Given a choice, many people would opt for longevity. However, the Shona understand that while some people are blessed with longevity, everyone is still mortal. There always comes a time when they will die. Sometimes, those who live long lives come to a point where they embrace their finitude and start wishing for death. It is common to hear a healthy old person wishing that death was overdue, and that should not be understood as suicidal, for it is only an acknowledgment that physical life should end at some point, and give way to spiritual life.

When such people die, their relatives normally accept their deaths as the will of God. Of course, they may perform the *gata* (consulting a diviner), but it would be merely ceremonial unless there is foul play that they suspect. If they consult a diviner to learn the cause of death, they are likely to be told that the cause was old age (*kukura*) or God (*rufu gwaMwari*). Even though people who die of old age are mourned, there is usually a common understanding among the mourners that the departed are better off dead than alive. The phrase that is often heard from the relatives of such a deceased is, *vanga vakura*, which can be translated as, he was too old. It is also uncommon that consulted diviners are likely to mention old age or God as a contributing factor to the very old person's death. Hence, God and old age can be used interchangeably as the cause of the death of geriatrics.

Natural Death

Some misfortunes or even deaths are believed by the Shona to be caused by nature or God in response to human disobedience. There are certain societal and religious norms that people are expected to uphold unwaveringly, and those who transgress may be punished by God. Such deaths or misfortunes are blamed on the victims themselves because they are seen as deserving them. For instance, the Shona believe that a man who commits adultery is likely to be struck by lightning as a form of punishment from God because God controls it (lightning).[10] A woman who has committed adultery may die of childbirth or her baby may refuse to eat and breastfeed, unless the unfaithful woman confesses her sins. Also, the people who disrespect the ancestors by working on the ancestral sacred day may also be punished in the same way. This ancestral sacred day is a day dedicated to the ancestors of the land, on which all the inhabitants of that land should rest in honor of the ancestors. No work is supposed to be done on that day. Murderers that have not been apprehended, may also suffer the same consequences.

However, natural causes of sickness are intimately related to Godly causes because they are seen as punishment from either God or the ancestors. So, ultimately, they are caused by God. They differ from Godly causes in that natural causes are a result of the victim's transgressions, and that they are meted out through nature. Godly causes are not a result of an individual's sins because God's time for them to happen would have come. Natural causes are punitive measures to compel individuals to uphold the moral standards of the community. In the eyes of the Shona people, transgressors of societal norms deserve to be punished, although, at times, the whole community may be affected by the punishment.

SPIRITUAL CAUSES

As has been alluded to already, the African universe is full of spirits, both good and bad. When a person becomes sick, both evil and good spirits are suspected until a diviner exonerates either group. If evil spirits

10. Bullock, *Mashona Laws and Customs*, 66.

are involved, the family of the sick person, with the help of traditional medical practitioners, may perform some form of exorcism or spiritual appeasement. If the illness is caused by any of the good spirits, the family of the ailing person may appease the aggrieved spirit if placatable. However, in cases where a good spirit has become notoriously malevolent, the family members have the option to ostracize it, in the same manner they would cast out an evil spirit.

Evil Spirits

Evil spirits include spirits that may be related to the living family members, nameless and unrelated spirits, and *zvidhoma*. *Zvidhoma* are the spirits of people who die as children, and are resuscitated by the witches so that they can be their own evil spiritual children. Although *zvidhoma* are spiritual, the witches treat them as if they were their biological and physical children. They may send them to run their malicious errands, some of which may result in the victimized people becoming sick or even dying. They are believed to participate in witches' ghoulish nocturnal parties where they devour human flesh, which they would have exhumed from the graves. According to Crawford, *chitupwani* or *chidhoma* is believed to be the spirit of someone who has died, and is then raised by the witches, which they use to strike other people.[11] Crawford thinks that the age of the dead person does not matter because witches can snatch the spirit of anyone that they want and change it into *chidhoma*.[12]

Although the *zvidhoma* phenomenon is not very common in other parts of Africa, Parrinder refers to the spirits of the dead, which are snatched away by witches on their way to the spirit world and are turned into ghosts.[13] These spirits are believed to be sent by their owners to beat up people. They can be deadly unless immediate intervention by traditional medical practitioners is sought. It seems that Parrinder is referring to the same phenomenon of *zvidhoma*, although the Shona do not consider them to be ghosts. Different Shona ethnicities refer to *zvidhoma* using different terminologies such as *zvishiri*, *zvitupwani*, *zvikara*, *zvovusiku*, and so on. For the Shona, ghosts are harmless spirits of the

---

11. Crawford, *Witchcraft and Sorcery in Rhodesia*, 118.
12. Ibid., 118.
13. Parrinder, *African Traditional Religion*, 133.

dead that may appear to have physical bodies, and are known to appear at certain places or areas.

The Shona also believe in the existence of nameless evil spirits, popularly known as *mamhepo*, which literally means "winds." These nameless spirits are ubiquitous and may cause misfortunes, illnesses, and death. Evil spirits can be exorcized by traditional medical practitioners if they have taken possession of an individual. According to Gelfand, these strong destructive "winds" can be eliminated by consulting a diviner, who then drives medicinal pegs into the soil at the four corners of the affected village or homestead. These medicinal pegs would prevent the evil "winds" from entering the homestead.[14] Magesa reports of some malevolent spirits, which he describes as the spirits of the people who were not accorded a conventional burial, and spirits of children who would have died before going through initiation.[15] For him, these spirits may be responsible for bringing disorder and disharmony in families. He advocates for their expulsion from their families of origin, for they are good for nothing.

Avenging Spirit

The Shona demand moral uprightness from all the people, and anyone found wanting in this respect is liable to punishment by the community or the spirits. Certain violations of the moral and religious codes of conduct go undetected by the societal leaders but can never escape the never-failing scrutiny by the spiritual eyes of God or the ancestors. In some cases, the punishment comes from the spirit of the offended person. Hence, offenses such as disrespect and neglect of one's parents, murder, and failure to pay what one owes to others are offenses that attract the wrath of the *ngozi* (avenging spirit).

According to Aschwanden, the Shona word *ngozi* is derived from the word *njodzi*, "meaning danger, sorrow, misfortune."[16] Bourdillon defines *ngozi* as an angry, difficult to appease, and terrifying spirit, which "attacks suddenly and harshly," causing death and serious illness among the relatives of the person who would have offended it.[17] The spirit may

---

14. Gelfand, *An African's Religion, The Spirit of Nyajena the case of the Karanga*, 72.
15. Magesa, *African Religion*, 176.
16. Aschwanden, 38.
17. Bourdillon, 233.

be of a person who was murdered, or a person who died before receiving his remuneration, or that of a mother who was disrespected by any of her children, which comes back to haunt the perpetrator in search of justice. The relationship between the Shona people and *ngozi* is contextual. To the spirit's family, *ngozi* is considered a good spirit seeking justice and reparations for a wrong done, but for the perpetrator's family, it is a malignant spirit, which chastises even the innocent. Hence, *ngozi* is probably the most feared spirit among the Shona peoples.

There are several types of *ngozi*. Gelfand states that there are four types of *ngozi*, namely, murdered person, unpaid servant, marital spirit, and ill-treated parent; the most vengeful and unrelenting being that of a murdered person.[18] Although there are other ways of dealing with *ngozi*, Gelfand asserts that "the cure lies in making adequate recompense to the descendants of the murdered person."[19] Usually, the family of an individual who is seriously ill, or who has died, consults a diviner who mentions *ngozi* as the culprit. This consultation of a diviner is necessary because of two challenges. First *ngozi* may delay its attack for generations, as Daneel has noted.[20] At the historical point at which the attacks start, those who knew about the murder or ill-treatment of a laborer would have died. Usually, they would not have told anyone of the murder. Second, sometimes the murder is only known by the perpetrator, who may have kept it a secret. In this case, the family learns about it from a diviner, who, most of the times, is successful in encouraging the perpetrator to confess about the murder.

Symptoms of *ngozi* attacks include serious illness, unexplainable deaths, misfortunes, and mental disorders. Daneel thinks that mental disorders are the most frequent symptoms of an avenging spirit.[21] Bourdillon, quoting Crawford, claims that the family of the aggrieved spirit may try to enforce the payments of the compensation by raising or awakening the spirit of their aggrieved family member against the family of the offender.[22] They may provoke the spirit by performing rituals at the grave of the deceased as per the instructions of a diviner.

---

18. Gelfand, *Shona Rituals with Special reference to the Chaminuka Cult*, 153.
19. Gelfand, *An African's Religion, The Spirit of Nyajena the case of the Karanga*, 70.
20. Daneel, *Old and New in Southern Shona Independent Churches*, 135.
21. Ibid., 135.
22. Bourdillon, 225.

There are several remedies that those affected by an avenging spirit may employ to counteract the situation. Daneel explores three possible solutions.[23] According to him, the family being tormented by *ngozi* may, through the assistance of a traditional medical practitioner, redirect the wronged spirit back to its people. It is believed that a powerful diviner can instruct the spirit to attack its own people. Second, the diviner may instruct the family of the perpetrator to pay compensation to the relatives of the deceased. This compensation can be in the form of cows, goats, cash, or even human beings, particularly a wife. The woman who is given away as recompense for *ngozi* is required to live with the family of the murdered person. One of her responsibilities is to sweep the hut built for the *ngozi*, closer to the home of the deceased's family homestead. If the compensation involves beasts, at least one of them is slaughtered to propitiate the aggrieved spirit. Daneel asserts that some families accept the compensation begrudgingly because of the vindictiveness of *ngozi*, which can easily afflict its own people with disease if something is not done properly.[24] The third remedy, which a diviner may recommend is an exorcism of the angry spirit. According to Daneel, this exorcism can be performed by the families of the perpetrator and victim together, while standing on either side of a river. A goat is then sacrificed in the running water to cool the spirit.[25]

The other type of *ngozi* is that of the spirit of an aggrieved mother. The *ngozi* of a beaten or scolded parent brings illness, not death. This *ngozi* can be appeased by paying compensation to the relatives of one's mother. Bourdillon alleges that the compensation may include the humiliation of the offender who should dress in rags and beg for the grains needed to brew beer for a feast in honor of the aggrieved spirit of the mother. Some Shona ethnical groups call this shaming ritual, *kutanda botso*. It should be noted that the Karanga of Nyajena do not have the option of *kutanda botso* but may oblige the offender to pay compensation to his mother while still alive, or to her relatives, if the mother is dead. In like manner, among other Shona ethnicities, an offending husband may be required to live in his deceased wife's hut, while performing household chores therein as a form of punishment.

---

23. Daneel, 138.
24. Ibid., 38.
25. Ibid., 139.

The other type of *ngozi* involves the spirit of an unpaid worker who would have been aggrieved by the lack of remuneration for his labor, and comes back seeking justice. This type of *ngozi* can be appeased by the payment of compensation, although it is claimed that sometimes it is difficult to locate the relatives of this type of *ngozi*. This challenge comes from the fact that in the past, some of the domestic workers in Zimbabwe were foreigners, whose relatives were not known. In such cases, diviners would assist the victims in tracing and identifying the relatives of the offended spirit.

Crawford postulates that among the Budya of Mutoko, a murderer could prevent the deceased from becoming *ngozi* by performing some rituals soon after the murder. He claims that one of the ways to prevent the effects of *ngozi* was for the perpetrator to eat the *muputi/mutimwi* (waist medicinal string) of the murdered person. Alternatively, the murderer could eat the blood from the victim's private parts, little fingers or toes, ears, heart, or tongue.[26] This ritual was believed to prevent the murdered person from becoming *ngozi*.

Ngozi should be prevented at all costs because its attacks are not necessarily directed at the perpetrator but other family members. Hence, it divides the family as members accuse each other of having caused the *ngozi* attacks. In some cases, different family members may begin to seek medication secretly, and by so doing directing the attacks to another family member. Those family members may also do the same until he who has the strongest traditional medical practitioner triumphs. The Shona consider this way of dealing with the avenging spirit unhelpful because it does not resolve the issue but worsens it by tossing the *ngozi* around, which makes it more malevolent.

Ancestors

The Shona define ancestors as the deceased spiritual and invisible members of a family, who would have been initiated into ancestorhood and invited back home through several rituals performed by their family members. Mbiti paradoxically calls them, "the living-dead," who he defines as the departed of up to five generations, who are "in a state of personal immortality, and their process of dying is not yet complete."[27]

26. Crawford, 88.
27. Mbiti, *African Religions, and Philosophy, Second Edition*, 81, 82.

They are still people and have not yet become things, because they are interested in the affairs of their families, they symbolically share food with family members, are recognized by their names, and they participate in family activities and rituals.[28] They are dead because they died, and were buried, and no longer possess the physical human body. They may reveal their presence and needs through dreams, visions, or diviners, as Anderson has put it. Although they are in the spiritual form, they continue to be active in family affairs.[29]

Not everyone can become an ancestor after death, for there are qualifications and disqualifications that the deceased should have fulfilled or avoided respectively, during his physical life. One should have been married, and presumably begotten children. Among the Shona, these children would be responsible for performing the *magadziro* (making an ancestor ceremony), a ritual, which incorporates the deceased's spirit back into the family as an ancestor. Even though the spirit of the deceased and perhaps other family ancestors may demand the *magadziro* ritual, they can only demand it from the offspring of the deceased. That is why marriage is crucial among Africans.

In addition to that, one should have lived a long and fruitful life, which does not necessarily refer to the number of years lived, but also to having descendants who would inherit one's name. A long life is a sign of blessedness and fulfillment among the Shona. Mbiti claims that a spirit remains an ancestor as long as there is a member of the family who remembers it.[30] Once remembrance ceases, the spirit stops to be an ancestor and drifts into the world of nameless spirits. Opoku, with reference to his observation of the Akan of Ghana, states that for the deceased to become an ancestor, he should have lived a fruitful, long, worthy of emulation life, and would have died a good death. According to him, people who die from suicide, accidents, violence, lunacy, dropsy, leprosy, and epilepsy are disqualified from becoming ancestors.[31] The same qualifications and disqualifications are echoed by Ikenga-Metuh, who also maintains that the deceased should have lived a life of acceptable moral standards.[32] It appears that Africans think that if the spirit of a person who would have

---

28. Ibid., 82.
29. Anderson, *Zion and Pentecost*, 181.
30. Mbiti, *African Religions, and Philosophy*, 2nd Edition, 83.
31. Opoku, *West African Traditional Religion*, 36.
32. Ikenga-Metuh, *Comparative Studies of African Traditional Religions*, 147.

died of any of the tabooed deaths is allowed to come back home as an ancestor, he may cause one of the family members to die the same way or by the same disease.

Ancestors do have several responsibilities. Gelfand says that ancestors protect their family members from harm; hence they merit the title, "guardian spirits."[33] They can safeguard the well-being of their relatives because they see what the living members of their families cannot. In addition to that, they do have the ability to defend them. Quarcoopome, writing from a West African perspective, asserts that ancestors are "guardians and policemen of public and private morality, and unseen presidents at family meetings," who are the intermediaries between their living family members and the divinities.[34] In support of that Mbiti holds that "ancestors are guardians of family affairs," ethics, traditions, and other activities, and as such, they are the "invisible police officers" of the people.[35] Africans believe that ancestors are very capable of being police officers of morality because they can see what humans cannot see. They do not only apprehend transgressors of societal norms, but they also judge and mete out punishment to them. Parrinder affirms that ancestors are concerned with everything that affects their families, particularly health and fertility.[36] They also own the land, which they make fecund by providing the rain. Olupona postulates that ancestors also assist in holding families together.[37]

Ancestors are at the center of African spirituality, and there have been debates as to whether they can or cannot cause sickness and death to one of their own family members. On the one hand, some scholars believe that ancestors can cause serious harm to their family members if aggrieved. According to Olupona, "a certain amount of unpredictability is a characteristic of all ancestors," for they can be vengeful spirits if offended. Several things can offend the ancestors. Gelfand asserts that ancestors can be annoyed if one of the family members decides to go away to live in town or elsewhere, far away from the rural home, for one should remain in the village where his umbilical cord is buried.[38] Living away from

33. Gelfand, *Shona Religion, with Special Reference to the Makorekore*, 51.
34. Quarcoopome, 139.
35. Mbiti, *African Religions, and Philosophy*, 2nd Edition, 82.
36. Parrinder, *African Traditional Religion*, 59.
37. Olupona, "Spiritual Beings as Agents of Illness," 167.
38. Gelfand, *An African's Religion, The Spirit of Nyajena the case of the Karanga*, 62, 63.

home may prevent the family member from attending ancestral rituals at home, and this neglect of rituals may cause him to forget his family traditions. In the past, if going to live away from home could not be avoided, ancestors had to be told about it and asked for their protection.

But it should be noted that ancestors do not just punish people randomly. Gelfand contends that a family that "leads a good clean life, according to the tenets of its faith, the *vadzimu* (ancestors) are unlikely to trouble it."[39] In support of that, Magesa insists that ancestors bring misfortunes upon their own families for two reasons.[40] First, the punishment would be good for the order of the universe. Second, the disciplinary measures would be good for the well-being of the people and their communities. For Magesa, the penal measures, though painful, are intended to correct the attitude and behavior of their descendants.[41] He claims that the afflictions from ancestors are the deserved consequences of some family members' misdemeanors.

Echoing the same sentiments, Kayode contends that ancestors do not just punish good people, but the neglectful and disobedient.[42] Those who neglect their family and communal responsibilities are likely to face the wrath of the ancestors. He claims that their punitive measures are more severe for the people who violate the prescribed discipline and ignore the duties they do owe to their family members and the community.

According to Mbiti, ancestral anger can be ignited by several offenses such as rendering improper burial to the departed, neglect to offer ancestors food and libations, and failure to observe their instructions.[43] Those who perform their family and communal duties have no reason to fear and resent ancestors. Chavhunduka mentions incest as one of the causes of ancestral anger.[44] He claims that the aggrieved ancestors may withhold the rains, which may bring about the indiscriminate suffering of both people and animals. In the case of a drought, even innocent people are bound to suffer because of the transgressions of an individual. That is why, in African societies, everyone is supposed to be his brother's or sister's, keeper.

39. Gelfand, *Shona Religion, with Special Reference to the Makorekore*, 52.
40. Magesa, 50.
41. Ibid., 80.
42. Kayode, *Understanding African Traditional Religion*, 19.
43. Mbiti, *African Religions, and Philosophy, 2nd Edition*, 83.
44. Chavhunduka, 59.

It looks like the majority of scholars concur that ancestors may punish their family members to enforce the moral standards of the African society. However, some scholars strongly disagree that ancestors directly cause sickness, misfortunes, or even death. Such scholars argue that ancestors do not directly cause misfortunes, but merely withdraw their protection, leaving their family members vulnerable to attacks from the evil spirits and witches. According to Gelfand, the Shona do not believe that *mudzimu* (ancestor) can kill or cause the death of a relative.[45] For him, if a death is not from natural causes, it should be attributed to witches and *ngozi*, and never to ancestors. In fact, there is no much evidence that ancestors ever cause death because they usually relent even if they are not appeased.

It appears that ancestors may not directly cause sickness or death of their relatives, but their withdrawal of protection endangers their family members, who are then exposed to attacks by witches and evil spirits. Therefore, they too may be guilty of complicit for the misfortunes that befall their family members. Although ancestors can be appeased easily, they would have caused pain and suffering in the first place. It should be noted that sickness of any kind weakens the ailing person, and may expose him to more diseases in the future.

Alien Spirits

The Shona believe that some sicknesses are caused by alien spirits (*mashavi*). These are spirits of people who die away from home and are not accorded proper burial rites, and of those who are disqualified from becoming ancestors, which seek recognition among strangers. Gelfand defines *mashavi* as spirits of foreigners who die and are buried in a strange land, which "wander around the country searching for suitable mediums or hosts to possess."[46] Daneel affirms Gelfand's definition of *mashavi* by referring to them as "spirits that come from afar, from underground, from the deep pool or merely from distant places."[47] The bottom line is that *mashivi* are spirits of people who are unrelated to the hosts.

Bucher mentions the controversial phenomenon of animal *mashavi*. It is believed that the spirits of animals such as baboons may possess

---

45. Gelfand, *Shona Religion, with Special Reference to the Makorekore*, 124.
46. Gelfand, *Shona Rituals with Special reference to the Chaminuka Cult*, 121.
47. Daneel, 128.

people and impart on them some of their natural traits.[48] Since *mashavi* are not ancestors, they are not readily accepted by their hosts. Usually, they impose themselves on the chosen hosts and eventually persuade them to accept and offer them rituals in exchange for certain talents and gifts. Bucher calls this acceptance of alien spirits "accreditation," which may take some arm-twisting of the host by the desperate spirit.[49]

There are many types of *mashavi*. Daneel identifies the *jukwa* alien spirits which have rainmaking capabilities.[50] These are believed to have originated from Matonjeni, which was the shrine of Mwari. According to Chigwedere, the Zungu *shavi* originated from the Portuguese.[51] Gelfand claims that the Mazungu *shavi* has its origins in the people from Mozambique, who died in Mashonaland.[52] The Zungu *shavi* bestows hunting and healing skills on its host. Madzviti *shavi* is said to have arisen from the Ndebele warriors who died away from home, during their raids. Gelfand lists many other types of *mashavi*, such as Masongono, Bveni, Zvipenzi, Murozvi, and Shangana. Each type of alien spirits conveys particular gifts, such as hunting, farming, healing, divination, or fighting, unto its host.[53] The anti-social alien spirits may pass on undesirable gifts such as stealing, witchcraft, laziness, and many other harmful traits to their hosts.

It is believed that before the alien spirits find a willing host, they are aggrieved because of several reasons. First, they may have perished in distant places and could have been laid to rest there. Second, since they died in faraway places and buried among foreigners, they might not have been accorded proper burial rituals as befitting their own traditions. Third, it takes some doing for such spirits to find a willing host, and that is why they have to pressure the intended host to accept them. As a matter of fact, very few people are ready to pay homage to *mashavi* unless they are promised some rewarding talents such as healing, hunting, divination, among others. So, to announce their desire to possess an individual, and to enforce their acceptance, alien spirits usually cause sickness to the chosen person. If the chosen person is still a child, as is

48. Bucher, *Spirits and Power*, 89.
49. Ibid., 89.
50. Daneel, 129.
51. Chigwedere, *From Mutapa to Rhodes 1000 to 1890 A. D.*, 58.
52. Gelfand, *Shona Rituals with Special reference to the Chaminuka Cult*, 121.
53. Ibid., 121–125.

sometimes the case, her parents may consult a diviner concerning the cause of the sickness. Usually, the parents are told about the *shavi* and the gifts that it intends to offer the host. They are also told about the type of ritual they should perform to accept the spirit. Once accepted, the host's health should be restored. She also is expected to receive the promised gifts soon afterwards.

It is believed that the *shavi* spirit does not cause death, and the illness is expected to go away as soon as the initiation ritual, which is attended by the family members of the hosts, neighbors, and a diviner is performed. Most of the *mashavi* are expected to possess their hosts at the acceptance ritual. Once accredited, the spirit should be appeased regularly. According to Rayner, the spirit has to be appeased by clothes, food, ornaments, and blood, in repayment of the special skills imparted on the medium.[54]

HUMAN CAUSES

There are basically two causes of sickness and death, which are caused by human beings, either on their own volition or under the influence of some spirits. The two causes are witches and *mhondi* (murderers). Most witches choose to be witches and to engage in witchcraft business. Likewise, most *mhondi* choose to murder people for one reason or another. However, the Shona believe that some of the people who become witches are coerced into the practice by some evil spirits. The same applies to *mhondi*, some of whom are also believed to operate under the influence of some spiritual forces. Although the Shona understand that these evil spirits may compel good people to harm others, the human perpetrators should be held accountable for the outcome of their actions. For the purpose of this study, this passage will only explore witchcraft.

Witchcraft

The commonest and most feared cause of sickness or death among the Shona, and perhaps among many other African ethnical groups is *huroyi* (witchcraft). According to Magesa, "In the African mentality, everything wrong or bad in society and in the world, and, most particularly, various

---

54. Rayner, *The Tribe and Its Successors*, 101.

afflictions, originate in witchcraft."[55] Technically, a person who practices witchcraft is called a witch if she is a woman, and a wizard if he is a man. However, most Shona people refer to either a man or a woman who practices witchcraft as *muroyi*, which is applicable to both genders. Hence, either a male or female *muroyi* is popularly called a witch.

There are two different, yet related conceptions of a witch among the Shona. First, the word "witch" can refer to any bad, envious, and individualistic person, as Chavhunduka has noted.[56] Bourdillon includes, in this category of witchcraft, selfish people and those who break serious taboos, particularly those who commit incest. Incest is considered to be so evil that only extremely evil people practice it.[57] So, anybody has the potential of becoming a witch, if one is to go by Chavhunduka's opinion. However, this kind of witchcraft seems to derive its meaning from the real witchcraft, which this passage explores.

Second, most Shona conceive of a witch as an extremely evil person, who harms others secretly and mysteriously by the employment of evil powers and harmful concoctions. Shorter points out that the witches' power is "essentially and implacably evil."[58] The Shona witch is different from the witches found among some ethnical groups in West Africa, where witchcraft is believed to be a vital force or potential that may manifest in the practicing of witchcraft if cultivated, as Magesa has observed.[59] Similarly, Evans-Pritchard alleges that among the Azande, witchcraft is seen as a substance in the body, which, due to certain favorable elements may manifest into full-fledged witchcraft. In this case, everyone has the potential of becoming a witch.[60]

Even though scholars may differ in their conceptions of witchcraft, most agree on the common characteristic of a witch. It is believed that both men and women may practice witchcraft, but the majority of witches are women. In support of this general claim, Parrinder asserts that witches are usually women, although men also engage in the trade.[61] Bourdillon and several other scholars concur that witches act secretly

---

55. Magesa, 182.
56. Chavhunduka, 86.
57. Bourdillon, 181–182.
58. Shorter, *African Culture and Christian Church*, 138.
59. Magesa, 182.
60. Evans-Pritchard, *Witchcraft, Oracles, and Magic Among the Zande*, 1.
61. Parrinder, *Witchcraft*, 138, 139, 143.

in the dark, desecrate graves, may kill people, and devour their victims' flesh.[62] Witches commit other heinous crimes such as harming their family members as an initiation ritual into the witchcraft trade, committing incest, and engaging in intercourse with spirits and animals. Bourdillon refers to these despicable sexual activities as "orgies," which involve witches, spirits, and familiars.[63] Elsewhere, Bourdillon claims that witches work in cohorts, attend nocturnal gatherings, where they perform contemptible rituals which include, "dancing naked, disturbing graves, eating human flesh," and engaging in other outrageous behaviors.[64] Concerning the eating of the victim's flesh by witches, Parrinder, writing about other African ethnicities, alleges that witches only eat the flesh symbolically, without harming the body.[65] He claims that they rather eat the victim's soul. However, among the Shona, the grisly devouring of human flesh by witches is believed to be real, not symbolic.

Gelfand postulates that witches become invisible when on duty, and may use animals such as snakes, hyenas, and owls during their bewitching errands.[66] It is believed that they can manipulate snakes, which they send to bite their victims. They may also ride on hyenas as they travel from one homestead to another. Witches can also change themselves into such animals. While most witches operate at night, there are also some witches that operate during the day. Such daylight witches clandestinely place harmful medicine along the targeted person's path or may poison the food of their victims. Elsewhere, this type of witchcraft would be referred to as sorcery. For the Shona, there is no clear distinction between sorcery and witchcraft, for all employment of evil to harm others is called witchcraft.

There are several methods of witchcraft acquisition among the Shona. Hereditary witches are those who inherit witchcraft from their parents or grandparents. Such witchcraft is usually passed on to one daughter by her mother.[67] Akrong alleges that in Ghana, witchcraft can

62. Bourdillon, "Witchcraft and Society," 176.
63. Bourdillon, *Religion and Society*, 189.
64. Bourdillon, "Witchcraft and Society," 176.
65. Parrinder, *Witchcraft*, 147, 149.
66. Gelfand, *An African's Religion, The Spirit of Nyajena the case of the Karanga*, 74, 75.
67. Gelfand, *The African Witch with Particular Reference to Witchcraft Beliefs and Practice
among the Shona of Rhodesia*, 26.

be inherited at birth or from a contaminated mother.[68] Some witchcraft is imparted on the recipient by a bewitching spirit. According to Chavhunduka, the bewitching spirit may be either of a relative or stranger who was a witch.[69] Since such witches practice witchcraft under the possession of the bewitching spirit, Bourdillon claims that they may not have awareness of their abominable activities.[70] However, it is believed that some of them may have weird dreams, which may alert them as to their possession by the bewitching spirits. Some may become aware of their activities after being identified by a diviner. Other people may acquire witchcraft through training or receiving instructions from a senior witch, as noted by Rayner.[71] It is also believed that people can purchase witchcraft from seasoned witches. In support of this belief, Haar, writing about Ghanaian witchcraft, says that men can purchase their witchcraft from those who already possess it.[72]

There are many other types of witchcraft in addition to the night witchcraft that has been described above. For instance, there are also agricultural witches who possess *divisi*, which according to Gelfand is the medicine that is mixed with soil and scattered in the field to enhance one's agricultural produce.[73] Furthermore, some witches use protective medicine called *rukwa*, which is used to safeguard the owner's properties from thieves. *Rukwa* is considered witchcraft because it endangers people who may steal the property. The Shona understand that stealing is evil, but it is a pernicious offense to endanger other people for stealing your property. Rodlach writes about the love potion as another type of witchcraft, which is believed to be added to the food of men who are suspected of having extra-marital affairs, and is believed to influence the behavior of such men. It prevents such men from falling in love with other women.[74]

There are several reasons that may compel witches to bewitch someone. It is believed that they may do that because of jealous, particularly when their victim is more successful than them, in agriculture,

---

68. Akrong, "A Phenomenology of Witchcraft in Ghana," 54.
69. Chavhunduka, 92.
70. Bourdillon, *The Shona Peoples*, 179.
71. Rayner, 87.
72. Haar, "Ghanaian Witchcraft Beliefs: A View from the Netherlands," 106.
73. Gelfand, *An African's Religion, The Spirit of Nyajena the case of the Karanga*, 79.
74. Rodlach, *Witches, Westerners, and HIV*, 89.

hunting, and other economic enterprises. Witches may bewitch a person who they hate because of reasons sometimes only known to themselves. Some grudge against one of the witches may spring them into action. Moreover, they may bewitch someone to devour his flesh at their nightly cannibalistic meetings.[75]

People can protect themselves from the effects of witchcraft. One of the preventive measures that the Shona employ is medicinal waist belts (*mazango*). In the past, these *mazango* were tied around the waists of almost every baby since it was believed that babies were extremely vulnerable to attacks by evil spirits and witches. Sometimes, people would use medicinal pegs, which they would drive into the soil around their homesteads to prevent witches and evil spirits from entering. Staying free of grudges may also help since most witchcraft accusations happen where there is social friction. Usually, people accuse their enemies of witchcraft. Resettling far away from the witch, exorcism, and expulsion of the witch are some of the protective measures that can be used by the Shona to prevent attacks.

Even though witches are believed to do their business secretly in the dark, there are ways used to identify them. Bourdillon claims that one's natural bodily disposition may lead to witchcraft accusations.[76] For instance, a woman of sulky disposition, morose demeanor, and reserved character may be suspected of witchcraft. Sometimes, the family of the victims may consult a diviner about the causes of sickness, and are then told of the involvement of a witch. In the past, most diviners readily named the witch, which became a criminal offense after the enactment of the Witchcraft Suppression Act of 1899.

Furthermore, some ordinary people claim to see witches in dreams and visions. In Zimbabwe, there is a group of diviners called *tsikamutanda*, who move from village to village for the sake of identifying witches. The identified witches, who profess the need to get rid of it, are then exorcised of their witchcraft for a fee.

There have been debates as to whether witchcraft as it is understood by the Shona, exists in reality, or as a mere figment of their imagination. Contributors to this controversy interpret the phenomenon from three primary angles. One school of thought argues that witchcraft does not exist in reality. The second school of thought, which is populated by

---

75. Bourdillon, *Religion and Society*, 189.
76. Bourdillon, *The Shona Peoples*, 185.

ordinary adherents of African Traditional Religion insists that witchcraft exists in reality, and its existence can only be ignored at one's own peril. The third school of thought belongs to those who are sitting on the fence. These are indifferent. They neither confirm nor deny the existence of witchcraft.

The people who argue for the existence of witchcraft provide evidence for their position. They argue that some people have confessed to being witches without being forced to do so.[77] These people would not confess to being witches if they were not. Crawford explores several confessions by witches concerning their nefarious activities, which they are said to have voluntarily given. He provides the names of the witches and their victims (dead and alive), and the vivid narratives of how they acquired witchcraft.[78] The people and scholars who hold that witchcraft is a reality take such confessions as irrefutable evidence for the existence of witchcraft. Bourdillon also affirms the evidence from the witch's confessions.[79] Parrinder, writing on a different forum, presents confessions by witches in which some claimed to have bewitched even their own children.[80]

Second, some people are believed to have been bewitched. According to Bourdillon, some people are said to have died after receiving threats by a witch.[81] Usually, these threats come after the witch would have been upset because of something. Some people are reported to have issued such threats when one of their family members was sick. In those threats, the suspected witches are dared to reverse the effects of their witchcraft or face retaliation by the one issuing the threats. Other people give such threats to retaliate for an evil done to themselves or one of their family members.

The third piece of evidence for the existence of witchcraft involves patients whose ailments may resist Western medicines. Bourdillon alleges that sometimes sickness and deaths which Western medicines and medical practitioners cannot cure or explain, respectively, occur.[82] Where there is no clear explanation as to the cause of sickness or death, some

---

77. Bourdillon, *Religion and Society*, 209.
78. Crawford, 45–58.
79. Bourdillon, *The Shona Peoples*, 174.
80. Parrinder, *Witchcraft*, 161–165.
81. Bourdillon, *The Shona Peoples*, 174.
82. Ibid., 174.

Shona people would perceive the involvement of witches. As a matter of fact, some people claim that the Western medical practitioners sometimes instruct them to take their ailing family members to the traditional medical practitioners when they suspect witchcraft as the cause of illness.

The universality of the belief in witchcraft, particularly in Africa has been offered as another vital piece of evidence concerning the reality of witchcraft. It has been argued that all these believers of witchcraft cannot be wrong. Supporters of this argument seem to subscribe to the philosophy that says the majority are likely to be right.

Finally, Chitakure argues that even though ordinary people cannot identify witches, there are specialists who can do that. The same can be said about Western health systems.[83] There are causes of diseases that can only be identified by those who are trained to do so using special instruments that are made to detect gems and other causes of illness. There is no reason to disagree with their diagnosis because they possess the knowledge to speak to that competently and authoritatively. In African Traditional Religion, traditional medical practitioners possess the knowledge and authority to identify sicknesses caused by witchcraft. They have the power to see what the ordinary eyes cannot. They are health specialists, and their diagnosis should be believed.

On the other hand, some scholars argue that witchcraft does not exist. They too have their own evidence to support their views. Shorter postulates that witches' confessions may not be used as evidence for the existence of witchcraft because some people may confess just to attain power.[84] Most Africans are afraid of witches, and they are likely to fear people who claim to be witches. The people confessing to be witches might not be witches at all.

In addition to that, Shorter contends that witchcraft accusations may be a psychological outlet for repressed "frustration and hostility."[85] Most of the time, people suspect their enemies of witchcraft, not friends. For him, there is a pattern of tension and conflict among the so-called victims and perpetrators of witchcraft. Therefore, what people claim to be witchcraft is just a way of venting their own frustrations.

Furthermore, since witchcraft can be practiced by people without their knowledge, there is very little defense if accused. If the accused

---

83. Chitakure, *African Traditional Religion Encounters Christianity*, 131.
84. Shorter, *African Culture and Christian Church*, 142.
85. Ibid., 140.

denies being a witch, the accusers are likely to point out that she practices witchcraft under the possession of a spirit, which prevents her from knowing her wicked activities. In support of that argument, Evans-Pritchard asserts that to deny that one is a witch is against the custom because it is possible to be a witch without knowing it.[86] This custom creates doubts in the accused because one can never be convinced of being guilty of some crime which one has no awareness of committing.

It has also been argued that since the majority of witches are women, some accusations may be a result of patriarchal marginalization of women.[87] According to Akrong, the women accused of witchcraft may be marginalized, ostracized, humiliated, tortured, or even killed.[88] Once they are accused of witchcraft, they have no one to empathize with them, when their human rights are trashed. People would feel that the accused women deserve punishment. So, it seems that these accusations are biased against women because they do not have the same power as men have.

Although doubts have been cast on the existence of witchcraft, many Africans still believe in its existence. Bourdillon asserts that, while the existence of witchcraft cannot be proved, its existence cannot be disapproved as well.[89] Perhaps, the biggest question is not about its existence or non-existence, but about the belief in its existence. Africans believe that witchcraft is the biggest cause of sickness, misfortunes, and death.

HEALING

Whenever one becomes sick, the Shona provide the sick person with medicinal herbs that are intended to cure him of his ailments. Almost everyone knows some of the common healing herbs that can be used. Most common illnesses are cured this way. However, when some sickness lingers on, or is so severe, the Shona usually consult a traditional healer for more effective medicines, and also to learn the cause of the sickness. If the sickness ends with death, the diviner is consulted concerning the cause of such an eventuality. The consultation of a diviner to inquire about the cause of death is called *gata*, and is sometimes required

---

86. Evans-Pritchard, *Witchcraft, Oracles, and Magic Among the Zande*, 59.
87. Shorter, *African Culture and Christian Church*, 140.
88. Akrong, 63–64.
89. Bourdillon, *Religion and Society*, 188.

before the performance of certain post-burial rituals, such as *magadziro* (Cleansing Ceremony), which will be dealt with in chapter 3.

Traditional healers are known by many different names, such as traditional medical practitioners, mediums, and derogatorily as "witchdoctors." The Shona call them *n'anga* or *chiremba*. *N'anga* can be classified into two major categories. Herbalists are those traditional healers who specialize in therapeutic herbs. Some would have acquired such knowledge from other herbalists. Others attain their herbal skills through the inspiration of the spirits that possess them. There are also traditional healers, who solely use spirits in their healing activities, and may have the ability to divine the cause of sickness or death. Their gifts are imparted onto them either by the ancestral or stranger spirits called *mashavi*.

Gelfand explores the different types of alien spirits and the skills that they give to their hosts.[90] The diviners can consult their *hakata* (bones), concerning the causes of sickness or death. Gelfand explains how these *hakata* are made and used to determine the cause of sickness or death. Some traditional healers can do both divination and healing. Bucher (describes divination as a process of putting questions to the *hakata* (dice) before they are thrown into the air, and falling to the ground.[91] Their significance can then be read from the position in which they land on the ground. There is no skill needed in throwing the *hakata* into the air, but in interpreting the meaning of their position as they settle on the ground.

For one to become a *n'anga*, one should be called by the spirit which wants to use him. Bucher holds that the spirit may call the host in dreams in which he sees the spirit instructing him to perform certain tasks.[92] In other cases, the chosen host becomes seriously sick. If the targeted host is a married woman, she may become temporarily barren. The family members of the sick person or barren woman may consult a diviner who is likely to alert them of the demands of the spirit. The family may consult more than one *n'anga*, until they are satisfied of the verdict. The healer is likely to tell them what the spirit will offer in exchange for its acceptance. They then perform a ritual in honor of the "invading spirit." If the spirit is a healer, the host eventually becomes a healer.

This chapter has reviewed the literature on the causes of sickness and death among the Shona people. The identified causes were explored

---

90. Gelfand, *Shona Religion, with Special Reference to the Makorekore*, 88–117.
91. Ibid., 117.
92. Ibid., 114.

under three major categories: Godly, spiritual, and human causes of sickness and death. It should be noted that when a Shona person is sick, the aim of his family is to assist him to recuperate naturally. This natural healing may be accompanied by the use of common herbs. If the sick person does not heal, or if he becomes seriously ill, his relatives are likely to consult a diviner to find out the cause of the ailment. The Shona may also seek the help of the traditional healer to cure the sick person. The Shona believe that most ailments can be cured using common herbs. However, at times, the sick person does not recuperate; he dies. If the sickness leads to the ailing person's demise, many rituals are performed to initiate the spirit of the deceased into the realm of ancestors, and the literature that deals with such rituals is reviewed in chapters 3 and 4.

CULTURAL CHANGES

Even though the above-explored Shona beliefs concerning the causes of sickness and death have changed, this section focuses on the changes that have taken place among the Karanga of Nyajena. The Karanga beliefs about the causes of death and sickness have significantly changed mostly because of the establishment of hospitals and the demonization of traditional practices by Christians. When a person is sick with what is considered a natural ailment such as influenza, most Karanga people look for herbs to give to that person. Ordinarily, these minor sicknesses are believed to come from God through nature. However, if the sickness lingers on or is very serious, the sick person goes to the clinic or hospital. Most patients do not try to go to the traditional healers first because witchcraft may not be suspected at this point. Most people now believe that there are biological and natural causes of sicknesses. They accept that mosquitoes cause malaria. They accept that cancer is one of the major causes of death. They also accept that some diseases are infectious. It seems that the natural causes have been accepted by most Karanga people thereby lessening the accusations on witches.

However, if the ailing person is taken to the hospital to receive Western medical care to no avail, the fear that the sickness might have been caused by witchcraft creeps in. The patient may be taken to a traditional healer, or his relatives may visit a diviner to find out the cause of his sickness. This consultation may be done when the person is still hospitalized. It seems that when sickness becomes more serious, the relatives are likely to go back to their traditions, which sometimes brings about tension between the Karanga traditionalists and Christians. This is prevalent among the people who live in the rural areas. If they consult a diviner, they are likely to be told that witchcraft, the avenging spirit, ancestors, God, or alien spirits are the causes of the sickness or even death. What this means is that, if the sickness is quickly cured after taking natural herbs, visiting the local clinic, or the hospital, the diviner may not be consulted concerning the cause. But if the illness becomes more serious, or the ill person dies, then the diviner may be consulted.

However, the diviner is not allowed to name the witch because of the Witchcraft Suppression Act Chapter 9:19: Ord. 14/1899, Acts 18/1989 (s. 11)., 22/2001, which outlaws the imputation of anyone for using non-natural means in causing disease in any person or animal. Despite the criminalization of naming witches, some diviners still do it, though they can face litigation if reported. Some Karanga use the traditional means of healthcare as a last resort. Even those people who refuse to go to the hospital when they are ill, they are likely to be taken to the hospital against their will by members of their families when the illness becomes more serious. At the hospital, the sick person and his family are told of the biological causes of the sickness.

It seems that the Karanga have benefited immensely from both the traditional and Western healthcare systems. Most of them always try both healthcare systems to their own advantage. However, some Christian ministers forbid their own followers to use both Western and traditional healthcare systems. Such churches believe in faith healing. Some members of these churches have been criticized for failing to immunize their children or using Western family planning methods. The participants named a few members of such churches who live in their villages.

On the other hand, some Karanga of Nyajena use all the three methods of healing namely, hospitals, traditional healers, and Christian faith healers. Those Karanga who are Christians, are reported to start with faith healing and prayers, and if the patient does not recuperate, they go to the local clinics or hospitals. There are at least four local clinics in Nyajena, namely, Guwa Clinic, Musvovi Clinic, Nyikavanhu Clinic, and Renco Mine clinic. There is only one government hospital called Muchibwa, which is the only referral center in Nyajena. If the illness cannot be cured at Muchibwa, the patient may be referred to Morgenster Hospital, which belongs to the Reformed Church in Zimbabwe. This hospital has more advanced medical equipment and acts as the hospital of choice for broken bones, pregnant women, and eye patients. However, some patients may be taken to Chiredzi Hospital, Masvingo General Hospital, or any other hospital deemed appropriate by their families and the medical practitioner who would have referred them.

If the patient becomes more seriously ill, he is taken to one of the major hospitals. If nothing changes, the family may use both hospitals and traditional healers. It looks like the Karanga of Nyajena are enjoying the best of the three worlds. This phenomenon may be called trite religiosity. He who has three ways of killing a cat stands a better chance of succeeding than the one who has only one method. The people of Nyajena have traditional healers, faith healers, and hospitals, and some use all at some point in their lives. It seems that the cultural changes experienced in this aspect are more beneficial to the people of Nyajena. The biggest challenge that was mentioned by the participants is that some people may delay taking the sick person to the hospital, while using traditional medicines to no avail. By the time they take the sick person to the hospital, it would be too late, and the patient dies.

Some of the interviewees in this study suggested that sick people should first go to the hospital, and if they do not become better, they should go to traditional and faith healers. However, other participants disagreed, arguing that both Western and African medicines should be tried simultaneously. While the Western medical practices have become more acceptable to the Karanga of Nyajena, there is still doubt as to the causes of sickness that Westerners give. One of my informants retorted, "Yes, there could be gems and viruses that cause diseases, but where do they come from? I believe that they are caused by witches and evil spirits. I think that we are talking about the same thing."

This study found out that many people still consider witchcraft to be the main killer of their relatives even though they know of bacteria, viruses, and other biological causes of sickness and death.

CONCLUSION

Whenever sickness happens, the Shona peoples' first reaction is to heal the sick person using common herbs, but if the sickness persists, they take the sick person to the hospital. If the hospital fails to cure the ailment, they usually consult a diviner to find out the causes of the sickness and the most effective remedies that can be used. If the sickness leads to death, again the diviner is consulted to find out the cause of the death. If a very old person dies, the consultation is still done. It has been noted that some of these rituals and understanding of sickness have changed because of the encounter between the Shona and people of other cultures.

Chapter 4

KARANGA PRE-BURIAL RITUALS

INTRODUCTION

THIS CHAPTER DEALS WITH pre-burial rituals, which refer to the rites that are performed before death occurs, particularly when the proximity of death is anticipated. Pre-burial rituals are performed from the time a person is grievously or terminally ill until the deceased's body finally leaves home for burial. These rituals include, but are not limited to *bembera*, divination (*gumbwa*), relocation of the terminally ill person to some other place outside the home (*kusengudza*), accompaniment or watching of the ill person (*kurindira*), visitation of the ill person (*kuvona mugwere*), burning of python fat, and the certification of death. Usually, the performance of these rituals can either be done by the family of the terminally ill person even without his consent or can be requested by the sick person if at this time, he is able to make such decisions.

The chapter builds on the process that began in chapter 3 by navigating the pre-burial rituals as they are performed, not only by the Karanga of Zimbabwe, but also by other Shona and African peoples. Although the study that resulted in the writing of this book was carried out among the Karanga of Nyajena, most of the rituals that are explored here are shared by most Shona ethnic groups. As has been alluded to earlier, the term Shona will also be used here. However, the term Karanga will be used when the ritual under discussion is exclusively practiced by the Karanga, and when discussing the cultural changes. Occasionally, the two terms, Shona and Karanga will be used interchangeably. Most of the rituals described here are performed for people who die or are buried at home. It should be noted that due to increasing urbanization in Zimbabwe, people who die at hospitals and in cities may not be awarded most of the death rituals described in this chapter. Since some of the bodies of people who die in towns are taken to funeral parlors, the undertakers who work there may use modern ways to deal with some of the rituals described in this chapter.

THE INEVITABILITY OF DEATH, AND IMPORTANCE OF RITUALS

It is incontestable that all human beings are mortal. They are born today, live their lives, and die tomorrow. It is true that human beings have progressed in mitigating the occurrence of certain undesirable things that may cause suffering and pain to themselves, but they have not yet managed to prevent the occurrence of death. To a certain extent, they can use medicines and other medical methods to delay its coming, but they cannot stop it from happening. Hence, death is inevitable, and at times, untimely. The inevitability and untimeliness of death neither make people accustomed to it, nor persuade them to embrace it as part of life. For many people, the fear of death is so great that most would attempt to evade it if given that option.

The fear of death stems from the fact that death marks the end of human physical lives, and heralds the beginning of another mysterious and supposedly everlasting life. Even though the existence of a more qualitative life after death has been peddled for many centuries by almost every religious tradition, such promises and assurances have failed to exorcize the adherents of such religions of their fears of death. In addition to that fear, most societies believe that the process of dying, and the transition from this physical to the invisible life are replete with many dangers that should be mitigated by the meticulous performance of death rituals. Consequently, "funeral ceremonies are the final and most dramatic" end to physical existence, as Goody has asserted.[1] In support of that, Thomas postulates that "death is the most sacred of all the rites of passage because it serves as the gateway to the afterlife, where one finally achieves

1. Goody, *Death, Property, and Ancestors*, 28.

the status of ancestor."[2] Moved by the same spirit, Mwandayi defines death as "the separation of the body and soul in which the material body takes a new state of decomposition while the soul due to its immortality continues to survive as a spiritual entity."[3]

Even though the Shona people believe that the human soul continues to live in a spiritual form after death, it is difficult to embrace the thought of dying because of the mysteries surrounding it, and the lack of indubitable knowledge of what happens after it. Of course, there could be another life as numerous religious traditions profess, but no one knows exactly if the quality of life in the afterlife would be the same as this physical life. Would people be conscious of their beings and relatives? Would they be able to consume food and drink beverages? Will there be marriage in the hereafter? Will there be sickness and pain? No religion can provide scientifically verifiable answers to these questions.

Furthermore, death is one of the "most disrupting phenomenon of all," as Mbiti has rightly observed.[4] It disrupts the orderly flow of life. It leaves gaps in family relationships. It sometimes whisks away loved ones without any warning. Death leaves a trail of trauma and grief wherever it visits. It changes lives, relationships, fortunes, and dreams. In affirmation to that, Fisher contends that the disruption brought about by death makes it an evil that interrupts the harmony of the family life.[5] Gundani echoes the same sentiments that death frightens both the family and the community, and it "shatters relationships that keep the family or clan going and stable."[6] When a loved one is taken away by death, the surviving family members and the community grieve, and are forced to learn to live without the deceased member of the family. If the deceased is survived by children, they may learn how to fend for themselves. Many things are bound to change because of the occurrence of death.

Imasogie believes that the lack of sufficient knowledge of what happens at the moment of death and the nature of the life after death makes it "a very solemn event fraught with danger for both the deceased and the living: hence, precaution must be taken to ensure that everything is done properly" regarding the rituals to be performed for both the dead person

2. Thomas, *African Traditional Religion in the Modern World*, 151.
3. Mwandayi, *Death and After-life in the Eyes of the Shona*, 56.
4. Mbiti, *African Religions and Philosophy*, 2nd Edition, 145.
5. Fisher, *West African Religious Traditions*, 95.
6. Gundani, "The Roman Catholic Church and The *Kurova Guva* Ritual in Zimbabwe," 198.

and the remaining family members.⁷ Pre-burial and other funeral rituals should be performed meticulously lest the spirit of the deceased or the ancestors are displeased. The displeasure of the spirits of the dead matters to most Africans because it sometimes produces dire consequences for the culprits and their families.

In addition to that, this scrupulous performance of death rituals is intended to assist the spirit of the deceased in crossing over into ancestorhood, for "Death is not the end of life, but a transformation of it. It is a profound crossing over of the soul from this world into the next," as Doumbia, Adama and Naomi have succinctly put it.⁸ In support of that, Wilson likens death to a journey to the ancestor world.⁹ Wilson writes, "A man, when he dies, is believed to join his ancestors. Until the end of the funeral rites, they say, he is on the way and if the ritual is not properly performed, he does not reach them. . . ."¹⁰ Now, if he does not reach the ancestors, there are repercussions—his spirit may come back to torment his family members until it is appeased. So, many Africans believe that prevention is better than cure.

Wilson has defined a ritual as "primarily religious action, that is, action directed to securing the blessing of some mystical powers."¹¹ It may also be performed to avert some punishment that is likely to happen as a result of some misgivings by the adherents of a given faith. For Gennep, funeral rites are accorded the greatest importance, and are most immensely intricate.¹² Shoko echoes the same sentiments when he postulates that outstanding honor should be accorded to the corpse, "to ensure the protection of the well-being of the people."¹³

WATCHING THE DYING PERSON

Watching (*kurinda*) a seriously ill person is one of the most important pre-burial rituals of the Shona. Wherever the dying person is being cared for, she should be watched constantly and closely. Mbiti, writing about

---

7. Imasogie, 62.
8. Doumbia and Doumbia, *The Ways of the Elders*, 149.
9. Wilson, *Rituals of Kinship among the Nyakyusa*, 18.
10. Ibid., 18.
11. Ibid., 9.
12. Gennep, *The Rites of Passage*, 146.
13. Shoko, *Karanga Indigenous Religion in Zimbabwe*, 85.

the Ndebele of Zimbabwe, says that the seriously ill person should never be left alone.[14] There always should be someone to keep watch on the ailing person. If the ill person is a man, his brother or oldest son should be the watchman. Mbiti gives two reasons for the need to watch the dying person constantly.[15] First, it assures the dying person of the perpetuity of his name through his sons. Second, since remembrance is crucial for the deceased's becoming an ancestor, the presence of the oldest son during the occurrence of death is a promise that the dying man would be remembered. This remembrance is believed to guarantee him of, and also prolong his ancestorhood. The intervals of watching should be frequent or even constant when the relatives of the dying person sense that death is around the corner.

The Karanga of Nyajena have several reasons for this close and constant watch of the dying person. First, the watcher takes care of the personal needs of the ill person. These needs include feeding, medication, cleaning, and sometimes just being present to accompany the dying person, depending on the nature of the illness and the state of the dying person. Bedridden patients are likely to need more personal care than those who can walk. The caregiver should be old enough to be able to assist the sick person go to the bathroom. In addition to that, the caregiver should be able to administer medications to the ill person as per the doctor's instructions. Furthermore, the caregiver should be able to cook food for the dying person, and assist her to consume it. Many dying people may have difficulties swallowing their food, and the one feeding them should be patient, caring, and prudent. Most of all, this accompaniment of the sick requires someone who has love, empathy, and respect for the dying person, and is dedicated to go an extra mile in providing for her needs.

Second, the watchperson also welcomes and hosts the relatives or villagers who visit the ill person. As has been explained above, many visitors are expected to visit the dying person. It should be noted that the traditional Shona peoples do not have patient visiting hours like Western hospitals do have. The Shona do not regulate the duration of the visits. So, people may visit the sick person whenever and as long as they want, and

---

14. See Mbiti, *African Religions and Philosophy*, 2nd Edition, 145. The Ndebele are not a Shona ethnic group. They migrated to Zimbabwe from South Africa around 1840 escaping the wrath of Tshaka, and occupied the area that became known as Matabeleland.

15. Ibid., 146.

should be allowed to see the ill person unless she is asleep. The person watching the dying person cooks food for the visitors. Some of the visitors may offer gifts to assist in the caring of the sick person, and the watch person is responsible for receiving them unless there are other elders of the family who can perform that duty. She may also listen to the advice visitors offer on how best the dying patient can be cared for. It is also part of her responsibilities to explain the nature and severity of the illness to the visitors, and may explain what the visitors are saying to the sick person and vice versa because the caregiver is likely to understand the blurred speaking or sign language of the sick person.

Third, most dying people are afraid of dying. Writing from a Western point of view, Backer, et al., assert that dying persons fear extinction, loss of things that they enjoy in life, the unknown, isolation and separation, leaving dependents without a breadwinner, and so on.[16] It is the responsibility of the watchperson to accompany, comfort, and help the dying to reframe their understanding of their impending demise. This fear of extinction may anger the dying person, or even drive her out of her mind. A dying person may cry, refuse to eat, and blame the caregiver of lacking love and kindness. Among the Karanga of Nyajena, she may accuse relatives of having bewitched her. The caregiver has to bear all the dying person's shortcomings and frustrations on behalf of the family, which is a mammoth task.

Fourth, among the Shona, this watching of the sick person is crucial because there are rituals that should be performed as soon as the sick person breathes his last, and these can only be performed if someone is present during the time of death. Bullock thinks that this final accompaniment could have been prompted by the fact that among some Shona ethnicities, an ill person was not allowed to die before sunset.[17] It was believed that the ancestors, who were supposed to receive the dead person would be most active after sunset. During the dying process, the dying person is believed to see the spirits of his ancestors, who are said to hold him by the hand, and lead him into the ancestral world. Consequently, the duty of the watchperson was to distract the ailing person from dying before sunset. Although Bullock's observation seems much plausible, he does not explain the methods that were used by such watchmen to keep death at bay until the acceptable time to die arrived.

16. Backer et al., *Death and Dying*, 27–28.
17. Bullock, *The Mashona (The Natives of Southern Rhodesia,)* 263.

Kuper, *et al.*, reporting their study of the Ndebele people, argue that while death could not be delayed, it could be hastened by slaughtering and sacrificing an ancestral beast.[18] This ritual was intended to prevent the sick person from dying during midday. Hence, if there was a reason to suspect that the ill person was likely to die during midday, the ancestors had to be persuaded to fast-track it so that it happened before midday. It is believed that the ancestors are not active during this time, and if the deceased is not warmly received, his spirit could be offended.

Some of my informants related a very strange ritual that may be performed if a dying person lingers on for a long time, and there is no hope of him recovering from the illness. In such a case, the ritual of burning python fat may be performed. The belief is that since a python does not die fast, anybody who would have touched its body during his active life, would also die slowly. So, the relatives of the patient may find some python fat, which they burn while the patient is inhaling the smoke. It is believed that if the slow, agonizing death is caused by having handled a python, the ritual of burning some python fat would fast-track the dying process thereby preventing the patient from enduring a long, painful death.

Fifth, the family elders or watchperson should be able to certify that the ill person has actually died. There are several signs of the approaching of death. There is loss of sensations. The arms and legs of the dying person become cold. Hence, the Shona use the phrase, *ava chando,* meaning, she is cold. Breathing and heartbeat cease. The eyelids and mouth of a dead person may open involuntarily. The eyes become fixed in a certain position. When all these signs happen, it is likely that the person would have died. At this point, the watchperson should notify others. It is encouraged that as the nearness of death is sensed more relatives should be present for the moment of death.

Last, the watchperson should notify others of the occurrence of death by wailing or just letting others know. This notification is crucial because funeral notifications and arrangements should begin as soon as death occurs to enable relatives living faraway to attend the funeral on time. In most rural areas, there are no funeral parlors or hospitals with mortuaries. So, burial arrangements should be made as soon as possible to prevent the corpse from decomposing before burial. So, someone has to be present during the dying moment to be able to alert others. In the

---

18. Kuper et al., *The Shona and Ndebele of Southern Rhodesia,* 101.

past, a quick notification of the occurrence of death was crucial because the Shona used emissaries to notify relatives living in distant areas. The emissaries needed more time to travel to such places.

THREATENING THE WITCH

When a family member becomes seriously ill, and the relatives have tried all forms of medication available to them to no avail, the Karanga of Nyajena perform a ritual known as *kutema bembera*. It refers to the public announcement of having the knowledge of the identity of the witch who is causing the illness. The name of the witch, though known by the family of the sick person, is not openly mentioned at this gathering. The purpose of this threatening of the witch is to encourage the witch to give the ill person an antidote (*kuworonora*). This phenomenon of trying to get the witch to withdraw the wizardry is also reported by Crawford among the Shona of Mwenezi.[19]

The ritual involves the family of the ill person secretly consulting a diviner or more than one diviner to identify the causes of the illness. If they are told that witchcraft is involved, and at times, the name of the witch, they do not just approach the witch to force him to withdraw his witchcraft. They share the news with the village head, who is supposed to call for a village meeting. Three things happen at this meeting. First, the villagers are notified of the serious illness of one of the villagers. In most cases, most villagers would be privy to this information, and would have already visited the sick person. The emphasis of this announcement is on the seriousness of the illness. Second, the village head and the head of the family of the ill person notify the villagers that they know who the witch is or are if many. This claim is intended to make the witch vulnerable. Third, they offer the witch an opportunity to reverse the effects of the witchcraft (*kuworonora*). Sometimes, a time frame for the reversal of the effects of witchcraft is mentioned. Usually, a threat is made to the effect that if the ill person is not healed within a certain period of time, either the name of the witch would be revealed to all the villagers after a public consultation of a diviner, or there would be a nefarious retaliation.

My informants claimed that *kutema bembera* usually yields positive results. Once the involved witches know that their identities are known, and can be revealed, they are likely to give the ill person some witchcraft

---

19. Crawford, 267.

antidote. However, sometimes, the ill person dies even after *bembera* has been performed. Some people claim that if the ritual is performed too late, the ill person may not be saved. The ritual should be performed as early as possible to enable the witches to reverse the effects of witchcraft before the person is irreversibly ill. One of the challenges of *bembera* is that it leads to speculations that may be wrong, and may create unnecessary tensions in the village. In some cases, innocent villagers are likely to be suspected of witchcraft, and may have their good standing damaged.

GROUP CONSULTATION OF A DIVINER

The Karanga of Nyajena refer to the group consultation of a diviner to find out the identities of the witches involved, as *gumbwa*. It should be noted that there are other Shona ethnicities that do not perform this ritual. *Gumbwa* is performed when the illness becomes more serious, and the ill person is not responding to all kinds of medications. The leader of the family of the patient may request the village head to send all the adult villagers to a diviner to find out the causes of the illness. Normally, the family of the ill person would have already consulted a diviner secretly, and would have been told who the witch is. This information would have been shared with the village head already.

There are four reasons for this public group consultation of a diviner. First, it is intended to have the witch identified in his presence. That identification would remove the burden of explaining what the diviner would have said to the witch and other villagers. If the accused person does not agree with the diviner, he may not blame the relatives of the sick person for having been accused of witchcraft. Second, the diviner usually asks the witch to give the ill person a witchcraft antidote to reverse the effects of witchcraft. The witch is commanded to do this in the presence of other villagers so that they can act as witnesses. Third, *gumbwa* is intended to shame the witch by pinpointing him as the cause of the sickness in the presence of other villagers. Fourth, it makes the accused person the public enemy of the villagers. From that time on, he becomes the first suspect whenever someone becomes sick in the village.

Usually, several diviners are consulted, and these should live in faraway places to prevent them from relying on their prior knowledge of people who are consulting them. Hence, the villagers may consult as many as four diviners until they are convinced of the findings. In some cases, where the culprit confesses to his nefarious activities as soon as the first diviner pinpoints him as the witch, only one diviner may be consulted. But if the culprit keeps refusing to accept responsibility over the illness, more diviners may be consulted. If about three diviners have been consulted, one after the other, and the same witch has been apprehended by all diviners, the head of the delegation may decide to go back to the village and try to persuade the witch to reverse the effects of witchcraft.

Be that as it may, some informants mentioned some villagers who had refused to take part in such a ritual citing their allegiance to Christianity. Usually, there is nothing that the village head can directly do to punish villagers who refuse to go for *gumbwa* because of the Witchcraft Suppression Act that has been mentioned in the preceding chapter. However, in the past, refusing to go for *gumbwa* was tantamount to confessing to being a witch. In fact, very few daring villagers would refuse to accompany others for *gumbwa*. If you have nothing to hide, you should not refuse to go for *gumbwa*. However, if the apprehended witch is an old person, who because of old age cannot accompany others for *gumbwa*, it is the responsibility of the village head, in the presence of many witnesses, to call for a gathering of all villagers, and reveal the name of the witch.

It should be noted that *gumbwa* is used as a last resort after other methods to heal the ailing person would have failed. The intention is not to shame the witch but to coerce him to give an antidote to the bewitched person. It is believed that the ritual has helped in apprehending witches, and forcing them to withdraw their attacks on the sick person.

RELOCATING THE SICK PERSON

In the past, the relocation (*kusengudza*) of the sick person was very common among the Karanga of Nyajena. The ritual involves removing the sick person from his normal home, and resettle him elsewhere. He can be taken to a healer's home, which would make the diviner's care of him a lot easier. The sick person may be relocated to a relative's home. Among other Shona ethnicities, in the past, a small hut constructed outside the homestead of the sick person could be used for this purpose.

There are reasons for performing this ritual. *Kusengudza* is intended to remove the sick person from the vicinity of the witches who would have caused his illness. That way, the witches will not be able to monitor the sick person's deteriorating health, and cause some more harm. Although witches can fly and ply their business far away from home, there is a general belief that they normally operate in their neighborhood. If they do not know the location where their victim lives, it is believed that they may not be able to continue harming him. The relocation also removes the sick person from the evil spells or harmful objects, which might have been planted in his home or house by the witches. In addition to that, the relocation is intended to allow the sick person to breathe fresh air outside his own home. Moreover, it removes him from the evil spirits, which may be responsible for his ill health. If he is relocated to the diviner's home, it may save the sick person from the tear and wear of being carried to and from the diviner's place.

CONFIRMING DEATH

As soon as the dying person breathes his last, the person keeping watch should immediately bend the arms and legs of the corpse. Aschwanden claims that the folding of some body parts is intended to prevent the spirit of the deceased from fighting since only upright men can fight.[20] In the past, some Shona ethnic groups had some ways, which they used to certify that death had indeed occurred. Bullock asserts that some cold water would be sprinkled on the dead person to find out if he would not react.[21] Where cold water was not readily available, they would use some incense called *mbanda*, that they would burn to produce smoke that would choke and jolt the dying person if he were still alive. If the water or *mbanda* smoke failed to jolt the dying person, then they would declare him dead. This verification was very important because burying an unconscious person would anger his spirit and the ancestors of the family. Aggrieved ancestors would punish the members of the family.

Kuper, Hughes, and Velsen have a different explanation of the same phenomenon.[22] They claim that the purpose of sprinkling the dead person with water and forcing him to "inhale the pungent smoke made by burning certain herbs," was an attempt to resuscitate him, not necessarily to verify his final demise. The verification of the occurrence of death is important because other rituals, which can only be performed as soon as a person dies, may be difficult to perform if delayed.

20. Aschwanden, 230.
21. Bullock, *Mashona Laws and Customs*, 42.
22. Kuper et al., 101.

CULTURAL CHANGES IN SHONA PRE-BURIAL RITUALS

Karanga pre-burial rituals have changed in one way or the other. Although *bembera* and *gumbwa* are still practiced, particularly in rural areas, it has become illegal to name the witches because of the Witchcraft Suppression Act originally passed in 1899, which criminalizes the claim by anyone to be able to identify a witch or accuse anyone of witchcraft. Even though the relatives of the ill person still consult diviners and the Christian "prophets," and may perform *bembera*, usually, no names are mentioned because of the fear of being reported to the police for accusing someone of witchcraft.

However, some cases were reported in which some diviners are said to have openly named the witches, and were arrested only to be released after being reprimanded by the law enforcement agents. Hence, most diviners are careful not to mention the name of the witch. Some were reported to have used certain indirect ways of letting the villagers know the identity of the witches.

In addition to that, some villagers refuse to be involved in the distant consultation of a diviner (*gumbwa*) citing their belief in Christianity. Since Zimbabweans have the freedom of worship, such people may not be coerced into getting involved in *gumbwa*. In the past, there were consequences for refusing to participate in *gumbwa*, such as the expulsion of such a villager from the village, which is no longer possible in Zimbabwe because village heads have very limited power.

Another change involves the consultation of faith healers or "prophets" instead of diviners, which was reported to have become fashionable in Nyajena. Although faith healers are also bound by the Witchcraft Suppression Act, they are favored because they are Christians, and purport to use Christian healing methods. This popularity of faith healers seems to be the fruit of a colonial mindset, which makes some Shona people think that anything that purports to be Christian or Western is qualitatively superior to anything African.

It was also reported that the *kusengudza* ritual had significantly changed. Before the coming of urbanization in Zimbabwe, the Karanga had only one home—the rural home. So, the patient would either be taken to a traditional healer or a relative's home for *kusengudza*. At times, they would build a makeshift hut for the dying person outside the home. But with the colonization of Zimbabwe by the British South Africa Company in 1890, and the beginning of industrialization and urbanization, the Karanga, like any other Shona ethnicity, started migrating to towns and mining or farming compounds where some of them purchased or rented houses. In some circumstances, their employers provided them with accommodation near their working places.

For instance, before Zimbabwe's independence in 1980, animal husbandry was a big thing in Nyajena. There were two large commercial animal ranges closer to Nyajena, namely, Makosi River Range (owned by Anglo-American Corporation) and Nuanetsi Range. There was also Renco Mine, which at its peak employed more than a thousand workers. There were also Triangle, Mukwasine, and Chiredzi Estates, which produced sugarcane and cotton. Most people who got employed in these places maintained their rural homes where the rest of their families lived, but would have a new home in towns, or on the farms or mining compounds. In some cases, the dualization of homes was necessitated by the fact that some mining compounds did not allow women to be residents.

Urbanization brought some changes to the *kusengudza* ritual. Instead of taking the dying person to a relative's home, now, some Karanga people take him either to his rural or town home, depending on where he is living at the period of his sickness. Also, very ill persons are taken to hospitals, and this cultural change shall be discussed in detail under burial rituals.

The participants in this research reported that the ritual of visiting the ill person is still significant in Nyajena. However, since many people die at the hospital, it has become increasingly difficult for the relatives to visit the ill person. There are some reasons for this. First, the hospital might be far away from the homes of some of the relatives. Second, hospitals have regulations concerning the visiting of patients. All the people interviewed during the fieldwork for this work noted that the number of visitors at the hospital is limited, and visiting times are sometimes limited to only two, one-hour visits per day. This stipulation has made it almost impossible for a family watchperson to accompany a dying relative constantly. The people dying at the hospital may die alone or in the company of strangers. This change will be explored in detail under burial rituals.

There have been questions concerning the existence of witchcraft itself. Even though most Shona people believe that witchcraft exists, some people argue that some accusations of witchcraft are false. Sometimes, people accuse their enemies of witchcraft, and these accusations are at times, mutual. This view confirms what Shorter observed in East Africa concerning witchcraft accusations occurring in communities where there were tensions and conflicts, and usually between equals, such as co-wives, neighbors, rival suitors, and so on.[23] Hence, it seems that the Karanga of Nyajena no longer quite believe that all reported witchcraft cases, are true, and have to be taken with a pinch of salt. This perspective is different from the past, where once a person was accused of witchcraft, and confirmed by the word of a diviner, she would be deemed a *bona fide* witch.

CONCLUSION

Although there are changes in the understanding and praxis of most of these rituals by the Karanga people, when sickness become serious, they are likely to try both traditional and Western ways of restoring a sick person's health. When a relative is seriously ill, some people exclusively rely on Western medicines until the patient's demise. Some other people rely on traditional health systems, exclusively. There is a third group of Africans that use both Western and African health systems. These methods may be employed one after the other or concurrently. Whatever the people do to restore the health of the dying person, and whatever the cause of illness that they believe, all is done to chase away death. However, a time always comes when the relatives of the dying person have to face the reality, and accept that the final demise of the ill person has arrived, and has to be embraced stoically by both the dying and the family members.

---

23. Shorter, *African Culture and Christian Church*, 141.

Chapter 5

Karanga Burial Rituals

INTRODUCTION

This chapter deals with burial rituals, which are by and large, a continuation of the pre-burial rituals. The Karanga of Nyajena in particular, and the Shona in general, have numerous rituals, which are performed between the moment the ill person is pronounced or certified dead, and the time the corpse is carried out of the house for burial. These rituals, by far, outnumber the pre-burial and post-burial rituals. They include the folding of hands and legs, closing of eyes and mouth, wailing, announcing death, payment of the death token, washing and dressing of the corpse, body viewing, resting the body on the way to the grave, the forbidden time of burial, farewell speeches, lowering the body into the grave, the people who are not allowed to attend the burial, the direction faced by the corpse, putting soil and stones onto the grave, the sweeping of the grave area after burial, and the placement of the *mutarara* branch on the grave.

In addition to general burial rites, the Karanga have special rites for the burial of certain people. For instance, there are some special rituals involving the burial of a fetus or a pregnant woman, an unmarried woman or man, and burial by proxy. Although burial by proxy is no longer as widespread as it might have been in the past, it is still practiced. The phenomenon of the shadow of the deceased demands special rituals as well. It should be noted that, even though these rituals are generally practiced, Shona ethnic groups may differ in the significance that they accord to them. Some of the rituals may have been abandoned as shall be explored under cultural changes.

Burial rituals are important to the Shona people. As has been observed by Goody, death rituals, in some way, control grief by providing a standardized way of grieving.[1] Hence, the bereaved know very well that they should express their grief within the acceptable communal grieving standards. It should be noted that it is somehow misleading to think of burial rituals as clearly distinct from pre-burial rituals because some of them overlap, and concurrently run as shall be discussed in this chapter. The divisions in this book are principally for academic and clarity purposes, and might not be very practical.

FOLDING HANDS AND LEGS

As has already been mentioned in chapter 4, the dying person should never be left alone. There should always be an adult family member to watch and care for the dying person. Among the Karanga of Nyajena, the appropriate person for this sacred responsibility is a close, mature relative of the dying person. If the dying person is a man, his son, wife, or brother should shoulder this sacred and solemn responsibility. However, where only daughters are available, one of them or more, can take over this responsibility. If the person on the deathbed is a woman, one of her daughters, sisters, or even mother, can carry this responsibility. This watching of the dying should be constant if the ill persons are displaying signs of the approaching of death. Even though death can come like a thief, under normal circumstances, its arrival can be predicted to a large extent. The signs of its approaching are sometimes subtle but related everywhere. Sankar has listed ten signs of the approaching of death. These are: the loss of sensation, motion, and reflexes, legs and arms becoming cool, more time spent sleeping, confusion about time and place, sight failure, loss of bowel and urine control, increase in oral secretions, restlessness, acute loss of appetite, and irregular breathing accompanied with a rattle in the throat and some periods of no breathing.[2] One does not

---

1. Goody, *Death, Property, and Ancestors*, 34.
2. Sankar, *Dying at Home*, 150–151.

necessarily exhibit all the above-mentioned signs. Only a couple or a few of them may signal the arrival of the end of physical life.

Once death has occurred, the first ritual to be performed is the folding of hands and legs of the departed. This may be performed by the watcher or any other relative who is present at home during the occurrence of death. Most of my informants told me that the Karanga have ways of certifying death. If breathing has completely ceased, the heartbeat has stopped, the eyelids are rigidly open, the jaws are relaxed, the arms and legs stretched, and eyes are staying fixed, then death is likely to have occurred. At this point, the watcher or any of the adult relatives at home immediately folds the legs and arms of the deceased. The arms and hands may be placed on the side of the body. The legs are folded to have the knees face the direction of the face. This ritual should be performed before the corpse becomes rigid. However, if the dead person is going to be buried in a coffin, as what usually happens these days, the hands may be placed on the sides of the body or folded and placed on the chest of the deceased. In this case, the legs are not folded, but just placed close to each other if they would have spread apart during dying.

This ritual is very significant. First, the body is folded to resemble the position and shape of a baby while it is still in its mother's womb. Death is seen as the beginning of a new life in Mother Earth's womb; the ancestral realm, which is symbolized by the soil. The grave will be the new womb in which the deceased will live until he is reborn or transformed into an ancestor. This rebirth is facilitated by the making of an ancestor (*magadziro*) ritual that will be discussed in detail under post-burial rituals. In addition, the folded position is full of potential and vitality.

Second, in the past, people were not buried in coffins. According to Chitakure, in the past, the folding of legs was mostly beneficial to the gravediggers because the length of the grave was determined by the length of the corpse.[3] The folded legs would also determine the length of the bier (*bwanyanza*) that would be used to carry the body to its final resting place. A similar *bwanyanza*, but not necessarily the same, would have been used to carry the same person during the *kusengudza* ceremony. The smaller the body, the shorter the grave to be dug, and the lesser the labor expended. If the legs and arms were not folded before the body became rigid, the tendons had to be cut to allow the folding. Bullock reports that among other Shona ethnic groups, the body was laid on its side, and

---

3. Chitakure, *African Traditional Religion Encounters Christianity*, 61.

the arms and legs were bent upwards.[4] Nowadays, most people only fold the arms of the corpse and not the legs because it has become almost standard to bury people in coffins, which are usually of standard length.

Third, ancestors are unpredictable, and sometimes vindictive. Although all the death rituals should be performed meticulously, the living family members have to prepare for any eventuality that may arise because of anything that may aggrieve the spirit of the deceased during his last days. Hence, the bending of legs and arms is done to incapacitate the deceased in case he wants to fight his family members because of an offence of omission or commission. The belief is that, in real life, only people with outstretched legs and arms have the greater potential to fight. By folding the deceased's arms and legs, he is incapacitated just in case, he wants to fight back.

CLOSING OF EYES AND MOUTH

The closing of the eyes and mouth is performed simultaneously with the folding of the arms and legs. The closing of the eyes and mouth may take several attempts until they permanently close. Some of my informants reported of several deceased relatives whose mouths kept opening until burial. In such cases, relatives should keep checking the mouth and eyes of the deceased to close them if they have opened involuntarily.

Sometimes, a person dies in the absence of the watcher or at night when the watcher is asleep, and the occurrence of death is discovered long after *rigor mortis*. If the body is already stiff, warm water and a towel may be used to relax the muscles so that they may be flexible. If the warm water does not help, a scarf or piece of cloth may be tied around the head and below the chin of the departed in order to close the mouth. The scarf should be removed when it is determined that the mouth remains closed. If the eyelids keep opening, some warm water may be used to relax them. In addition to that, a coin may be placed on the closed eyelids for a while to keep them closed. However, the coin used should not be too heavy because it may force the eyeballs down into the sockets, something which should be prevented from happening.

The ritual closing of the mouth and eyes of the deceased is significant. First, it is intended to prevent the soil from getting into the eyes and mouth of the dead person during burial. The corpse would have

---

4. Bullock, *Mashona Laws and Customs*, 43.

been washed, and allowing the soil to get into the mouth of the deceased would be counterproductive. In addition to that, since death is seen as a long sleep, the eyes and mouth should be closed as in a normal sleep. Furthermore, the ritual is performed to prevent the corpse from scaring the mourners. A corpse with closed eyes and mouth is less scaring than one whose mouth and eyes are wide open.

WAILING

As soon as death has been ascertained by the senior relative present during its occurrence, wailing may begin. Normally, women are expected to cry out loudly, and at times, saying some consolatory words concerning their loss, or indirectly accusing the witches who would be suspected of having caused the death. Men are expected to cry silently, or not to shed any tears at all. Men should be brave and courageous, and crying does not paint a good picture of a brave man.

Questions have been asked concerning the genuineness of funeral wailing. Rayner gives three possible motives for the wailing.[5] The wailing might be genuine and out of the sorrow of losing a family member because death would have robbed them of a friend, father, mother, daughter, son, or guardian. Further, the wailing may be a result of trying to satisfy the custom since women are expected to weep when someone dies. Moreover, it may as well be induced by the fear of being suspected of welcoming death, and this suspicion may lead to the dreaded accusation of witchcraft. Whatever the reason for wailing, it is one of the most important death rituals among most African ethnical groups.

The ritual wailing serves several functions among the Shona. First, it serves to notify the neighbors of the occurrence of death. If the dying person is being watched by a woman, she may make others aware of the death of the sick person by bursting into wailing, which unlike other African ethnicities, such as the Nyakyusa of Tanzania, will continue intermittently until after the burial.[6] Writing about the Nuer people, Evans-Pritchard reports that although women are expected to wail, it should be for a short time to inform neighbors about the death or burial of the deceased.[7] Once the neighbors have been made aware of the

---

5. Rayner, 65.
6. Wilson, 30.
7. Evans-Pritchard, *Nuer Religion*, 114.

occurrence of death, women are expected to stop crying. Among these African ethnicities, it seems that the wailing is mainly a communication method to notify neighbors of the occurrence of death.

It is different among the Shona peoples, where wailing can go on for several days after the burial. In the rural areas, all villagers would have known of the seriousness of the illness, and in most cases, anticipating the final demise of the ill person. Most, if not all villagers, would have visited the dying person once or more times during the course of his illness. So, once the neighbors hear the wailing from the home of the ill person, they quickly rush over there. As they arrive at the threshold of the home of the deceased, women may also join in the wailing, at times, throwing themselves about, and saying words of anguish or accusation. Sometimes, the deceased himself is blamed for having run away from his family. "Why have you run away from us?" Also, the remaining spouse may be asked, "What have you done to her or him?" Usually, such utterances are not considered to be accusations of witchcraft but just expressions of shock and grief.

Second, the wailing, questioning, anger, and desperation when death occurs are normal stages of grief and dealing with it, as Pine has noted.[8] It is believed that wailing is therapeutic. The tears are believed to wash away anguish and anger. Among the Shona, wailing women are allowed to express their grief that way because that ritual has to be performed. However, the women who would have already recovered from their wailing are expected to support and console other women, lest they injure themselves. Sometimes, the women who accuse certain people of having caused the death during wailing are reprimanded by others.

It is also claimed that the amount of wailing signifies the amount of love the mourners had for the deceased. The greater the love for the deceased, the louder and longer the wailing. However, mourners are known to wail at the top of their voices even if they did not like the deceased. Of course, close relatives are expected to cry more and louder. Also, if the death was unexpected, the wailing is louder to signify the shock being experienced by the mourners. If a bad or very old person dies, although wailing is still expected, it may not be as loud as for a relatively younger and good person. Among some African ethnicities, professional mourners do play an important role. They are said to be hired and paid for their services. Among the Karanga of Nyajena, the mentioning of professional

---

8. Pine, "Dying, Death, and Social Behavior," 37.

mourners is frowned upon as unacceptable. A dead person should be mourned by his family and neighbors, not unrelated hired mourners.

ANNOUNCING DEATH

As soon as death is certified to have occurred, all the family members and the community should be notified without delay. One of the rituals associated with the announcement of death is the wailing that has been explored above. Goody, in his exploration of death rituals among some ethnicities of West Africa, gives a tripartite method of the announcement of death.[9] The immediate wailing of women that follows the death of a person is intended to notify the people living in the surrounding areas of the occurrence of death. At this point, those who respond to the wailing only know a little about the death in question. The wailing would be followed by the playing of the xylophone using a particular tune that identifies the dead person with a particular gender, for there are distinct tunes for men and women. Finally, messengers would be sent to those relatives who live in distant places, and they would announce the name of the deceased. So, wailing alerts villagers about the occurrence of a death, then the xylophones identify the sex of the dead person, and finally, the messengers mention the name of the deceased person. Of course, in most cases, the neighbors already have their suspicions of the identity of the deceased person if he has been unwell for a long period.

Likewise, in the past, the Shona used wailing and drums to inform the neighbors, and emissaries to notify relatives living in distant places. According to Gelfand, some relatives should receive formal information about the passing on of their relatives even if they live in the vicinity.[10] For instance, in the past, some Shona groups were supposed to inform the father-in-law of the death of his son-in-law using a gift of a hoe if he (father-in-law) were not present at the time of death. It was a common practice that close relatives would be summoned if someone were dying. If a hoe were not given, any other relevant token of informing him would be acceptable. If he were not formally notified, he was likely to refuse to attend the funeral to register his disappointment.

Also, the *sahwira* (official family friend) was supposed to be among the first to be appraised of the occurrence of death since he would be one

9. Goody, 51.
10. Gelfand, *Shona Rituals with Special reference to the Chaminuka Cult*, 184.

of the sacred practitioners during the burial of the deceased. His duties would include among other things, making light of the death by telling jokes about the dead person and the living family members, and also receiving his body, and laying it to rest in the grave. Bourdillon claims that among some Shona ethnicities, the *sahwira's* antics are therapeutic, for they relieve the people of their grief.[11] In fact, the *sahwira* was supposed to be present during the death of his friend, but if unavailable, he had to be notified as soon as possible.

It is important that the emissary be an adult who knows a thing or two about making death announcements. If the departed has not been seriously ill, or if the relatives were not aware of his illness, they need to be prepared for the shocking news. According to the participants in this study, the announcer does not just tell them of the demise of their relative. He may start by notifying them of the seriousness of the illness. He may also mention that the ill person would not make it. And when he feels that the one being notified is ready for the bad news, he should tell him about the death. Whenever possible, the announcement of death should be made slowly and carefully. This stage-by-stage announcement of death is done to lessen the effects of shock on the one being told. According to Praagh, writing from a different worldview, the shock may include total disbelief of the sad news, paralysis, and numbness.[12] To avoid hurting the one being told about the death, it is encouraged to first make him sit down, and prepare him for the bad news. If a woman dies, and her own relatives have to be notified, a token of the notice of the death may be paid. Of course, transport costs may be covered by the son-in-law if the relatives of the deceased woman live far away from the place of the burial.

Letters and telephones could also be used to announce the occurrence of death to family members who live away from home. Again, the process of notification in stages should be followed to avoid shocking the one being notified. This change has been made necessary by the migration of people to other places, far away from their family homes. In addition to letters and telephones, people's deaths may be announced on radios and televisions.

Even though there are several channels and means of conveying the sad news of death, it should be noted that it is the responsibility of everyone who has been made aware of someone's death to pass the sad

---

11. Bourdillon, *Shona Peoples*, 201.
12. Praagh, *Healing Grief*, 12–13.

news on. So, those people traveling to other places after a death has occurred are expected to propagate the news. Everyone should know about it as soon as possible. One of the significances of this quick spread of the sad news is to prevent people from encountering misfortunes (*mashura*) associated with not being aware of the death of their relative.

In all these forms of announcements, euphemisms about death are used instead of direct language. Ordinarily, the one announcing death is not expected to say, "X has died." For instance, the Karanga may use, "*atisiya*" (she has left us), "*ashaika*" (she has disappeared), "*hakuchina*" (she is no longer there), "*atungamira*" (she has gone before us), *azorora* (she has rested) and many other death euphemisms. These euphemisms are intended to dignify the process of dying. They also explain the Karanga understanding of death. The dead is now invisible and has gone to the realm of the ancestors. *Atungamira* alludes to the acceptance of death, and the awareness that all human beings will follow. The dead has just gone before us, but we will all follow. It is important to bear in mind that death notices are delicate and should be announced with utmost respect to the deceased, while taking all precautions that the living relatives being told of the death are psychologically prepared to receive the devastating news.

Nowadays, there are additional means of communicating the occurrence of death. Radios, emails, and cellphones may be used to convey the message of someone's demise to the relatives. However, the use of these other alternative methods of communication does not override the use of traditional methods. Once they hear the word, all the family members and neighbors begin to gather at the home of the deceased. Everyone who is able is expected to attend the funeral because failure to do so might be construed by the spirit of the deceased as a sign of disrespect. Most close relatives try to arrive at a funeral before the burial of the deceased, and if they are late, the burial may be delayed enabling their late attendance.

WASHING AND DRESSING OF THE CORPSE

The washing of the dead body is one of the most significant death rituals among most Africans. All Shona ethnical groups perform the ritual washing of the corpse. Normally, among most Shona ethnic groups, the body is washed and wrapped in a white cloth or a blanket, or just clothed in new clothes, and laid on a reed mat. Nowadays, a blanket may be used instead of a cloth. It seems that wrapping in white cloth is ubiquitous in Africa. Goody reports it happening among West African ethnic groups, particularly the LoDagaa. He writes: "When the old women have anointed the body, they take a length of white cloth and wind it around the waist of the dead man."[13] Among the LoDagaa, this white cloth would have been purchased using the money obtained as death gifts from previous deaths. While the wrapping of the body with a white cloth is a common phenomenon in Africa, its significance has rarely been explored. Among the Shona, the official ancestral colors are black and white sewn together, and it might be that the white color is very significant.

However, Aschwanden claims that among the Karanga of Ndanga in Bikita, a black cloth, not white, is used to wrap the corpse.[14] Taboos concerning the color of the cloth exist. Muchemwa maintains that no red linen should ever be used to wrap the corpse because of two reasons.[15] First, red symbolizes blood and the destruction of life. Second, the Shona believe that red attracts lightning, which can be a natural or human cause of death.

Usually, the closest family members such as sons and brothers (for a man), and sisters (for a woman), perform this ritual. According to Goody, among the LoDagaa of West Africa, it is usually women advanced in age or who have reached menopause who shoulder this responsibility.[16] Childbearing women are not allowed to perform this ritual, to protect them from the many physical and spiritual risks, which are associated with death. These risks include sickness, death, and bad luck. According to Muchemwa, the corpse should be washed starting with the head, which he equates to how children are normally born with the head coming out first.[17]

Chitakure holds that this ritual bath does not need to be a full wet bath, but just symbolic.[18] Hence, some people may use a wet towel to target organs of the body that are usually affected by sweat. These may include, but not limited to, armpits, between the legs, private body parts, eyes, and behind the ears. Among other African ethnicities, herbs may

---

13. Goody, 69.
14. Aschwanden, 232.
15. Muchemwa, *Death and Burial Among the Shona*, 33.
16. Goody, 56.
17. Muchemwa, 33.
18. Chitakure, *African Traditional Religion Encounters Christianity*, 61.

be mixed with the bathing water as Doumbia has observed among West Africans.[19]

This ritual is performed before the corpse is presented for viewing, and transported for the subsequent burial. The most common practice is to wash it as soon as possible before the arrival of mourners. The Karanga use a bucket or dish with warm water in which a towel is dipped. In the past, *gambe* (large piece of broken clay pot) was used. The wet towel with soap is then used to clean different parts of the body such as the face, nostrils, mouth, armpits, private parts, back, and neck. The ritual is performed by a close relative of the deceased.

Ordinarily a woman's body is washed by women, and a man's body by men. The ritual washing can also be performed by nephews (*vazukuru*). The dish, soap, and towel used may be taken for personal use by the person who would have washed the corpse. Some participants said that the dish and towel may be given to the mother of the deceased. Other participants maintained that the dish, soap, towel, and remaining dirty water may be placed in the grave during burial. The water is particularly important because if it gets into the hands of evil people or witches, they may use it to prevent the deceased from becoming an avenging spirit if the departed would have died aggrieved. Once the washing is done, some body lotion such as Vaseline may be applied to the body. Finally, the corpse is dressed. In the distant past, an animal hide would be used to wrap the body. After cloths were introduced by foreign traders such as the Arabs and Portuguese, some white cloth was used to wrap the body. Nowadays, the corpse may be dressed in the deceased's best clothes, or even some church attire, as shall be discussed under cultural changes.

There are several reasons for washing and dressing the body of the deceased. Muchemwa contends that the symbolic bathing of the corpse serves the purpose of making the deceased's spirit clean and acceptable to the ancestors.[20] The washing of the body is believed to symbolize the cleanliness that is required by the ancestors. The dead is on a journey to a new home, and he should be dressed in a presentable way to avoid embarrassing his ancestors during reception in the ancestral realm. If the deceased is dirty, he may not be received in the ancestral realm, and his spirit may come back to haunt his family members.

19. Doumbia and Doumbia, 150.
20. See Muchemwa, 32, 33.

Also, this washing of the dead body symbolizes the spiritual rebirth. At birth, a child is bathed before it can meet the general members of the family. The same child is clothed in clean clothes. The bathing is like getting rid of the old form of life, and embracing the new. Other religious traditions such as Christianity, use water for baptism and exorcism. Since the dead are in the process of attaining a new life, they should have a clean body, and smart clothes.

In addition to that, Muchemwa claims that the washing of the corpse resembles human social lives, for people do not receive visitors or "attend a social gathering" while not clean.[21] Since death is like a journey to a new place, one must be presentable to his hosts. The ancestors, who would be waiting to receive him, expect him to be appropriately dressed. Also, the mourners would be scandalized if the deceased were to be dirty and clothed in dirty clothes.

Another reason for washing the corpse is that a dying person may lose bowel and urine control because of the involuntary relaxation of the body muscles. Consequently, if there is waste in the colon or bladder, the dying person may soil himself involuntarily. This human waste may stink badly. Hence, there is always a need to wash the corpse as soon as possible, to prevent the bad smell from offending the mourners.

In addition to that, water is believed to cool the dead person's anger, lest he attacks his living relatives. The Karanga are extremely careful not to offend the spirit of the deceased in any way. Consequently, they perform every ritual meticulously. However, the Shona believe that mistakes of omission or commission that may offend the deceased can happen. To counteract a situation where the offended spirit of the deceased comes back to punish its family members, they wash the body to cool the spirit's anger in advance. This cooling of the spirit is a preventive and conditional action.

MARKING AND DIGGING THE GRAVE

The digging of the grave is initiated by the ritual of *kutara guva/kutema rukawo/ruhau*, which means the symbolic marking of the grave. The marking of the deceased's final resting place is one of the most significant rituals among the Shona peoples. The grave is dug on the day of the burial starting early in the morning until it is finished. Hence, the marking and

21. Ibid., 32, 33.

digging of the grave may be classified under pre-burial rituals. It has been placed under burial rituals because it is the preparation of the final resting place for the dead person, and is more intimately connected to burial itself than to the preceding rituals. Mwandayi says that this ritual is supposed to be performed by a close relative who is chosen by the family of the deceased because the grave would be the house of the deceased, and no one is given a house by a stranger.[22] *Kutema rukawo* is almost similar to the ritual that is performed when a Shona man wants to build a house. Usually, his father or guardian is supposed to drive a peg into the soil on the spot the house would be built as a sign that he has given him permission to construct the house, and also to invite the ancestors to bless the place. However, if the father of the deceased is not available any other authorized relative may perform the ritual. A married woman's grave should be marked by her own relatives. The husband and her own children are not authorized to mark her grave.

The *kutara guva* ritual should be performed early in the morning. The authorized person uses a hoe or pick to mark the boundaries of the grave, or may dig the place where the grave should be dug for about three times, while saying a short prayer, such as, "this is the place where we are making you a home." This symbolic digging resembles the modern-day groundbreaking rituals. Where a close relative is not available, a person of the same totem may be authorized to mark the grave. Also, in cases, where adult relatives are not available, a young child of the deceased, under the guidance of an adult, may perform the ritual. Women, too, may perform the ritual if all male relatives are unavailable.

If the departed is a woman, it is one of her own relatives who should mark the grave. Her husband or children are not qualified to mark the grave since she is not related to them through totem. Chitakure contends that "If the grave is not marked by the authorized relative of the deceased, her spirit may become a *ngozi* (avenging spirit), and would come back to haunt her husband's family including her own children."[23] Chitakure further alleges that the ritual of *kutara guva* is sometimes abused by greedy parents who refuse to mark the grave until they are offered all the outstanding bridewealth for their deceased daughter.[24] The ritual of *kutara guva* for a married woman complicates the burial process if no sufficient

---

22. Mwandayi, *Death and After-life in the Eyes of the Shona*, 202–203.
23. Chitakure, *African Traditional Religion Encounters Christianity*, 106.
24. Ibid., 106.

bridewealth was paid for her because a married woman is supposed to be buried at her husband's home if she has born children.[25] So, if her family is aggrieved because of one thing or another, the family members may refuse to perform the ritual of *kutara guva*, until the amount of money or number of beasts that they demand is paid. Some may delay the burial as long as they can or until their demands are met. This tactical delay would be challenging to enforce if the burial were being done in their own home because the son-in-law and his family could easily leave before the burial. If the relatives of the deceased woman refuse to mark the grave, the spirit of the deceased woman may come back as an avenging spirit to haunt her husband's family. Since most Shona people fear the avenging spirit, members of the bereaved man's family pool up resources to pay up the remaining bridewealth. This pooling up of resources shows that a woman is married to the whole family, not just her husband. Hence, if her spirit becomes an avenging spirit, it attacks the extended family indiscriminately.

Once the ritual of *kutara guva* has been performed, other diggers may begin the digging. Ordinarily, most men who are not closely related to the deceased should be at the grave site to assist with the digging, but it is the young adults who perform the task. The male elders who are present during the digging may give directions as to how the grave should be dug. Some Shona groups may offer beer to the gravediggers to cool their thirst since their job is very demanding. At this point, women are at home performing other rituals such as wailing, receiving guests, singing, cooking, and dancing. According to Gelfand, in the past, if the men finished digging the grave earlier than the burial time, it was supposed to be guarded by at least two men, while the rest could go back home where other people were gathered.[26]

Even though the standard depth of a grave is about six feet, most Shona people use their eyes rather than a tape measure to determine its depth. According to Evans-Pritchard, the grave is supposed to be deep enough to prevent hyenas and other animals from snatching away the body.[27] It seems that many African groups follow this rule. If the corpse is defiled in any manner, or eaten by wild animals, the spirit of the dead would come back to haunt the family.

---

25. Wilson, 13.
26. Gelfand, *Shona Rituals with Special reference to the Chaminuka Cult*, 185.
27. Evans-Pritchard, *Nuer Religion*, 145.

DEATH TOKEN

Mourners are expected to contribute some money or food or both to the bereaved family as a death token (*chema*). Gelfand refers to *chema* as a "farewell present."[28] There is no stipulation as to the amount to be given, and there is no single method of paying the *chema*. Rayner says that the monetary gifts are placed in a bowl that is situated close to the head of the corpse.[29] Bourdillon writes that the *chema* was just a small coin that would be offered to the dead, and was usually accompanied by a few words by the giver.[30]

Muchemwa contends that in bygone times, *chema* could be paid using goats, bracelets, fowls, and other items of value, and that some givers introduce themselves to the departed as they present their gift to the deceased.[31] Others report that there is usually a family member who is appointed to collect the fee. The bereaved family appoints one of the family members, particularly one who is literate and trustworthy to receive and record the mourners' monetary contributions. Sometimes, mourners offer food in addition to money. Usually, neighbors bring maize meal and vegetables, and these are received and documented by the women in charge of the provision of food to the mourners. In addition to money and food, men may assist with the fetching of firewood and water that will be used throughout the funeral. In some Nyajena villages such as Machimbira and Mavuka, they do have standing committees whose treasurers receive burial contributions on a monthly basis, in order to assist bereaved families in times of death. *Chema* is expected from all people who come to perform the ritual of commiserating with the bereaved (*kubata mavoko*), even if they arrive long after the burial.

Among the LoDagaa of West Africa, if not all *chema* is used at the funeral of a person, the remainder should be kept, and should be used at the subsequent funerals in the same family. It should not be spent on other needs except funerals, lest the ancestral spirits are upset. For the Karanga, *chema* can be used for any other use that the bereaved family deems necessary.

The contribution of *chema* is a symbol of the Karanga *hunhu* (good behavior), which compels villagers to unite and assist each other in times

---

28. Gelfand, *Shona Rituals with Special reference to the Chaminuka Cult*, 185.
29. Rayner, 65.
30. Bourdillon, *The Shona Peoples*, 200.
31. Muchemwa, 35.

of need. Death is believed to be a blow to everyone in the community. Sometimes, the bereaved may not have enough food to feed the mourners so, they need assistance. The money contributed is also a symbol of farewell to the deceased. In real life, people would have exchanged many gifts, and *chema* is the final gift to the departed. Furthermore, *chema* is a symbol of loss and sorrow for having lost a human being. It is a token of mourning. Some of the interviewees in this study emphasized the point that if one wishes others to assist in the event of a death in one's family, one must also be willing to assist others in times of their need. *Chema* is like an insurance policy from which bereaved families are likely to get assistance in times of need.

BODY VIEWING

When the body is ready for burial, and all the burial preparations have been made, it is brought outside the house and placed closer to the door in which the mourning was performed. In the past, a funeral carrier made of tree bark and two poles (*bwanyanza*) was used to transport the body to the grave. During burial, the stretcher or mat is destroyed and placed in the grave, but only after the body or coffin is completely covered with the soil. Nowadays, a coffin or just a reed mat may be used. Once the body is placed outside the house, the family ritual leader then invites the mourners to come by to view the deceased. This ritual is for all mourners who do not have a nervous disposition that may prevent them from performing it. As mourners pass through the head side of the deceased, they may momentarily stop, bow, and say a few words silently. In the past, body viewing was only for adults, for children and pregnant women were not allowed to view the body or even to attend the burial because it would pose some danger to their health.

    Body viewing is intended to allow the mourners to bid farewell to the deceased. My informants contended that the final goodbye resembles what the same people would have done—coming to see the newly born baby. At this point, the viewers may say a few words to the deceased who is believed to be around in the form of a spirit. It gives them an opportunity to ask for forgiveness if they would have wronged the deceased during his lifetime. More so, body viewing brings about closure to the mourners, and helps them to overcome grief. Here, the mourners' doubts, fears, and disbelief about the death are either debunked or confirmed depending on their state. They realize that death has occurred, and the deceased is gone for good, at least, physically.

TRANSPORTING THE CORPSE TO THE GRAVE

When the time for burial arrives, the body is placed on a bier (*bwanyanza*), which is made from two poles and tree bark, a job which Bourdillon apportions to the sons-in-law.[32] The bark and the poles would be broken and placed in the grave during burial. Nowadays, most people are buried in coffins, and again, it is the sons-in-law's responsibility to carry it to the grave. Among some Shona ethnicities, the corpse should exit the house through a hole that is made at the back of the house for the reason of confusing the spirit of the dead if it wanted to come back before the appropriate time and rituals. This arrangement seems to suggest that the spirit of the dead lacks conventional wisdom of looking for the entrance. Bendann has reported the same practice of carrying the corpse by some "other way than the ordinary door" as a common practice among Asian cultures, whose "main object may be to prevent the dead from finding his way back."[33] For Aschwanden, this exiting the hut through an opening at the back is intended to prevent those carrying the bier from being stricken by death as they exit, for it is believed that as the body is being carried out through the door, death might enter through the same door way.[34]

The body may be carried around the homestead, and the *varoora* (daughters-in-law) may purify the hut in which the corpse was. Mwandayi offers two reasons for taking the corpse around the hut.[35] First, it enables the deceased to bid farewell to his habitation. Second, it is done to confuse the spirit if it wanted to come back to haunt its family members. Gelfand reports of some Shona groups that offer a goat (*nhungamiri*) to the spirit of the dead and other ancestors.[36] This goat is supposed to lead the procession to the grave, where it would be slaughtered later. The Karanga of Nyajena do not perform this ritual.

---

32. Bourdillon, *The Shona Peoples*, 201–203.
33. Bendann, *Death Customs*, 57, 60.
34. Aschwanden, 254.
35. Mwandayi, 212.
36. Gelfand, *Shona Rituals with Special reference to the Chaminuka Cult*, 186.

As soon as the body exits the house, a procession is formed, and the bier is carried with the head of the deceased facing the grave. In the past, young children were not allowed to take part in the funeral procession, lest the corpse would make them blind. It looks like this taboo was intended to cushion the children from witnessing the fragility and limitedness of human life. Doumbia Adamma and Naomi assert that among some West African ethnicities, women and children should avoid the route the funeral procession would have taken to the grave, for a couple of weeks after burial. Anyone who violates this taboo may become ill.[37] However, it might be difficult to tell if the violators became ill or blind in reality.

As the funeral procession marches to the grave, the bier should be placed on the ground for ritual resting for a couple of times. There are no stipulations concerning the number of rests or the distance between rests, but the Karanga of Nyajena suggest two or three times. They claim that resting and turning of the corpse is performed for two reasons. One of the reasons is to confuse the spirit of the dead so that it does not find its way back into the home if it ever wanted to return prematurely. The spirit's coming back into the home should wait until the required rituals that guarantee its safe return are carried out. The other reason is that it gives the participants some time to observe some silence, while clapping and ululating, in honor of the deceased. However, as shall be noted later, nowadays, most corpses are transported to the grave by vehicles, and the resting ritual is not performed until at the actual grave.

Bullock asserts that the length of the distance between resting spots does not matter, but the resting itself.[38] Once the ritual leader is satisfied with the distance traveled, he may instruct the people carrying the bier to rest the corpse. Gelfand suggests that about every 20 yards, the bier should be placed to the ground, and the position of the body is then changed, with feet pointing to where the head was.[39] However, the bier carriers should remember to have the head of the corpse face the grave after the last stop. Mwandayi holds that since the Shona understand death as a journey, there is a need for the spirit of the deceased to rest just like other sojourners do.[40]

---

37. Doumbia and Doumbia, 152.
38. Bullock, *Mashona Laws and Customs*, 44.
39. Gelfand, *Shona Rituals with Special reference to the Chaminuka Cult*, 186.
40. Mwandayi, 212.

After the final stop, the bier or coffin may be carried straight to the grave where it is placed near the grave. It should be noted that there are taboos concerning burial times. Burial should be either in the morning or afternoon. Mwandayi quoting Muchemwa, stipulates the acceptable burial times as between 4:00 am and 12:00 noon, or 2:30 pm and 10:00 pm.[41] He asserts that the principal reason for observing these times is to honor the ancestral working and resting schedule, who are supposed to receive the spirit of the dead after the burial. In other words, the spirit of the deceased should arrive in the ancestral world during their working hours to facilitate its warm reception. This specification of burial times seems to be post-colonial since there were no watches before the arrival of the colonists in Zimbabwe or many other African States. During that era, time was reckoned by just looking at the position of the sun, moon, or some stars, or the crowing of the cock. So, the forbidden burial time would be referred to as, "midday," rather than some specific times. This practice of resting the corpse is tied to the idea that the spirit of the dead does not leave his body until the body is buried. Even after that brief visit to the world of ancestors, the spirit is believed to come back to the grave from where it would be invited to come back home later as an ancestor. In Nyajena, any disregard of the burial time taboo attracts a fine from Chief Nyajena. It is believed that disregarding that taboo angers the ancestors of the land, who may punish the whole community by withdrawing the rain, or allowing the people or animals to be struck by diseases.

EULOGIES

Just before burial, speeches eulogizing the deceased may be given. Only close relatives are given an opportunity to give these speeches about the deceased. The village head, even if not related to the deceased, is always allowed to give a speech, either at this time, or at the end of the burial. Usually, he announces the sacred resting and mourning days in honor of the departed and ancestors. Sometimes, the family ritual leader may also invite the debtors who are owed anything by the dead to let him know what they are owed by the deceased. This information is crucial and should be shared publicly. The speeches are a tribute to the dead, which chronicle his good deeds and relationship with the community.

---

41. Ibid., 210.

Occasionally, someone may say bad things about the dead, but the norm in Nyajena is to lavish praises on the dead person. Speeches concentrate on the positive side of the deceased as informed by the Karanga philosophy of *wafa wanaka* (the dead has become good). This philosophy is intended to persuade the living to make peace with the dead because he is no longer present to either defend himself or make amends. Furthermore, *wafa wanaka* philosophy directs the mourners to take this time to think of the good things the deceased would have done. However, *wafa wananka* can mean that the dead has escaped the sufferings of this world, and should not be ridiculed. Ordinarily, people talk about the evil that other people do all the time, and sometimes, do not give a thought to the good that other people do. The graveside eulogies are intended to give mourners an opportunity to think of the good that the dead would have done to the community or to individuals.

LAYING THE BODY IN THE GRAVE

When everything is ready, and perhaps after a few speeches, the body is placed in the grave. Among some Shona peoples, the *sahwira* will be among the people who perform this job. Among others, the sons-in-law are expected to lay the body into the grave. Gelfand states that the body is laid on the reed mat (*rupasa*), and a wooden pillow (*mutsago*) is placed under its head.[42] He further alleges that in the past, no singing was allowed during this most solemn time.

Some Shona ethnicities place some food supplies, money, drinks, and other gifts into the grave for the spirit of the deceased and other ancestors who would welcome him into their realm. Bullock notes that if the deceased is a woman, pots, water-pitchers, and spoons, are placed in the grave, but only a drinking cup for a man.[43] Among most Shona groups, these utensils are placed onto the grave not inside, and are intended for the use of the spirit in its new life. These utensils are supposed to be cracked if the person being buried was good, but should not be cracked if he was of ill-repute. The cracking of utensils may signify the length of the stay the spirit will have to endure before being allowed to come back home as an ancestor. It seems the spirit of a good person is offered cracked utensils so that it aspires to quickly come back home where

---

42. Gelfand, *An African's Religion, The Spirit of Nyajena the case of the Karanga*, 81.
43. Bullock, *The Mashona (The Natives of Southern Rhodesia)*, 268–269.

the utensils are uncracked. The spirit of a bad person is offered uncracked utensil for it to go for good. However, bullock argues that the utensils are cracked to signify that, while the utensils were needed in the past, they would not be needed in the future.[44] Among other African groups, Mbiti has observed spears, bows and arrows, stools, snuff, and other things being put into the grave if the deceased is a man.[45] He claims that the weapons are intended for the dead man's use in the ancestral world.

The direction to which the body should face is dictated by the cultural identity of the person being buried. This direction could be East, West, South, or North. Bullock suggests that the body should face the direction from which the ancestors of the deceased would have come.[46] This suggestion is based on the Bantu Migration theory, which says that the Shona are not the indigenous inhabitants of Zimbabwe—they migrated from the North. Also, inside Zimbabwe, the Shona continued to migrate from one place to another. Hence, the direction referred to here, may refer to that of the founder of their current clan.

Mbiti reports that the Ndebele bury their corpses facing the South because that is the direction from which they came.[47] Mbiti further alleges that among the Ndebele, the side on which the corpse lies, depends on the gender of the deceased—men lie on their right hand side and women on their left. In support of that, Bourdillon asserts that among the Shona, the normal burying side for men is the right, to prevent the deceased from killing people using his right hand assuming that the dead person is right-handed.[48] Muchemwa alleges that if the corpse of a man is laid in the grave on its left side, the spirit will come back to strike "with inexorable force and it will bring trouble after trouble."[49] While several scholars concur concerning the side on which male and female corpses should lie in the grave, Aschwanden begs to differ by stating that among the Karanga of Ndanga, Bikita, a woman should be buried on her right and a man on his left.[50] The rationale behind this being that, during hu-

---

44. Bullock, *Mashona Laws and Customs*, 43.
45. Mbiti, *Introduction to African Religion*, 2nd Edition, 120.
46. Bullock, *The Mashona (The Natives of Southern Rhodesia)*, 268.
47. Mbiti, *African Religions and Philosophy*, 2nd Edition, 146.
48. Bourdillon, *The Shona Peoples*, 203.
49. Muchemwa, 34.
50. Aschwanden, 255.

man conjugal intimacy, men favor to lie on the left-hand side, and women on the right-hand side.

Among the Karanga of Nyajena, in the coffin, the body should be laid on its back, with the face turned to the East or upwards. The East direction symbolizes the good things and the light, which come from the East. Other participants of this study said that the body was to be laid on its side depending on the gender of the deceased. A woman should be laid on her right-hand side, and a man, on his left-hand side. If the husband and wife are buried in the same burial place, as is normal in the rural areas, their graves should be placed side by side. Again, the man's grave should be on the left-hand side, and the wife's grave on the right. This is done to honor the normal sides that different genders use during procreation. It is assumed that if the couple is being intimate in a side-by-side position, the man usually operates from the left-hand side of the bed, and the woman from the right-hand side of the bed. If is also believed that even where a man favors to perform the 'sacred games' from the right-hand side of the bed, when the adult games are over, he is likely to go back to the left side to sleep. Furthermore, the side on which the body is placed in the grave is symbolic of the work that the departed will perform in the ancestral realm. The deceased would become an ancestor, and one of the significant duties of ancestors is to bring about the fertility of the land, animals, and human beings. So, the side on which he or she is laid is symbolic of the sexual act, in which the land, people, and animals receive fertility.

COVERING THE GRAVE WITH SOIL AND STONES

When the body has been placed in the grave, the elderly relatives are requested to throw a little soil into the grave. Some elders may perform the ritual for family members who are not present during the burial. This ritual is intended for the elderly who would have not been active in the digging of the grave, and for the absent relatives because every relative should manually assist in the burial of the departed. As the appropriate mourners throw a pinch of soil into the grave, they may utter a little prayer.

It is also intended to prevent misfortunes from happening to those relatives who are not present during the burial. These freak accidents are called *mashura/manenji*, which are a means of communication by the spirit of the dead to the family member who may not know that death has occurred. In his research among the same people, Gelfand reports that the objective of throwing these handfuls of soil into the grave is "to prevent *manenji* (an accident or misfortune) happening to any relative who is far away and cannot attend."[51] Furthermore, the ritual is intended to cast away evils and misfortunes that may attack the family, seemingly both present and absent. Once all who are willing to throw the soil have done so, the grave is quickly filled with soil using shovels and hoes.

As soon as this ritual is done, the undertakers may quickly fill up the grave with soil. If the grave would be plastered with cement in the future, it is left with a heap of soil on it, and no rocks are used to cover it. However, the head side of the grave is marked with a tall head stone, which is carefully planted to prevent it from falling down. If the family of the departed does not anticipate plastering the grave with cement in the future, the soil mount is covered with rocks. Care should be taken to see to it that all the soil that would have been removed from the grave be returned to the grave. As men are shoveling the soil back into the grave, women and older men begin to fetch stones to the grave. Once they reach the grave, a family member may line them on top of the soil mount that is already on the grave.

Each person should carry strictly one rock at a time. In Nyajena, carrying two rocks, or plates, or any other tools used during burial at the same time, is forbidden for three reasons. First, if the deceased were to come back as an avenging spirit, he would kill two people at a time, if two stones were carried at the same time, either by mistake or design. Second, in the event that the departed comes back to haunt his family, his spirit may team up with another spirit, and the consequences would be catastrophic. Third, if there is another family member who is sick, he or she may not survive the illness. So, to prevent such misfortunes from happening, only one stone, plate, or tool should be carried at a time. Where a scotch cart is used to carry the stones, they should be placed a few meters from the grave so that they can be carried one by one from that place by the mourners.

Some Shona groups may erect a fence around the grave using the branches of a tree called *mutarara*. Other Shona groups may place a branch of a tree called *chizhuzhu* on top of the grave. This tree branch would have been used to sweep the area around the grave. Muchemwa

---

51. Gelfand, *An African's Religion, The Spirit of Nyajena the case of the Karanga*, 81.

writes about the branch of *mutarara*, which is placed on top of the grave to ward off evil spirits.[52] Bullock believes that once the leaves of the branch have withered, (normally placed on a woman's grave) it is believed that the body of the dead person would have burst, and at that stage, the witches cannot devour it at one of their ghoulish meetings.[53] The sweeping is intended to find out if the witches would have desecrated the grave.

For a couple of days, early in the morning, the grave is inspected for witches' footprints, whose presence may be a sign that the grave was violated. After these mandated visits to the grave, most Shona peoples avoid the graves because of their respect for the dead, and to allow the dead to rest peacefully. In fact, some Karanga of Nyajena are afraid of graves, and may not sit on them or even point at them. Despite the fear of graves, some family members may return to the grave of their relative to clean the area or perform appropriate rituals.

PURIFICATION OF THE UNDERTAKERS AND THE HUT

It is believed that getting involved in the burial rituals makes the undertakers ritually unclean. Hence, all people who would have come in close proximity of the corpse should be purified. In the past, people would go to the nearest river to wash away their association with the death. Nowadays, among some Shona ethnic groups, the ritual cleansing is done at the grave using medicated water. Muchemwa claims that some Shona groups use a mixture of water, and crushed tree leaves such as *hazvieri, mushozhowa, musvisvinwa,* and *rugumudzambwa,* and *muzeze* is used to sprinkle the water onto the people.[54] In some places, the ritual cleansing is for everyone who would have been involved in the burial. However, the rest of the people may only wash their hands and faces using the medicated water, but those who would have come into close contact with the corpse have to completely wash their bodies. Chavhunduka holds that this purification is imperative because the spirit of the dead is "unpredictable and dangerous," and appropriate precautions must be taken.[55]

52. Muchemwa, 36.
53. Bullock, *The Mashona (The Natives of Southern Rhodesia),* 268.
54. Muchemwa, 43.
55. Chavhunduka, 58.

This ritual purification is also performed among other African peoples. Doumbia and Doumbia report about the ritual cleansing that takes place in a river or lake after burial by the Mande peoples of West Africa.[56] Of course, the Mande go a step further by leaving all the objects used during the burial beside the grave because of a couple of reasons. First, the objects are considered to pass on bad luck to anyone who touches them. Second, the objects are dangerous and may cause harm to anyone handling them. So, for the Mande of West Africa, it is not only the undertakers who are defiled by their close contact with the corpse, but also the objects used during the burial.

The hut in which the body lies also needs purification, which may be done using water mixed with medicines. Ordinarily, for most Shona groups, the purification of the hut is one of the many responsibilities of the daughters-in-law. According to Bullock, among other Shona ethnicities, traditionally, if the deceased were a woman, her hut was abandoned, and allowed to dilapidate because of disuse.[57] The possessions of a deceased woman may be sealed away in her hut or granary and should not be used until the inheritance ritual has been performed. If the widower is offered one of the sisters, cousins, or nieces of the departed wife, she may be allowed to use her huts and most of the belongings except cows. Normally, the cows if she had any, are taken by her father or male relatives.

BURIAL OF FETUS, LITTLE BABIES, AND PREGNANT WOMEN

Most Shona peoples believe that the death of either a full-term baby, which has not cut its first teeth, or fetus poses a lot of danger to the family and the community. Hence, some specific rituals have to be performed to appease the spirit of the deceased infant or fetus. According to Bullock, in addition to the above, in ancient times, the Shona got rid of babies such as twins and malformed children and those children who would have cut their upper teeth first.[58] Among the Karanga of Nyajena, the babies who cut their upper teeth first were not killed, but had their upper teeth removed to give way for the bottom ones to come out first. The teeth were

---

56. Doumbia and Doumbia, 52.
57. Bullock, *The Mashona (The Natives of Southern Rhodesia)*, 269.
58. Bullock, *Mashona Laws and Customs*, 46.

removed to evade the tribulations that would befall the community if such a situation were not remedied.

Rayner describes the death of a child who has not yet cut his first teeth as "abnormal, mysterious, and dangerous, particularly in the case of a woman who was having her first child."[59] In fact, Rayner contends that a child who has not cut his first teeth is not considered a human being, hence, the disposal of his remains is replete with danger.[60] Extreme precautions should be taken. Special rituals should be performed. For burial, their bodies are placed in a clay pot, and buried in running water or a swamp. Sometimes, burial along riverbanks is recommended. The burial in a swamp area or along the riverbanks is intended to cool the baby's frustration and anger for having died prematurely. If the baby is buried on dry land, it is believed that there would be a drought.

Gelfand alleges that if the deceased baby is still on breast milk, he would be buried with his face pointing upwards, and if this is not done, its mother would become barren.[61] It is believed that the spirit of the baby would block the mother's womb. Gelfand further claims that the river or stream on whose bank the baby was buried had to have flowing water throughout the year so that its spirit would be perpetually cooled. In addition to that, he postulates that still-born babies are placed in a clay pot and buried under similar conditions.

Aschwanden claims that among other Shona ethnicities the baby is buried in the river sand, in a *gambe* (broken clay pot).[62] For him, burying the baby in a broken jar is intended to make the baby believe it is still in its mother's womb. When the first rains come, the body is washed out of the jar by the water, and that symbolizes its birth. This ritual is intended to mislead the baby into believing that it is normally born just like other children. It also helps in cooling down its anger of having failed to make it into the world.

Among the Karanga of Ndanga, if a pregnant woman dies before delivering a baby, she too is supposed to be buried near a river. This ritual is believed to cool the spirit of the dead woman and that of the unborn baby in her womb. In the past, in Nyajena, if the pregnancy were advanced, say between seven and nine months, it was recommended to remove the

---

59. Rayner, 64.
60. Ibid., 63–64.
61. Gelfand, *Shona Rituals with Special reference to the Chaminuka Cult*, 187.
62. Aschwanden, 249.

baby from the mother's womb and bury them side by side in the same grave. It was tabooed to bury such a baby in its mother's womb, for it would spell disaster to the community.

The cooling of the spirit of the deceased baby or pregnant mother is crucial because it is believed that the death of an infant would have deprived the baby of a full life. So, the spirit is deemed angry and dangerous. When the rain season comes, and the river is flooded, the remains of the baby are going to be washed away and transported into the oceans far away from where the baby's relatives live. This washing away of the remains of the baby signifies the washing away of the possible dangers that may harm the family or community.

If due to any reason, a little baby or pregnant woman are buried on dry land, a ritual of cooling their spirits should be performed. One such incident was reported to have happened in one of the Nyajena villages. A young girl is said to have given birth to an unwanted baby, killed her, and buried her secretly in a shallow grave on dry land. When what had happened was eventually discovered, the young woman was arrested, and her parents had to perform a ritual to cool the spirit of the baby, and to avert the catastrophe that awaited the community. Beer was brewed, and some of it was taken to the place where the baby was secretly buried. Also taken to the grave was a calabash full of cold water, and a goat's blood. These were poured at the baby's burial place to cool her spirit. Even if the mother of the deceased baby were present, she would not be allowed to eat the meat of the sacrificial goat or drink the beer, as a form of punishment.

In Nyajena, only women who have gone past child-bearing age are allowed to conduct the burial of fetuses or babies who die before cutting their teeth because they are no longer capable of bearing babies. The mother and all men are not allowed to attend. If the mother attends the burial, or show any affection towards the dead child, she may not be able to conceive again. Men may help in the digging of the shallow grave but have to leave the actual burial to the elderly women. Normal mourning rituals such as *kukanda chibwe* or *kubata mavoko* are forbidden. Public commiserating with the bereaved parents is not allowed. If the deceased baby is a girl, she is laid on her right-hand side, and if a boy, on his left-hand side, symbolizing the normal sides women and men lay on during their intimacy. The burial should be performed early in the morning when it is still cool. No one should visit the burial place again. The bereaved mother should avoid the exact spot at which her baby was buried as long as she can remember to prevent the spirit of the baby from recognizing and causing harm to her.

BURIAL OF YOUTHS AND UNMARRIED PEOPLE

In bygone times, the burial of unmarried persons was different from that of babies and other adults. This group included all who died before marriage or before begetting children. The Karanga feared that the spirits of such people were likely to be aggrieved because of the unfruitful life led, and would come back into the family to cause harm. There were rituals that were performed or omitted to prevent the departed from seeking recognition as ancestors. For instance, Gelfand notes that as the corpse of such a person was being transported to the grave, the body was not turned around as would be done to the body of a person who was married.[63] Since time immemorial, there is no *magadziro* (making of an ancestor ritual) for the unmarried. Here, the assumption is that the unmarried person has not begotten children. It should be noted that, a person who has begotten children out of wedlock can become an ancestor. Hence, the issue is more about having born a child rather than having been married.

Bullock asserts that such deceased unmarried people would be buried with a symbolic wife or husband depending on their gender.[64] The symbolic spouse or child could be an animal, roofing pole, grinding stone, or any other symbol appropriately representing a spouse or child. The spirits of those who died without marriage or begetting children would not be invited to become ancestors as Mbiti also observes.[65] In support of that, Chitakure claims that if one died before marriage, the cleansing ceremony, which is intended to make the spirit of the dead an ancestor would not be performed.[66] The main purpose of the cleansing ceremony is to initiate the deceased into ancestorhood. As an ancestor, one's principal responsibility is to protect one's family, and without having one's own family, there is no need of becoming an ancestor. Consequently, the spirit of an unmarried person is disqualified from enjoying the status of ancestor. However, that does not mean that such a spirit is accursed.

---

63. Gelfand, *Shona Rituals with Special reference to the Chaminuka Cult*, 192.
64. Bullock, *Mashona Laws and Customs*, 46.
65. Mbiti, *African Religions, and Philosophy, 2nd Edition*, 148.
66. Chitakure, *African Traditional Religion Encounters Christianity*, 80.

In Nyajena, an unmarried man or woman is buried with a rat inserted into his or her rectum to signify his or her child or wife. If the deceased is a spinster, she can be buried with a *citrillus lanatus* (*shamba*) tied to her back, representing her child or husband. Some families bury a bachelor with a sausage fruit (*mveva*) representing his wife or child. In the past, a different sausage fruit would have been used during the boy's puberty to ritually lengthen his manhood. Gelfand, who did his research in Nyajena reports that, in the past, a stick was inserted into the anus of an unmarried boy or girl during burial.[67]

A special prayer is said to tell the deceased not to come back as an ancestor. The Karanga fear that if a person who dies single is allowed to become an ancestor, he may haunt his relatives because of his frustration for having died without being married. So, the spirit of the departed is told not to come back home as an ancestor because anyone who dies before marriage or having begotten a child is automatically disqualified from ancestorhood. The status of being unmarried is some sort of self-disqualification because the ritual of *magadziro*, which makes the spirit of the deceased an ancestor should be performed by one's own children or grandchildren. It is believed that such disqualified spirits may find appeasement among unrelated people and may become alien spirits.

BURIAL OF CHIEFS

Chiefs occupy a special place of authority and responsibility among Shona peoples. Before the colonization of Zimbabwe in 1890, and a few years after that, chiefs, by virtue of being religious and political leaders of their communities, wielded much authority and power, and deserved much respect from their subjects. Consequently, the death of a chief was a matter of greater concern and secrecy for his family and subjects. When a chief was dying, he was taken away from his home and resettled at a traditional healer's place. His illness, relocation, and subsequent death was kept secret by his close family members. If he died, his closest family members would clandestinely burry him, and would not announce his death until after about a month, and would publicize it at a time when they felt that his body had decomposed. Gelfand states that among some Shona ethnicities, only the nephews and grandchildren of the chief were

---

67. Gelfand, *An African's Religion, The Spirit of Nyajena the case of the Karanga*, 89–90.

privy to the information about the chief's demise and his subsequent burial.[68] Waiting for the decomposition of the corpse was intended to prevent contesting houses from invading the grave to obtain a piece of the corpse for malicious purposes. When the time to notify the public about the death of the chief arrived, they would tell the people that "the mountain had fallen."[69] Soon afterward, there would be a staged public burial of the deceased chief at which a bull was killed, and its skin stuffed with material sawn to resemble the human form, which the family would present for burial as if it were the chief's body.

According to Bullock, in those bygone times, the Makorekore and Watonga Shona groups, mummified the corpse of their chiefs by sealing and drying it in a special hut built for that purpose outside the home.[70] Some close relatives would be tasked with the watching of the corpse and the removal of the maggots, which were carefully preserved, for they were believed to carry the spirit of the dead chief. These maggots were eventually buried together with the corpse of the chief. At the time of burial, a bull would be killed, and its hide would be used to wrap up the corpse of the chief for burial. Usually, the burial was in a cave, where his body was placed in a sitting position, sometimes among other mummified corpses belonging to his family. Once a chief was buried in a cave, the hill would be considered sacred. However, a chief could also be buried in a grave.

The Makorekore are also said to have believed that the dead chief would transform into a lion spirit (*mhondoro*). In anticipation of the *mhondoro*, the grave in which the chief was buried was not completely sealed. A small opening was left, and it was through it that the lion (*mhondoro*) was seen every night by the meticulous watchers, in and out of the grave. When the watchers thought that the lion was big enough, they would seal off the opening after the lion would have gone out of the grave, to prevent it from reentering. That ritual would force the spirit of the dead chief to have the lion as its permanent host, until at the point when it was reincarnated into a spirit medium. Hence, such a spirit medium can also be referred to as *mhondoro*.

In the past, among the Karanga of Nyajena, the death of Chief Nyajena was a very solemn occasion, which was kept a secret for a about a month. The chief's body was sometimes, mummified, and buried in a

---

68. Gelfand, *Shona Rituals with Special reference to the Chaminuka Cult*, 203–204.
69. Ibid., 204.
70. Bullock, *Mashona Laws and Customs*, 45.

cave, in a sitting position. In Nyajena, two sacred hills, namely, Chimbete and Marevesa, are believed to have been the burial places of the founding chiefs. The two hills are mentioned in their totemic poems. The ancestral spirits of the Nyajena chiefs are referred to as, "vari Chimbete, vari Marevesa, (those in Chimbete hill, and those in Marevesa hill).

However, nowadays, the chief is buried in his own village, in the cemetery where his close relatives are buried. His body is not mummified. It is reported that when the previous occupant of the throne of Chief Nyajena died, the resting days were extended to one month. In the past, if the chief died during the rainy season, the sacred days on which the people of Nyajena should rest, could be postponed until the following Winter. This postponement was intended to allow the people to work in their fields, lest they failed to harvest any crops. The successor to the dead chief is not immediately named until after a few months or even years. In the meanwhile, a close relative or even son of the deceased chief would be asked to perform the chiefly responsibilities. It should be noted that the appointment of a chief in Zimbabwe, has become politicized, and involves District Administrators, and even government officials. Consequently, the jostling for the chieftainship by authorized families may delay the appointment of a chief indefinitely. In Nyajena, the competition is more intense because chieftainship is rotated among the aristocratic families, whose heads may not agree about the specific family to succeed the deceased chief.

THE SHADOW

A mysterious phenomenon called the shadow (*bvuri*) has been reported among the Karanga of Nyajena and other Shona ethnic groups. It is believed that a human being has two shadows—the white shadow and black shadow. The Karanga believe that once a person dies, the white shadow should disappear. If it does not vanish as expected, it is assumed that the spirit of the dead person is aggrieved. This anger might have been caused by some error of omission or commission in the performance of the death rituals, or might have been caused by witches. In addition, the anger may be a result of the ill-treatment the dead person would have been subjected to by one of his relatives during his last days of life. Furthermore, the white shadow may appear to warn the family that the corpse would have been tampered with, by the witches. It is a warning that something is not right, and has to be rectified before the body is laid to rest. Moreover, it is believed that witches can try to change the corpse into an evil spirit before burial. Finally, they may try to devour corpse before it is properly secured in the grave. Hence, the appearance of the *bvuri* is a clarion call by the deceased that something is not right, and that the family has to be vigilant.

This appearance of the shadow may be triggered by the arrival of the witch or culprit at the funeral. If the shadow is a warning to the family about the arrival of the perpetrator, they must take necessary precautions and remedial actions before he causes more harm to the spirit of the deceased. They may choose to confront and interrogate him in order to extract a confession from him.

Aschwanden, who carried out his study among the Karanga of Ndanga, Bikita, Masvingo, offers comparatively explanations for the phenomenon of the shadow.[71] He claims that his informants told him that the white shadow is a symbol of a man's soul and it should either become invisible or vanish at death. When it does not vanish, it has several meanings. First, something might have gone wrong in the carrying out of death rituals. Second, the appearance of the white shadow may be caused by the spirit to delay its burial to allow someone very dear to the dead to arrive, and would disappear as soon as the person arrives. Third, if the deceased is a woman, the white shadow might be a sign of her anger against her husband if he abused her during her physical life. In this case, the husband must compensate the father or guardian of the departed woman for the white shadow to disappear. Fourth, the white shadow may be a sign that the death was caused by a murderer, and if he is present, he should confess his wrongdoings to facilitate the vanishing of the shadow.

Among most Shona groups, there are several methods used to resolve the appearance of the white shadow. The family of the deceased, if they already have a suspect, may confront the perpetrator, and if he confesses, he is asked to pay a fine of the admittance of guilt. In cases where witchcraft is suspected, Aschwanden says that all the relatives are gathered into the room where the corpse is kept under constant surveillance by close relatives.[72] Once everyone is in the hut, all are requested to exit the hut one by one, slowly. As they exit, someone will be watching the shadow closely. It is believed that the white shadow immediately

---

71. Aschwanden, 236.
72. Ibid., 236.

disappears as soon as the culprit walks out of the room. In that way, the bereaved may identify the witch, who is then confronted to extract a confession of his evil doing.

In addition, *varoora* (daughters-in-law), may be asked to scold the deceased for the white shadow to disappear. This scolding can only work if the appearance of the shadow is caused by the anger of the deceased because of some ritual that would not have been done appropriately. The *varoora* can bully the spirit into forgiving its family of the wrong done. Although ancestors can be scolded to spring them into action, at this point, it is believed to be extremely dangerous to scold the deceased. Consequently, *Varoora* should shoulder this responsibility because they are not related to the dead by blood, and the spirit of the deceased cannot attack them because of the insults. As the *varoora* are performing the ritual of scolding the dead, others are busy watching the shadow. Once it disappears, the scolding should cease immediately, and the *varoora* should thank the deceased for listening to their pleas.

If all other remedies do not work, the close relatives may need to consult a traditional medical practitioner to learn the cause of the displeasure, and the remedy to be used to appease the spirit. Once the cause of the appearance of the white shadow is dealt with, and the spirit of the deceased is appeased, it should disappear. The disappearance of the shadow brings much relief to the family of the deceased because it would be disastrous to bury the body before the shadow disappears.

It should be noted that once the white shadow has appeared, it does not go away until the issue that would have caused it is resolved. Failure to resolve it may cause some misfortunes happening to the family or community because of the displeasure of the spirit.

The appearance of the *bvuri* is very significant. It shows that the dead are still conscious of their surroundings. They know what is happening to them and to their lifeless bodies. They can still communicate with their families, albeit differently. This communication saves the family from future misfortunes, which may happen to the family if they were not resolved before the burial. The quicker the resolution, the better the relationship between the deceased and his family, and the more peaceful the future.

MUTARARA BRANCH AND SWEEPING AROUND THE GRAVE

When the grave is completely covered with stones, a branch of *mutarara* tree (*gardenia Ternifolia*) may be placed on top of the grave. In cases where the grave is dug a day before burial (which should be avoided in Nyajena), the *mutarara* branch is also used to cover the grave opening overnight. The people of Nyajena do this for four reasons. First, the ritual symbolizes that the physical life has ended, and the deceased has entered the spiritual realm. In the past, in Nyajena, the same branch could be placed on the threshold of a witch's house to communicate that she was no longer wanted in the village, and had to vacate her home. Likewise, the placement of this branch on top of the grave signifies the end of the physical life, and the beginning of a new life in the spiritual realm. Although the deceased is expected to come back home, later, as an ancestor, in the spiritual form, his bodily form is not welcome. So, the *mutarara* branch is used as a fence to prevent the deceased from coming back in the bodily form.

Second, the branch is intended to invoke the spirit of the deceased to rise as an avenging spirit to fight the people who are being suspected of having caused his death. So, this branch may not be placed on the graves of people where witchcraft or any other foul play are not suspected. It is believed that the withering of the leaves of the branch should remind the spirit of the deceased to wake up and attack the people who would have caused his death. The spirit can do this as an avenging spirit, and would only relent after compensation has been paid.

Third, the branch is intended to prevent wild animals from digging the grave or playing on it. Although the grave is deep enough and well secured with stones to prevent wild animals from digging up the body, some animals may try their luck. If any signs of the grave having been tampered with are detected, even if caused by wild animals, it may cause a lot of anxiety and fear. Whatever damage would have been done by animals, would always be attributed to witches. Hence, protecting the grave helps in preventing unnecessary anxiety and fear if something happens to it.

Fourth, the Karanga do not use *mutarara* for firewood because it has some mystical powers. They believe that it can chase away evil spirits. By placing it on the grave, they believe that it drives away evil spirits that may want to harm the spirit of the departed, which at this moment is believed to be extremely vulnerable to evil spirits. This vulnerability of the spirit is believed to be caused by its close association with its undecomposed body. Once the body decomposes, the spirit is believed to gain more power, and if it qualifies, it can be promoted to ancestorhood.

THOSE NOT ALLOWED TO ATTEND THE BURIAL

It is important to point out that, in the past, many African ethnicities forbade young children and pregnant women to attend burials. In addition to pregnant women and children, among some Shona ethnical groups, one of the twin brothers or sisters was not allowed to attend the burial of the other twin. Among other Shona ethnicities, the remaining spouse was not allowed to attend the burial of his or her spouse.[73]

There were two reasons for this sanction. It was believed that children and pregnant women could easily be affected by whatever would have caused the death, and the evil spirits, which are believed to roam the homestead and burial place during this period. These evil forces would be trying to snatch away the spirit of the dead. The witches would be trying to steal the body before it is secured in the grave. When they fail to do that, as they most of the times do, they look for vulnerable people—pregnant women and children, among the mourners. Therefore, the women and children should be protected from such possible attacks. If the deceased were one of the twins, it was believed that the evil spirits that would have caused the death of one twin, would mistake the surviving twin sibling for the dead one, and would strike him. The twin sister or brother needed to be protected from a catastrophic mistaken identity that could happen.

BURIAL BY PROXY

Burial by proxy refers to the symbolic and ritual burial of the personal clothing, weapon, soil from the grave, or an animal's head in the place of the deceased whose body cannot be physically buried in the appropriate rural home cemetery. In the past, among the Shona, burial by proxy was prompted by many factors. First, there were people who died in foreign lands, away from their rural homes, and no one in their family knew about the occurrence of their deaths or the location of their burial places

---

73. Bullock, *The Mashona (The Natives of Southern Rhodesia)*, 264.

if buried at all. In such cases, relatives would wait for the return of the missing relative, but if he did not show up for a considerable period of time, they would consult a diviner, who would notify them of the occurrence of their deaths. According to Bullock, sometimes, the spirit of the deceased could come back home and would make one of the family members mysteriously sick.[74] His relatives would then consult a diviner, who was likely to confirm the demise of their family member.

Second, burial by proxy was also performed for people who would have died, and been buried in a faraway place. In this case, the relatives knew about the occurrence of death, and the place of burial, and one of them or more would have attended the burial. In colonial Zimbabwe, these burials were likely to happen in the newly established urban areas, most of which were situated far away from the rural home of the deceased person. Also, some people, because of their religious affiliation, were compelled to be buried in a church symmetry, far away from their rural homes. The representatives of the relative who would have attended the burial would take some of the soil from the departed's grave, and would bring it back home for burial.

Third, burial by proxy was also done for a person who would have died away from home, and whose remains had not been found. It was common for some people to die at the battle front, away from home, and their bodies were not transported back home for burial. A few of them would be buried by colleagues at the battle front in shallow graves, but others would be regrettably left in the open where their bodies were devoured by wild animals. There were also people who were attacked and devoured by wild animals either at home, or while hunting, and their bodies would not be available for burial. Usually, the family of the deceased would know about the occurrence of death, but they could not retrieve their bodies for burial.

Among the Shona, there are numerous forms of burial by proxy rituals, one of which is to take a piece of cloth belonging to the deceased, and bury it under a fruit tree such as *Muvonde* (sycamore tree) or *Muchakata* (*Parinari capensis*) at home. The place where the cloth is buried acts as the official grave of the deceased for purposes of rituals that require the family members to go to the grave. It seems that a fruit tree is conducive for this ritual because it symbolizes the fruitfulness of the person

---

74. Bullock, *Mashona Laws and Customs*, 47.

symbolically buried there under. Alternatively, the relatives could bury the departed's clothes or weapon under a fruit tree.

Bullock says that among the Budya, if someone died far away from home, and his body could not be transported to his rural home, the most senior member of the relatives attending the burial would take some soil from the grave of the deceased, and would tie it in a black cloth, which was then taken back home for burial.[75] The soil could be buried in a shallow grave at the rural home of the deceased, while being accorded most of the death rituals. Sometimes, the soil and the black cloth would be buried together with a black goat. As a result, the deceased would have two graves. The one at his home would be used for all ritual purposes by the relatives. The people believed that the spirit of the deceased would be living at the home grave, and not at the grave where his body would have been buried physically.

In some cases, if the deceased's body were not located, the family would collect a goat's head or bones from the veld, which they would bury as if they were burying their relative. The grave would become the official burial place of the dead and would be used for all ceremonial purposes involving that person.

Gelfand reports a slightly different version of the same rituals.[76] He claims that if a person died away from home and were buried there, some Shona ethnical groups would send a relative, even after the burial, to take a stone or a handful of soil from the grave. The soil or stone would be brought home for burial. A black goat would be slaughtered, and together with the stone, would be wrapped in a black blanket for burial. Alternatively, some people would get a small branch of a tree, beat the grave, telling the deceased that they were taking him home. The branch would be pulled for a while and then taken home for a second burial. This second burial of the deceased was compelled by the need to bury a relative at home, where ancestors would receive him.

Among the Karanga of Nyajena, if someone dies away from home, or buried in a faraway place, if his death or grave are not known, and if no burial by proxy ritual was performed, a fruit tree such as *muhacha* can be used for rituals relating to the dead. The tree would act as his burial place.

Burial by proxy rituals were performed to guarantee each dead member of the family a decent burial place at the rural home of the

---

75. Bullock, *The Mashona (The Natives of Southern Rhodesia)*, 272.
76. See Gelfand, *Shona Rituals with Special reference to the Chaminuka Cult*, 196.

family. This decent burial place would be among other deceased members of the family, and would facilitate the performance of other post-burial rituals such as *magadziro* because the new grave would be used for all other ritual purposes associated with that person. This burial shows the importance of the rural home for most Shona people. In the past, the rural home was the place where the baby's umbilical cord and its mother's placenta were buried. The place where the baby's umbilical cord and placenta were buried were considered sacred places for the owners because that is where they connected with the ancestors of the family. According to Doumbia and Doumbia, most West African peoples always tried to bury a dead person where he was born. Hence, in death, just like in birth, connection with the ancestors of the family was crucial.[77]

It is interesting to note that, although the Shona believe that spirits of the dead are not limited by space and time, in the case of burial by proxy, they seem to make the spirit dependent upon the living family members. The spirit cannot travel alone from its urban burial place, for it has to rely on the family representatives to bring the soil from its grave for another burial at home. It goes a long way to show the importance of sacred shrines, and the mutually beneficial interdependence between the dead and the living.

CULTURAL CHANGES IN BURIAL RITUALS

As has been mentioned in the preceding chapters, it cannot be denied that all cultures are dynamic. This dynamism may be a result of acculturation, which brings about mutual influences between cultures. In the encounter between Western and Shona cultures, some of the Shona ritual practices were demonized, abandoned, or replaced by Western practices. This section seeks to explore some of the cultural changes in Shona death rituals, and the benefits or setbacks of such transformations to the Shona people. These changes are explored from a postcolonial perspective, which argues that some of the important Karanga death rituals could be salvaged before they are completely lost.

---

77. Doumbia and Doumbia, 151.

From Dying at Home to Dying at the Hospital

Nowadays in Zimbabwe, unlike in the past, many people die at the hospital. In the traditional rural setting of the Shona society, before and soon after the colonization of Zimbabwe by the British South Africa Company in 1890, most terminally ill people died at home, surrounded, and comforted by close family members if available. Here, home refers to the traditional rural home, which every Shona person was entitled to. Up to now, most Shona people who have houses (*dzimba*) in urban areas, do have homes (*misha*) in the rural areas where, in most cases, their parents live. Occasionally, some patients would die at a traditional medical practitioner's home, while receiving treatment, or on the way to or from a healer's place of healing. Even in the case where a patient died outside his home, he still would be surrounded and comforted by his close relatives. It should be noted that some Shona people still prefer to die at home, but the number has dwindled. There is something sacred and consoling about dying in the midst of one's close relatives. Since death is like surrendering to the will of nature, and a complete acceptance of defeat, the accompaniment in those last moments of one's physical life, by family members assures the departing person of continual communion and love by the remaining family members.

Despite the unpopularity of dying at home among most Shona peoples, there are numerous advantages of dying at home. Duda, writing from a different society and context contends that in "dying at home we maintain the ability to choose our own way, whether it be a little decision like what time we eat, or a big one like whether or not to use life-sustaining techniques."[78] There is something therapeutic about being able to make decisions about one's healthcare. It is important for the terminally ill person to be able to choose what she wants to eat. In some cases, the dying person may have an appetite for some certain foods, and if she is at home, her family could make such foods available. Duda, goes on to list the numerous advantages of dying at home. She asserts that it is natural, and it enhances the quality of life because it maintains the respect and dignity of the patient, which makes her feel loved, wanted, useful, and normal.[79]

---

78. Duda, *A Guide to Dying at Home*, 60.
79. Ibid., 61.

Furthermore, Duda claims that "love is a very effective pain neutralizer."[80] At home, one has the freedom to "express feelings, of grief, anger, and love," which may be difficult to express in a hospital setting, where one has the feeling of being watched all the time. In fact, in the hospital, one is constantly kept under surveillance, for most hospital wards have surveillance cameras. It does not feel good to know that you are being watched all the time. This loss of privacy dehumanizes the patient. The loss of privacy is connected to the loss of human dignity. Duda rightly claims that in a hospital, the dying person can easily lose her dignity, humanity, and individuality by being referred to as "the patient in room 204B," instead of her real name. Of course, the hospital personnel use these code names for the protection of the patients' privacy, yet taking their dignity away by so doing.[81] At home, a patient has a name, which her relatives use to call her. She is allowed to make decisions concerning her care and future. She has dignity.

Duda also contends that at home, there is no "travel wear between home and hospital."[82] In Zimbabwe, the shuttling of the dying person between home and the hospital can be very expensive since most rural people do not own automobiles. Most have to hire private vehicles to transport their ill and deceased relatives. Even though public transport is almost always available, the trips may be very difficult and painful for the ill person because of the rough roads and overcrowded buses.

Sankar insists that the patient who dies at home is given autonomy, which helps her maintain her identity by being treated as a social being by the caregiver, and she defines a caregiver as the "person with primary responsibility for someone whose disability or incompetence makes him or her dependent on another to accomplish the task of daily living." [83] Usually, the caregiver is closely related to the dying person, which makes the dying person free to share his feelings and emotions. There is respect brought about by the relationship between the two. Mothers can take care of their ill husbands and children, or the other way around. Siblings can take care of their dying siblings.

These advantages do not imply that hospitals are not important—they are. To navigate the importance of the hospital, perhaps it

---

80. Ibid., 64.
81. Ibid., 60.
82. Ibid., 61.
83. Sankar, *Dying at Home*, 194.

is imperative, at this juncture, to explore how Western hospitals came into existence. Backer, Hannon, and Russell trace the earliest hospitals to the healing temples of ancient Egypt, which were then followed by the Buddhist public hospitals in India, and the Muslim hospitals in the East. Western hospitals, which began as inns eventually started taking in the homeless and the poor within the city to provide lodgings for them.[84] Eventually, they evolved into places where people suffering from acute illnesses were cared for, with the aim of returning them back home alive. Since many of these homeless people could not afford to hire private physicians, most hospitals started offering medication.

Corr, Nabe, and Corr quoting Simpson and Weiner, say that the word "hospital," comes from the Latin word, *hospitale*, meaning, a place of "reception and entertainment of pilgrims, travelers, and strangers."[85] So, initially, all that a good hospital could do was to provide a resting place, good food, clean water, and shelter. Backer, Hannon, and Russell argue that until the late 19th century, the appropriate place to die was the home, for hospitals were not quite organized.[86] They note that as hospitals developed and evolved, their goal was the provision of medical services to cure, ameliorate, and prevent diseases in individuals.

The introduction and establishment of hospitals in Zimbabwe in the 19th century, changed the way the terminally ill people were cared for. First, some of the hospitalized people could now die at the hospitals, where they would be receiving Western health care. This new development forced them to die away from their rural homes and relatives. This phenomenon has brought about challenges in the transportation of corpses back to the rural home where they should be buried. Although there are cemeteries at or near some of Zimbabwe's big hospitals, many Shona people feel obliged to bury the remains of their loved ones at their rural homes, where some of the already departed family members are laid to rest. This obligation brings about the challenge of transportation costs. Participants in this study concurred that transporting a dead body from the hospital to rural homes was expensive. For example, in Nyajena, many families have to pay exorbitant transport costs to bring the body of their deceased relative home. The average cost is at least one cow. Of

---

84. Backer et al., *Death and Dying*, 86.
85. Corr et al., *Death and Dying, Life and Living*, 2nd Edition, 201.
86. Backer et al., 86.

course, this transport cost could have been avoided if the patient had been allowed to die at home.

Second, another challenge encountered by people who die at the hospital concerns the unavailability of close family members during the final dying moments. In most hospitals in Zimbabwe, close relatives can only visit patients during stipulated visiting hours. Unless the patient is a young child, relatives are not allowed to spend the night watching their ill family member. The nurses and other medical personnel have that responsibility. Sometimes, the patient dies alone because the nurses on duty would be attending to other patients. In cases where patients die alone, the dying may feel lonely and abandoned. That is why some patients are said to express the wish to return home, and die there. So, it is likely that at the hospital, a sick person dies alone, or in the presence of the hospital personnel, who are not related to him.

Even if a sick person dies during the visiting hour when her family members are present, the medical practitioners on duty may ask the relatives to leave the room at the onset of death. In the past, the accompaniment by relatives during the last moment of life was mandatory, and would give the dying person an opportunity to say his last wishes to the family members present. It also showed him that the family had not deserted him in this crucial moment of his life. To worsen the matter, since close relatives are not present in the hospital ward when death approaches, the *kupeta* (folding of hands and legs) and closing of the yes rituals may not be performed properly.

The participants in this study reported other things that are missing at the hospital. Reflecting on the American health situation (and this can be applied to Zimbabwean hospitals as well), Chapman advocates for a healing hospital instead of a hospital that intends to cure.[87] He criticizes some American hospitals for lacking the loving, compassionate, and respectful service for patients. It is this type of service that leads to the healing of the patient, and if absent, the healing may not happen. Chapman alleges that in American hospitals, the patient is sometimes treated like a robot, and to some extent, dehumanized. Chapman claims that "Patient gowns and IV lines seem to signal that the patient has now become something less than a full-fledged human.[88] The hospitalized ill persons are often referred to with a variety of demeaning sobriquets such

---

87. Chapman, *Radical Loving Care*, 4.
88. Ibid., 5.

as "the gall bladder in 5028" (person with gall bladder disease) or "the frequent flyer" (regular visitor to the ER) or "the screamer" (disoriented patient who groans a lot). For Chapman, the use of terms like these in reference to patients are degrading and marginalizes them.[89] Normal human beings have names, and should be called by their names. The gowns that Chapman criticizes are open at the back and can easily show the naked body of the ill person, and this diminishes the dignity of the dying person. At home, things are different because patients are dressed in their own clothes.

Third, at hospitals, some of the important rituals that would normally be performed for the dying at home cannot be performed. According to Aiken, these death rituals are intended to acknowledge that life would have been lived fully by paying last respects to the dead, making it easier for the bereaved to express grief, offering a helping hand to the mourners, and allowing both the deceased and the bereaved to experience a rite of passage from one status to another.[90] In fact, in hospitals such rituals are not permitted. For instance, at Morgenster Hospital, and other major hospitals in Zimbabwe, the use of traditional herbs is not allowed. In addition to that, the causes of death explained by the Western medical practitioners are not compatible with what the Shona are used to. For instance, the hospital may explain how mosquitoes and cancerous tumors may have caused the death, but the fundamental question about why this person, at this particular time, is not answered. Why would a mosquito bite one person instead of another? Why would one person and not another, have cancer at that particular time? The traditional diviners can answer such questions.

Fourth, most hospitals in Zimbabwe are located in areas far away from the homes of the people. In the rural areas, most ill people are taken to mission hospitals, far away from the patient's home and relatives. This relocation prevents many family members from visiting the dying person. The dying person may feel isolated. Lawton writing about the American experience, contends that, ordinarily, patients complain that relatives have ceased to see or visit them.[91] This feeling can be made worse by being relocated to a hospital situated far away from the rural home. People may not have adequate bus fare to visit the dying frequently. Sharing the

89. Ibid., 5.
90. Aiken, *Dying, Death, and Bereavement*, 133.
91. Lawton, *The Dying Process*, 44.

same sentiments, Corr, Nabe, and Corr say that "Persons who are dying most likely are to be concerned about such matters as being abandoned, losing control over their own bodies and lives, and being in overwhelming pain or distress."[92] Although most hospitals can take care of the physical pain, they may not be able to deal effectively with distress and the feeling of being abandoned. This feeling is worsened when the dying patients are in hospitals far away from their homes, where their relatives cannot afford to visit them. Even if they are able to visit, the length of the visit is limited to just a couple of hours at most.

In addition to dying at the hospital, another huge cultural change concerns the burial of the deceased in urban cemeteries, unlike in the past, where all burials took place in rural areas. This phenomenon has been necessitated by two factors. First, during the federation of Rhodesia and Nyasaland (1953–1963), many immigrant workers came to work in Southern Rhodesia (Zimbabwe) from Nyasaland (Malawi) and Northern Rhodesia (Zambia). Most of these migrant workers bought homes in towns, and some of them never went back to their countries of origin. These urban dwellings became the only homes for some of those migrant workers. Sooner, some Shona people also bought houses in urban areas in addition to their rural homes, and sooner, some abandoned their rural homes.

Second, the industrialization and urbanization of Zimbabwe enticed many Shona people to leave their rural homes in pursuit of gainful employment in towns. Initially, mostly men worked and lived in the towns where they worked, while their families lived in the rural areas. Eventually, many men brought their families to towns to live with them. This movement of people from rural Zimbabwe into urban areas caused the abandonment of rural homes, which were initially left in the care of elderly parents if they were still alive. Nowadays, many people either rent or have purchased houses in urban areas, and no longer visit their rural homes if they still have them. The people who still want to bury their beloved ones at their rural homes, may be hindered by the cost of transporting the remains of the deceased, and also by the unavailability of their own homes there. In such cases, it becomes cheaper to conduct burials in urban cemeteries, closer to their new homes. As a result, many burials are conducted in towns since many rural homes have become dilapidated, abandoned, inaccessible, or are far away from the place of

92. Corr et al., 170.

death. Some of my informants reported that some people from Nyajena were being buried as far as South Africa because the bereaved families would have failed to transport the remains of their relatives to Nyajena.

There are numerous challenges of burying relatives in urban cemeteries. One of the challenges of doing so is that the corpse may be prepared for burial by strangers at the mortuary. The grave is usually dug by strangers, who in most cases, do not care for rituals such as marking the grave. Consequently, the departed is given a home for her final repose by strangers, which is against the customs of the Karanga people. Furthermore, the ritual of washing and dressing the body may not be performed by the relatives, but by the mortuary personnel, unless a special request for exception is made by the relatives of the deceased. In addition to that, the grave may be surrounded by strangers' graves, unlike in rural homes, where it is surrounded by the graves of relatives, who are expected to welcome the spirit of the deceased into the ancestral realm.

Benefits of Hospitalization

Now, it is over a century after the colonization of Zimbabwe, and forty years after Zimbabwe attained its independence from the British colonial masters. The passage of time and acculturation have also brought about significant changes in the care of dying people. When people become more seriously ill, they are sometimes transported to the hospital as has been explored above. Some of them would have been to the same or a different hospital before, and would have been discharged due to the worsening of the illness, so that they could receive palliative care at home. In the Western world, palliative care is recommended for terminally ill people, and is intended to give them comfort care such as pain management while waiting for their final demise. Corr, Nabe, and Cor describe palliative care as addressing the symptoms rather than the underlying causes of the illness, because at this stage of illness, it would have been decided that all possible medical interventions would have been tried, and no interventions may be capable of halting the disease.[93]

In other words, the goal of palliative care is mitigation rather than curing. Since most Shona people do not understand the goal of palliative care of patients, and are not properly trained to render that care, they may take back the patient to the hospital when they sense that death is around

93. Corr et al., 186–187.

the corner. Some families send back the dying person to the hospital with the hope that a healing miracle would be performed. The Shona have been made to believe that Western medicines can cure any ailment. Even though in some cases, some dying patients' health eventually improve at the hospital, most do not make it. Often, it is futile to take back the ill person to the hospital even though he may have been discharged from the same hospital to receive end of life care at home.

This mentality of relocating the dying person, who would have been discharged from the same or another hospital to receive palliative care at home, back to hospital should not be roundly condemned, for the hospital offers numerous advantages to the dying person and the caregivers. First, hospitals have advanced medical equipment and technologies that they use to empirically diagnose the cause of the patient's illness. The logic is that, if they can identify the physical cause of the illness, they can be able to treat and cure it. The relatives of the ill person want to give the patient the best chance of regaining his health, and they believe that the hospital can do that.

Also, there is a certain end of life care, which can be best given at the hospital. For instance, if the patient is unable to feed naturally, the hospital personnel may use nasogastric or intravenous feeding, which is impossible or too expensive and complicated to do in the rural home. The nasogastric tube is used to give the patient medication or liquid food via a tube inserted through his nostrils. Intravenous feeding is used for patients whose digestive system cannot absorb or accept food that is taken or eaten. This feeding is done using a tube inserted through one's vein. In this case, the hospital may provide care for the dying that can improve the quality of her final life to the bitter end.[94]

Second, at home, there may be no one to take care of the sick person because of other vital commitments. A dying person needs special attention and care, and if this is unavailable at home, then the hospital may be preferred. Even if there is a family member who is willing to take care of the dying patient, home-based care is not easy. According to Sankar, caring for the dying is an "emotionally charged activity," which may invoke deep grief, anger, and a feeling of helplessness in the caregiver.[95] As if that is not enough trouble, "the dying person may vent his or her anger by trying to control the caregiver, placing absurd and unrelenting demands

---

94. Duda, 62.
95. Sankar, 128.

on the caregiver, and retaliating furiously when these demands are not met."[96] So, the hospital is equipped with personnel that can deal with that anger by not taking it personally or offering counseling.

Third, if the patient dies at the hospital, most hospitals have mortuaries in which the body can be kept until transport and funeral arrangements have been made. The regulated temperature in mortuaries delays the decomposition of the corpse. This temporary storage of the corpse in the hospital mortuary has become more important among Zimbabweans because family members do not often live in the same place as they used to do in the past. It is even more complicated now because many Zimbabweans live in the diaspora, far away from home, and they are likely to take several days to arrive home for a funeral. Many young Zimbabweans have crossed the border into South Africa, where they seek greener pastures. Since all close family members should attend the funeral of a relative if they can, the relatives are able to wait for them, since the body would be at the hospital mortuary.

Fourth, in hospitals, there are qualified healthcare givers who are trained to minimize or even prevent the transmission of diseases. Sometimes, people suffer from infectious diseases, and it would be extremely difficult for the family to prevent the spread of such diseases at home. There is always the risk of contracting diseases, particularly if there are small children and the elderly at home. Also, there are many hazards at home that can endanger the health of the dying person or her family members. So, taking the terminally ill patient to hospital is seen by many Shona people as a way of protecting the family members from contracting the same disease. At the hospital, they have the right equipment and chemicals that prevent the spread of communicable diseases.

Although the preceding reasons for taking the dying person to hospital are compelling enough, there is yet a fourth reason that is profoundly significant. From a cultural point of view, this relocation of the seriously sick person to the hospital may be induced by the traditional relocation of the ill person (*kusengudza*) mentality. As has been explained in the preceding chapters, the dying person was relocated to another place, preferably a healer's home. This relocation was intended to take away the patient from the witches that might have bewitched him. In addition to that, it was also meant for the patient to receive treatment at a traditional healer's place. Furthermore, if the sick person were about to die, he was

---

96. Ibid., 131.

offered an opportunity to reflect on his impending journey, speak out his finally words, and die peacefully, away from the noises in the home. It was believed that dying people needed privacy and peace, which may be scarce at the hospital, where medical practitioners may come in and out of the ward as they please.

Defining Embalmment and its Benefits

In addition to the temporary storage of bodies in mortuaries owned by hospitals, some people take the corpse to funeral parlors, where they are embalmed (treated with chemicals that keep decay at bay), and where make-up may be applied to the deceased. Corr, Nabe, and Corr define embalming as, "the removal of blood and other bodily fluids from the corpse and their replacement with artificial preservatives that may help retard decomposition and to color the skin."[97] In affirmation of that, Mayer defines embalming as a "process of chemically treating the dead human body to reduce the presence and growth of microorganisms, retard organic decomposition, and restore an acceptable physical appearance."[98] Mayer classifies embalming into four categories: vascular embalming, which is performed by injecting the chemicals into the arteries, cavity embalming, which refers to the direct treatment of the body cavities such as abdomen, thorax, and so on, hypodermic embalming, which uses syringes and needles to inject chemicals directly into the tissue of the body, and surface embalming, where the embalming chemical is directly brought to the body surface to supplement vascular embalming.[99]

Embalming fluid is a solution used to preserve a corpse temporarily or indefinitely after death. Embalming fluids often "contain a combination of formaldehyde," chemicals like "methanol and ethanol, and water."[100] About eleven liters of the fluid is injected into the corpse through the collar artery and is distributed throughout the body via the circulatory system. Although preservation is temporary, it can last for weeks or even years. There are numerous benefits of embalming the body. For Mayer, it makes the body presentable, non-offensive, and acceptable by restoring its appearance, and slowing decomposition, which allow the bereaved

---

97. Corr et al., 285.
98. Mayer, *Embalming: History, Theory, and Practice, Fourth Edition*, 25.
99. Mayer, 27.
100. Ibid., 55.

enough time to gather or make important decisions pertaining to the burial.

The preservation of the body is very important to most Zimbabweans. Since an embalmed body can last long before decomposition, it gives time for the family members of the deceased to gather and make other funeral preparations. Many Zimbabweans live in the diaspora, and it takes a few days for some of them to travel back home. Also, some people die in the diaspora, far away from home, and may have expressed the wish to be buried in the country of their birth. Embalming facilitates the transportation of such deceased people from the country of death to Zimbabwe, or from urban to rural areas.

Challenges of Embalming

Even though the Shona have accepted the changes in their funeral and burial arrangements that were brought about by the embalmment of the corpse, still, embalming is not without reproach. Corr, Nabe, and Corr criticize embalming for putting more focus on the body as if it were still alive. Moreover, it is expensive, and the money used for the process can be used for the care of the living family members of the deceased.[101] In rural Zimbabwe, the biggest burial expenses are that of purchasing the coffin, providing transportation for the body, and the provision of food for the mourners. For instance, in Nyajena, the closest hospital is Morgenster, which is about two hundred or more kilometers away from the center of the Nyajena. Unless one of the relatives of the deceased has a truck to ferry the corpse, hiring one can be costly. Therefore, the money that is spent on embalming, which can be just cosmetic, in some cases, can be used to purchase the coffin and to meet the transportation expenses.

Also, embalming defies the natural order of things. It is natural law that after death, corpses should begin to decompose. This natural process of decomposition compels relatives to lay to rest the deceased as soon as possible. The Karanga believe that the deceased is transitioning into a new state of life, and this has to be facilitated by the performance of burial rituals. If these rituals are delayed, it means that the process or the journey of the deceased to the ancestral realm is also delayed. This delay may anger the spirit of the deceased and the ancestors unnecessarily.

---

101. Corr et al., 288.

Further, the chemicals used to embalm a corpse are said to be poisonous, and it is believed that some of them may cause cancer. In rural areas, people may handle the corpse without proper protective clothing or gloves, and this may put them at risk. The mourners may not wash their hands properly after burial, which may be hazardous. This exposure to harmful chemicals is exacerbated by the fact that, among many Shona ethnical groups, the body is supposed to spend, at least one night in the home of the deceased, and in most cases, members of the family spend the night in the same room with the corpse. The people may inhale the poisonous chemicals if there are any leakages from the body.

The other contentious issue concerns the removal of the human blood from the body during the embalming process, in order to replace it with the chemicals. Blood is part of the human body, and its removal undermines the integrity of the corpse. A corpse without human blood, may not be considered integral. This leads to the question, "can the spirit of an embalmed body become an ancestor?" If the answer is affirmative, is there no danger of the ancestor coming back home with a physical body, since the *magadziro* may be performed before the complete decomposition of the corpse? As if that is not confusing enough, the removed blood may be thrown away, or burned by the morticians, thereby desecrating it. Human blood is sacred, and should be given a burial befitting of human blood.

However, despite the setbacks outlined above, more and more Shona people appreciate the use of chemicals to embalm the body of a deceased family member, particularly those who die in hospitals or in towns. Half of the participants in this study felt that the advantages of embalming outweighed the disadvantages of not doing so.

CULTURAL CHANGES IN ANNOUNCING DEATH

The traditional Shona people had rituals concerning the announcement of the death of a relative, but most of these rituals have changed. For instance, the traditional use of the drum, blowing of a horn, or the use of emissaries to announce the occurrence of death is almost gone. Nowadays, some people use phones or social media such as Facebook and WhatsApp to announce the demise of their relatives. It cannot be denied that the use of phones has brought about several advantages to communication. In announcing the occurrence of death, the cellphone is cost effective and timesaving in the sense that one does not need to travel to announce the occurrence of death to relatives. Now, with many family members living far away from their traditional homes, the old way of announcing death would be costly because the emissary would need to fly to notify those relatives living outside Zimbabwe. The use of phones and social media has made things a lot easier.

Moreover, phones and the internet are faster. At the stroke of a key, a message is sent to all intended recipients wherever they are. This immediate notification of relatives and friends, of the occurrence of death, encourages the relatives to quickly make traveling arrangements to the burial place. They may also send their death tokens (*chema*) to assist in the burial of the deceased if they are unable to attend the funeral physically. If social media is used, the messages sent may keep going as they are forwarded by the recipients until every family member is notified. Hence, within a short period of time, most people are likely to get the news about the deaths of their relatives. Timely notification of death to relatives is crucial among the Karanga to avoid freaky accidents or misfortunes (*mashura*), which are caused by being unaware of a relative's death.

However, this advancement in the announcement of death has brought about several challenges too. Announcing death on social media or phone, as has become the custom, usually lacks the traditional protocol of death notifications. In the past, the emissaries who were sent to announce the occurrence of death were skilled in the proper manner of making such life-changing announcements. If the death to be announced had happened suddenly, and the relatives had not been notified of the illness of the deceased before he died, the emissary would begin the announcement by psychologically preparing the recipient to receive such a message. Instead of announcing the death suddenly, the announcer would hesitate by talking of the serious illness of the deceased as if he were still alive. If the listener were standing or working, he would be asked to sit down. When the announcer felt that the relative was psychologically prepared to receive the bad news, he would tell her of the death of the relative. In addition to the careful and considerate announcement of death, the announcer played the role of a counselor.

On the contrary, the use of social media does not prepare the relatives to receive the sad news of the demise of their family members. Sometimes, pictures of the deceased are posted on social media (if death has happened suddenly in an accident) before the relatives have been notified. This way of announcing death is not only disrespectful to the deceased, but also traumatic to other family members. It shocks them, and may leave many questions unanswered since the context of the death is sometimes missing. In this study several informants reported many cases where a family member had died in an accident, and the family of the deceased had learnt about the tragedy on social media, which was very traumatic.

While the use of modern communication methods cannot be avoided because of various advantages, which they bring, there is a need for a new ethic in the protocol of announcing death. People who announce deaths should have concern for the wellbeing of those to whom they are breaking the news.

BURIAL IN URBAN CEMETERIES

In modern times, the deceased may be buried in an urban cemetery as has been already mentioned above. Normally, the people who live and die in the rural areas are likely to be buried there. However, there have been instances in which someone who dies at his rural home, is brought to an urban cemetery for burial. In like manner, some people who die in town are transported to their rural homes for burial. But if someone has a house or home in town, he is likely to be buried in an urban cemetery. There are advantages of doing so. First, the urban cemetery may be closer to the deceased's home, and this may significantly cut the transportation costs of both the corpse and the mourners. Second, most urban areas are easily accessible, and burying a relative there enables most relatives who live in urban areas to attend the funeral. The cemetery is also accessible to funeral parlor buses that are usually used to ferry mourners to and from the cemetery. Most people in urban areas are employed in one way or the other, and traveling to rural areas may force them to take off days. Now, if the burial is done in town, closer to where they live, they may attend the funeral and then quickly go back to their work. Third, the family of the dead does not worry about gravediggers and undertakers because they are provided by the city or the funeral home albeit for a nominal fee depending on the cemetery chosen.

However, burial in urban areas has its own challenges. Since the grave is dug by strangers, there is no marking of the grave (*kutara guva*) ritual, which is an integral aspect of the Karanga burial rites. Unlike in real life, here the dead is given a home by strangers. Even though a relative may offer the home (grave) to the deceased at the time of burial, the place is not chosen by the relatives, and the new home is not dug by close relatives. The ritual of resting the dead on the way to the grave may not be performed since the coffin is transported to the cemetery in a vehicle.

Further, in the urban cemetery, the dead is buried among strangers. There might not be any single relative buried in the same graveyard. For the Shona, it is crucial that the newly departed be received and initiated by her own ancestors, who most of the time, are buried in the same family graveyard. Although ancestors are not limited by space and time, the Shona think that the rural home is their abode of choice, and the deceased is likely to join them faster if buried at the rural home cemetery. Some people are concerned about the welfare of the spirit of the deceased in the cemetery among strange spirits. Most of the time, these graves are closely packed together that the mourners may have to step on foreigners' graves, which is tabooed by the Karanga of Nyajena. Moreover, urban graves are not covered by rocks as would happen among several Shona ethnicities. Consequently, the soil that is used to cover the grave may be washed away by the rains, or spread out by wild animals, which is another cause for concern.

Another significant challenge is that many Karanga people were either born in the rural area or at hospitals when their parents were still living in the rural areas, and their umbilical cords were buried at their rural homes. So, if the deceased's body is buried in an urban cemetery, far away from where the deceased's umbilical cord is buried, the connectedness of that individual with one's roots, ancestors, and God is disturbed. On top of that, when relatives, who may have failed to attend the funeral come to see where their relative was buried, they may not perform the ritual of *kukanda chibwe* because of the unavailability of small stones in towns, or the forbiddance of placing stones on graves by City Council bi-laws. Furthermore, there is an increase in the use of flowers for people who are buried in towns. Although flowers are very significant to many other cultures, some Karanga people may not find them as significant and durable as pebbles. It does not appear helpful to offer flowers to a departed parent who would not have appreciated them during her physical life. One does not begin to appreciate flowers after death if she never appreciated them before dying. The placing of flowers on the graves of relatives may not replace that of *kukanda chibwe* (placing the pebble).

THE USE OF COFFINS

In the past, the Karanga of Nyajena used the bier (*bwanyanza*), which was constructed by the sons-in-law (*vakwambo*) or nephews (*vazukuru*) using two poles and tree bark, to transport the corpse to the grave or to relocate a sick person. The body would eventually be laid on a reed mat for burial. A wooden pillow was used to rest the head. But this has also changed among the Karanga. Most corpses are now buried in coffins, particularly in urban cemeteries. However, in the rural areas people are not pressured to bury deceased relatives in coffins, but most do. Most of the participants to this study did not recall anyone who was buried without a coffin in their rural villages. In one of the villages in Nyajena, a businessman was said to have been buried without a coffin because the people who were supposed to bring it had delayed, and the body was fast decomposing. In another village, an elderly woman was said to have been buried without a coffin because she had told her family that she did not want to be buried in a coffin. Her main argument was that she would be suffocated in a coffin. Of course, she would not be buried alive, but she is said to have talked about it as if she would be buried alive. There were also a few reports where some corpses were buried without coffins because the relatives could not afford to purchase coffins. But these are a few exceptions because it has become almost normative to place bodies in coffins for burial.

There are several advantages of burying corpses in coffins, and transporting them in vehicles. If the burial place is far away from the home of the deceased, the use of a vehicle to transport it is imperative. If the deceased is being laid to rest in an urban graveyard, a vehicle has to be used to transport his remains to the burial place. In addition to that, a coffin is easy to handle by the undertakers, particularly when they place the corpse into the grave. This easy handling may prevent the spread of infectious diseases. Further, most coffins are decorated and nice to look at, and they indeed console the bereaved.

However, there are also challenges caused by the use of coffins, to the traditional Karanga persons. First, coffins are expensive, and their use may deprive the family of the deceased of the little money that is available, and could have been used for something else. Whether one is buried in an expensive coffin or without a coffin, burial is burial. Once the grave is filled with soil, what remains, and is visible to the people, is just a hip of soil, not the expensive coffin or casket. So, where people struggle to make ends meet, and the law allows it, it is wiser to avoid the use of a coffin.

Further, in the coffin, the body has to face upwards so that the mourners can see the face of the deceased, and this may violate the traditional direction to which the dead body should face. These directions are important because it is believed that the ancestors, which will receive the deceased's spirit can be located in such directions. It is also believed that if the departed is buried facing a wrong direction, he may lose his way to the world of the ancestors. Facing the right direction makes it easier for the spirit to find its way, or locate the realm where ancestors of its family are residing.

SOIL THROWING AND THE USE OF STONES

Among the Karanga of Nyajena, and several other Shona ethnical groups, the ritual throwing of soil into the grave has been Christianized, and its religious significance transformed. Nowadays, the ritual is usually led by the pastor who recites the popular phrase, *"ivhu kuvhu, dota kudota, guruva kuguruva,"* which can be translated as, "soil to soil, ashes to ashes, dust to dust." Here, Christians are referring to the presumed origin and destination of the flesh—the soil, from which the body of the first man is believed to have been created by God.

The Karanga traditional mourners understand this ritual differently. It is performed to indicate an individual's manual involvement and contribution in the burial of one's relative. The ritual is intended for old relatives who cannot actively and manually assist in the digging or covering of the grave with soil, and the carrying of the stones. The ritual is also performed on behalf of the family members who would have failed to attend the funeral. This ritual would prevent the absent family members from encountering *mashura*. *Mashura* means inexplicable and freaky misfortunes that may happen to the family member who may not have attended the funeral of the deceased relative. *Mashura* are also said to happen if the family member has not been notified of the death of a relative. Those relatives who cast the soil on behalf of absent family members may utter a word or two on behalf of the absent member. So, although this ritual is still performed by the Karanga, its significance has radically changed. Instead of performing it as proof of manual involvement of the older members of the family and those who are absent from the burial, it has now been given a Christian meaning. This Christian ritual was reported to be carried out even when burying non-Christian persons. It should be said that the Shona ritual of *kukanda ivhu* has nothing to do with the Christian mythical origin or destination of human beings, and neither should replace the other.

Another cultural change involves the Karanga ritual of placing stones on a grave. In urban cemeteries and some rural graveyards, stones may not be put onto the grave because cement will eventually be used to plaster the grave. One of the advantages of using cement is its durability. Unlike stones, which can be scattered by animals, plastered graves are more durable and appealing to the eye. Also, it has become custom, particularly in urban cemeteries, to use a cross instead of a headstone, to indicate the position of the head. The cross may be used instead of a headstone even if the deceased were not a Christian. This indiscriminate use of Christian symbols shows how the encounter between Christianity and Karanga traditional Religion has affected the latter.

Another cultural change concerns the permission of children to attend the burial of relatives. One of the advantages of allowing little children to attend the burial rituals is the bringing of closure to them. The other advantage is that children begin to grapple with existential questions and challenges, and may acquire the knowledge of performing some of the rituals. However, young children can be traumatized by seeing the corpse of their departed relatives. If the person would have died of an infectious disease, children may be more vulnerable to catching the disease than adults. Hence, allowing or compelling children to attend burials may have long-lasting adverse effects on them.

BURIAL OF FETUSES AND BABIES

Most women give birth at Western hospitals or clinics, particularly when delivering a baby from their first pregnancy. Unfortunately, a few of these babies may die at the hospital, where they are disposed of in the manner suitable to the hospital concerned. In most cases, in Zimbabwe, such deceased fetuses or premature babies are incinerated, which has its own advantages and disadvantages. One of the strengths is that there are no burial costs, and it prevents the spread of infectious diseases.

However, the incineration of fetuses and premature babies is against the Karanga culture. Traditionally, such deceased babies are supposed to be buried along the riverbanks or in wetlands to cool the anger of the babies. Now, burning them makes them angrier, assuming that heat affects them. Their anger may affect their mothers and the communities in which they live. In addition to that, the disposal of such babies at the hospital is not done by older women, who have reached menopause, and are traditionally authorized to handle such delicate burials. As if that is not bad enough, burning reduces these babies to nothing, yet the Karanga believe that the babies are not nothing since they have a spirit, which deserves to be treated with respect. This may endanger the persons who are in charge of the disposal of such babies or the mothers.

MARKING THE GRAVE

Another cultural change involves the Shona ritual of marking the grave. As has already been explained, this ritual should be performed by a close relative of the deceased. Although many Shona peoples still believe that this ritual is very significant, it is difficult to perform it if the deceased is buried in an urban cemetery. In most urban cemeteries, the grave is dug by undertakers employed by city councils. Hence, the deceased is offered a home by strangers. Even if the son-in-law has not fully paid bridewealth for his wife, her relatives cannot use the ritual of marking the grave as leverage in the negotiation of the payment of the arrears because the grave is already dug, and the burial can go on whether they boycott it or not. Also, in urban graveyards, the grave is likely to be surrounded by strangers' graves. Of course, family members may be buried in the same cemetery, but far away from each other.

DEATH TOKEN CHANGES

The payment of the death token (*chema*) has significantly changed. As has been said earlier, *chema* was originally just a small coin, perhaps the equivalent of twenty cents or less. There was usually a small basket or plate placed in the hut where the deceased was being kept. Mourners would place their coins in that plate. Eventually, most Shona peoples started contributing food items such as mealie meal, vegetables, salt, bread, and any other type of food that may be needed during the funeral. As time went on, communities started making monthly contributions, which would be used to assist in the burial of any contributing member or his or her family member. For instance, in Machimbira's Village, in Nyajena, the contributing members are not required to contribute to the *chema* being paid during the funeral, for they would have already paid their *chema*. The *chema* being paid during the funeral is only intended for the mourners who would not have contributed to the revolving fund. However, the villagers are still required to contribute mealie meal in addition to the monetary contributions that they would have done before the funeral in question. If a non-contributing villager or her dependent dies, the other villagers do not use the pooled-up resources to assist at the funeral as they would do for a contributing villager. However, they are expected to pay the voluntary *chema*.

Another new aspect of *chema* takes place on social media. This has become popularized by the fact that many Zimbabweans now live in the diaspora. This movement of Zimbabweans to other countries increased around the year 2000 at the beginning of Zimbabwe's economic meltdown and the political violence. Many Zimbabweans started looking for greener pastures in other countries. It is said that there are millions of Zimbabweans living in other countries. Unfortunately, some Zimbabweans die in those countries, and most of the time, their remains are expected to be transported back to Zimbabwe for burial. Sometimes, the relatives or just well-wishers of the deceased cannot afford the cost of transporting the corpse back to Zimbabwe. Some of them set up go-fund me accounts on social media in order to raise money to assist the family or friends of the deceased in meeting the transportation of the body expenses. This is a new kind of *chema* whose contributors may not be relatives or neighbors of the deceased, but well-wishers.

These new forms of *chema* have several advantages. For example, the community that makes monthly *chema* contributions will always have enough money to assist in the event of a member dying. Villagers do not have to worry about failing to pay their *chema* when needed because they would have contributed already. The social media Go-Fund-Me *chema* appeals enlarge the catchment area by inviting even strangers to contribute. This phenomenon emphasizes and strengthens the unity of all humanity, and the need to assist each other whenever necessary.

CONCLUSION

Cultural and religious transformations are inevitable in every society because no culture is static. However, every society should seek to maintain its cultural identity. So, whatever cultural change happens, it should not lead to cultural amnesia. Every culture, though open to cultural transformation caused by its encounter with other cultures, there should always be some cultural constants that remain the same. These cultural constants give each cultural group its identity and integrity. However, people are likely to cherish and maintain the cultural constants if they know their significance. Hence, this chapter has attempted to explain the significance of some of the Shona death rituals to encourage Karanga people be proud of their own rituals even if they appreciate other people's cultures.

Like every cultural change, there are both advantages and disadvantages in most of the changes discussed in this chapter. Where advantages of practicing certain Shona death rituals outweigh the borrowed rituals, it is advisable for the people to stick with their traditional rituals. However, where the borrowed rituals have more strengths, it would be foolhardy to refuse to embrace them. What is wrong is to fully embrace another people's cultural practices at the expense of one's own. Allowing or aiding the demonization and trashing of one's culture is an admittance to one's inferiority as a human being. The people you assist to trash your culture, will trash you just like they did to your culture. The disrespect of one's own culture is tantamount to the disrespect of one's very being. A people that runs away from its cultural heritage loses its cultural identity and integrity in the same process. A people without its own culture ceases to be. The death of a people's culture is the death of that people.

Chapter 6

KARANGA POST-BURIAL RITUALS

INTRODUCTION

POST-BURIAL RITUALS REFER TO all the prescribed solemn ceremonies that are performed from the time the grave in which the deceased has been laid to rest is completely covered with soil and, or stones, until several years after the *magadziro* and inheritance ceremonies. Even though ancestral rituals continue to be performed intermittently as long as the spirit remains an active ancestor, most of the subsequent ceremonies are not closely associated with the death of the ancestors being honored. In Karanga cosmology, post-burial rituals are profoundly significant just like pre-burial and burial rituals. First, they are the means through which the newly and recently deceased of the family or community are initiated into the invisible and spiritual realm in which other ancestors reside. Second, post-burial rituals assist the relatives of the departed to cope with their heartrending grief of losing a family member. Writing from the Western point of view, Pine identifies five stages of grief that the bereaved should be assisted to come to terms with, namely, disbelief of the occurrence of death, questioning why death has happened, the onset of anger, the exacerbation of anger tinged with desperation, and finally reaching some form of resolution.[1] Praagh expands grief stages into the following seven: paralyzing shock, denial, bargaining, anger directed to

1. Pine, "Dying, Death, and Social Behavior," 38.

those one feels caused the death, feeling guilty of having failed to save the deceased, sadness or depression, and finally, accepting the reality of death.[2] Third, they clearly display the interdependence and communion between the deceased and their living family members. On the one hand, the deceased may not enter the spiritual realm peacefully unless certain rituals such as *magadziro* are performed. On the other hand, the living family members depend on the ancestors for protection, inspiration, good health, intercession, economic prosperity, and family unity.

Post-burial rituals explored in this chapter include, cleansing of the mourners, the consultation of a diviner about the cause of death, placing the stones on the grave, resting or sacred days, commiserating with the bereaved, making of the ancestor, distribution of personal belongings, distribution of estate, cleansing of tools, and the cleansing of weapons, among others. However, it should be noted that the rituals are not necessarily celebrated in this order or one after the other, for some may be celebrated concurrently. In addition to that, the praxis, and timing, and significance of the rituals may differ from one Shona ethnical group to another. Although the rituals explored here are performed by most Shona groups, this study relied heavily on the Karanga of Nyajena.

CLEANSING OF THE UNDERTAKERS

Several Shona ethnicities have varied cleansing rituals for the mourners and tools in which sacred water, sometimes, mixed with herbs is used. However, some Shona groups, such as the Karanga of Nyajena have no special medicated water used for the cleansing of undertakers and mourners. Undertakers or mourners do not go to the river to cleanse themselves with running water. The absent of herbal medicated water among some of the Karanga of Nyajena does not mean that they do not cleanse their gravediggers and mourners. In Nyajena, at the end of the burial, after closing speeches have been given, some ordinary water is provided for the people to wash their hands before they leave the grave. It seems that the washing of hands is more for hygienic purposes than ritual purposes. The undertakers and the mourners who would have handled the grave soil, coffin, and stones need to wash their hands before they return to the home of the deceased, where, in most cases, food would be served before the dispersal of mourners. Soap can be used if available, and this washing

2. Praagh, *Healing Grief,* 13–25.

is a sign that the Karanga of Nyajena are more concerned with hygiene than ritual praxis.

However, some of my informants asserted that although the Karanga of Nyajena do not seem to attach any ritual significance to the washing of hands after burial, the practice has some ritual significance, which might have been superseded by the emphasis on personal hygiene instead of ritual significance. The water that remains from the washing of the hands by the mourners is usually sprinkled around the grave, after sweeping the area. This sprinkling of water is meant to clear the surrounding ground of any footprints. This sweeping and sprinkling of water around the grave would enable the bereaved to detect if the witches or other forces of darkness would have tried to desecrate the deceased's grave.

It is also believed that the washing of hands by the undertakers and other mourners is also intended to ritually cleanse them from the effects of handling a dead body. A corpse is considered ritually unclean because of two things. First, it carries the disease that would have caused the death. The disease may be biological or spiritual. The Karanga are aware that infectious diseases may be spread through the handling of dead bodies. The disease has to be washed off the hands that would have handled the corpse and objects associated with the departed relative. Likewise, evil spirits that may have caused the death are believed to stay outside the grave, roaming the surrounding area. They may attack the mourners, or follow them to their homes, particularly those who would have come into close contact with the corpse. Second, the Shona believe that death causes some "darkness" in the family and home of the deceased, and this darkness is personified by the corpse itself. Anyone coming into the proximity of the corpse becomes ritually unclean. Hence, the washing of hands by the mourners simultaneously removes infections from their hands, and cleanses them of the deleterious spirits responsible for the death.

Furthermore, the sprinkling of the remainder of the water on the area surrounding the grave is intended to cool the deceased. This cooling should be understood in two different but related ways. First, the water cools the deceased, who at this time, is believed to be angry and extremely vindictive. Second, the Shona believe that the uninitiated dead experience extreme bodily heat because of the areas through which they pass. Hence, the sprinkling of water around the grave is intended to cool the spirit of the dead, which may desperately need this cooling. More so, other family ancestors, which attend the burial invisibly, would have traveled from their various abodes, passing through hot areas, which may make them very thirsty. They too need cooling, and to quench their thirst.

In addition to that, the washing of hands is a sign to the departed that he should not seek to punish the mourners because they would have completely disassociated themselves with his demise. It is a declaration of one's innocence. In the past, one would whisper the following words as she washed her hands: "*Usanditevera, handisini ndakakuuraya*," which can be translated as, "Don't follow me, I am not the one who caused your death." Before the spirit of the dead is cleansed, all that can be associated with his burial should be left at the grave including the dirt from the soil. The tools used are taken home, but would be cleansed during the *doro remvura*. Even at home, the deceased's personal belongings, should not be touched or used until a ritual of cleansing the belongings (*kubata nhumbi*) has been performed. The communication from the washing of hands is loud and clear; "Please, do not follow us back into the home. Even the soil that is associated with your grave, we leave it here." This declaration is important because the departed should remain in his new home; the grave, or should venture into the ancestral realm, but not his original home, until a ritual to welcome him back into the home is performed. It is very interesting to note that an almost similar practice is also found in Western cultures, where the estate of the deceased is not shared or used until the estate is distributed according to the will of the deceased, if available, and the laws of the land that govern the distribution of such properties.

Although the ritual is still practiced by many Shona people, among the Karanga of Nyajena, it is not mandatory, and many bereaved families no longer request the mourners to wash their hands soon after burial. However, most undertakers must wash their hands out of necessity—to remove the dirt they would have handled. Also, the tools used during burial are not usually washed unless the soil would have been damp to necessitate the cleaning of tools. This omission has been attributed to the sequence of events at most burials in Nyajena. Under normal circumstances, food is served soon after the burial, and all the people should wash their hands before eating as per custom. Consequently, some mourners see no need to wash their hands at the grave because they should wash them again at the home of the deceased before having their meal. Unlike the washing at the grave, which is done in a twenty-liter container, the washing at home is done individually. So, the dictates of personal hygiene may have compelled some mourners to forego the general washing of hands at the grave, and embracing the individual washing at home just before the meals.

CLEANSING OF TOOLS

Among other Shona groups, the washing of hands is also accompanied by the washing of tools that would have been used during the burial. Most Shona ethnical groups believe that the washing of the tools that would have been used during the burial has religious significance. The Karanga of Nyajena perform a cleansing ritual a few weeks after the burial, which they call *doro remvura* (beer of water) or *masukafoshoro* (cleansing the tools or shovels). Even though its main purpose is to thank the undertakers by providing them with beer and food, the ritual does have religious significance. Certainly, it cannot be just a token of thanking the gravediggers and all who would have assisted during the burial. Gelfand asserts that in the past, at the *doro remvura*, a sacrificial goat or ox was "sacrificed as a compensation for the flesh of the body" which the mourners could not consume.[3] Nowadays, the slaughtering of a sacrificial beast is no longer mandatory. If *mashopeshope* to find out the cause of death has already been done before this ritual, the outcome would be revealed to the people during this gathering.

The significance of the ritual can be derived from its title. It is also called *doro remvura* because it acts like water that would have been used to cleanse the gravediggers and other mourners on the day of the burial. Since some families do not perform the ritual cleansing immediately after the burial, the *doro remvura* ritual is intended to cleanse them. It is the beer that does the work of the cleansing water. It also quenches the gravediggers' thirst because of the hard labor of digging that they would have endured on the day of burial. The gravediggers' ancestors also take part in the beer drinking. Bullock contends that it is intended to quench the thirst of the friends and relatives who would have assisted in the burial of the deceased, and it gives the family an opportunity to set a date for the inheritance and *magadziro* rituals.[4] In support of that, Bourdillon gives several functions of this ritual. For him, it marks the official end of the mourning period although close family members may

---

3. Gelfand, *An African's Religion, The Spirit of Nyajena the case of the Karanga*, 82.
4. Bullock, *Mashona Laws and Customs*, 44.

continue to mourn until after the *magadziro*.[5] Moreover, it allows the family members of the departed an opportunity to gather again as they did at his funeral, and talk about the affairs of the family. On top of that, this coming together avails to them an opportunity to learn the cause of death from the *gata* delegates. Besides, they may also share the estate of the dead or decide for its safekeeping until further notice. Furthermore, the care of the deceased's family may also be discussed at this ritual. Finally, the ritual is intended to cool the spirit, which may begin to assist its own people although it is not yet a full-fledged ancestor until the *magadziro*. According to Rayner, the goat that may be slaughtered at this ritual is food for both the invisible and visible family members and their neighbors.[6]

Mbiti, reporting about the Ndebele people, writes of a similar ritual called the washing of hoes ritual.[7] This could be the ritual from which, the Karanga's *masukafoshoro* (washing of shovels) is derived. Mbiti observes that at this ritual, all the implements that would have been used during the burial are washed with beer.[8] In addition to that, some medicine is given to all the children in the family to protect them from the harm that might be caused by their proximity to the corpse. Mbiti claims that it is not only the human participants that are defiled by their close contact with the corpse during burial but also the objects that are used in the digging of the grave[9]. They, too, need to be cleansed.

The contemporary Karanga nomenclature for the ritual, *masukafoshoro*, which may have been influenced by the Ndebele ritual of cleansing the hoes, is very telling. The term, *masukafoshoro*, is a compound word coming from Shona words, one of which is derived from the English language. *Masuka* comes from the verb *kusuka*, which means cleaning, and *foshoro* is a Shona derivative of the English word, shovel. The tools that would have been used during the burial become defiled by their close contact with the dead, and they also need cleansing. These shovels and other tools would have been cleansed on the day of the burial, but still need ritual cleaning in which beer, and occasionally, a beast is sacrificed. This term is an indication of the changes happening even in the names of

---

5. Bourdillon, *The Shona Peoples*, 208.
6. Rayner, 66.
7. Mbiti, *African Religions and Philosophy*, 2nd Edition, 147.
8. Ibid., 147.
9. Ibid., 147.

Karanga death rituals. Some people advocate the use of the original name of the ritual, *doro remvura*, because *masukafoshoro* distorts the significance of the ritual. But I think that *masukafoshora* is also self-descriptive and tremendously significant.

Since the Shona believe that any close contact with the corpse may defile people, Mwandayi contends that apart from cooling the spirit, the *doro remvura* also purifies the burial participants from the defilement caused by their close contact with the corpse during the burial.[10] While those who would have participated in the burial would have been cleansed either by washing in the river or using the medicated water at the gravesite, they still need more cleansing, and this time, using beer. While they are not expected to wash their bodies with the beer, the mere partaking in its drinking purifies them. For that purpose, anyone attending the ritual, even if not an ordinary beer taker, should at least take a sip of the beer, and then pass the container to the seasoned beer takers.

An interesting point has been raised concerning this ritual. Since this beer is to quench the thirst of the gravediggers, some of my informants have argued that the spirit of the deceased, which is believed to be thirsty at this period, can also partake in the beer drinking. This point has been refuted by other informants who argue that, since the deceased is not yet an ancestor, it cannot partake in the drinking of the beer, which is held in its home. The newly deceased member of the family can only come back home, and be offered rituals after the *magadziro* ceremony, which initiates him into ancestorhood. It is likely that other ancestors of the family take part in the *masukafoshoro* beer drinking since they are not tabooed from coming home.

COMMISERATING WITH THE BEREAVED

Commiserating with the bereaved, which is known as *kubata mavoko*, is one of the most pervasive post-burial rituals among the Shona. The Shona verb, *kubata*, means to touch, hold, or handle, and the noun, *mavoko* means hands. Therefore, *kubata mavoko*, literally means holding or touching hands, a practice which refers to the ritual greeting of the bereaved by mourners while they say a few words of condolences or empathy. In fact, this ritual begins as soon as a person dies, and continues throughout the performance of all other burial rituals, until well after the

---

10. Mwandayi, 213.

burial. Hence, it can also qualify as a pre-burial or burial ritual. It can take place at other places, away from the home of the deceased.

There are ethnical variations in how the *kubata mavoko* is done. In Nyajena, all the people who arrive at a funeral should greet all the mourners who would have arrived there before them. Although formal greetings are expected at any gathering, *kubata mavoko* is accompanied by a few words concerning the occurrence of the death. One can use any of the following: "*nenhamo dzakuwirai, nedzoi, nematambudziko, nedzinoparadza*" This is a way of acknowledging the occurrence of death and the grief it causes upon the remaining relatives and the whole community. The one being greeted responds by saying, "*dzakavonekwa,*" meaning that death or misfortune has been experienced. When all the people who are sitting outside the house in which the deceased's body is lying have been greeted, the new arrival, then gets into the hut in which the corpse and the next of kin are. The same ritual greeting is exchanged. The close relative of the departed may briefly explain how the deceased would have died, the nature of his disease, and his last words. Sometimes, the person manning the corpse responds to the ritual greeting by extending her hand to offer a greeting, or by sobbing, without saying a word. The sobbing becomes more intense and louder if the new arrival is a close family member.

This ritual is performed throughout the funeral whenever a new arrival appears. The ritual is also expected of those relatives and villagers who would have missed the funeral. Whenever they have an opportunity to visit the family of the deceased, they should perform the *kubata mavoko* ritual. If the deceased were a close family member, they may also perform the *kukanda chimbwe* on the following morning of their arrival. While *kukanda chibwe* is for close family members only, *kubata mavoko* is for everyone. It can be done by people who live far away from the home of the deceased to relatives of the dead, wherever they meet them.

Kubata mavoko is a very significant ritual. First, a greeting is a sign of solidarity and a commitment to engaging in peaceful interaction with the one being greeted. *Kubata mavoko* is a sign that the mourner comes in peace, and would like to share the sorrow that the bereaved family is experiencing. In life and death, the human person belongs to the community, and because of that, the community shares the sadness and sorrows of having lost a member.

Second, *kubata mavoko* is a declaration of one's intention to attend a funeral and assist during the funeral, in any way possible. It signifies that the mourner has come for nothing else except paying her last respect to the departed. The new arrival should declare this intention as soon as she arrives at the funeral. It should be declared to each individual who is already at the funeral because the whole community would have lost a member, and is affected in one way or the other. The intention should continue to be declared whenever a new mourner arrives. Therefore, throughout the funeral, mourners are reminded of the purpose of their gathering—to pay their last respects to the dead, to commiserate with the bereaved, and to assist the bereaved, particularly during the burial, in any way possible. Of course, they may talk about other issues, or drink beer, yet they always remember the cause of their gathering. In situations where some mourners get carried away by other issues, they are usually reminded not to forget the reason for their gathering. *Tisakangamwa zvatavunganira pano* (Let us not forget why we are gathered here) is the phrase often used to remind the mourners of the purpose of the gathering, particularly if some of them seem to forget the cause for the gathering.

Third, *kubata mavoko* allows the new arrival to register his presence at the funeral by presenting himself both to the deceased and the closest relatives of the deceased who are present. Every relative and neighbor of the deceased are expected to attend the funeral. Those who fail to attend without any grave cause are frowned upon or even condemned. Since there is no official attendance register at funerals, this ritual allows everyone to know people who would have attended the funeral. Also, the close relatives of the deceased will always know the attendees of their beloved's funeral because all *kubata mavoko* must end in the hut where they are watching the corpse.

Fourth, the *kubata mavoko* greetings are intended to move both the bereaved and the mourners from a state of denial to that of acceptance of the occurrence of death. The occurrence of death to a close family member is not only devastating but also shocking. One of the characteristics of this shock is the denial that death has happened. This denial may hold the bereaved captive, hopping that the deceased would not have died. The ritual greeting tries to convince those family members who have not yet accepted the occurrence of death to realize that, indeed, death has taken place. Every time they respond, "*dzakavonekwa*," they are in fact, professing that the death is real, and that it has actually happened. This constant reminder of the reality of death forces the bereaved to talk about death, cry, and share their anguish. It is in this crying and sharing of anguish that denial turns to acceptance, and grief begins to heal.

Finally, it is believed that the ritual is intended to confuse evil spirits that may have accompanied the people coming to attend the funeral. Although most of such spirits are good, there could be evil spirits accompanying mourners, and these should not be allowed to find their way into the hut in which the departed's body is kept. The greetings that are done before one enters the house in which the remains of the departed are stored are intended to confuse the evil spirits or even to chase them away before the new mourner presents herself into the house in which the corpse is. In addition to that, the ritual confuses the harmful spirits if they intended to attack the close family members of the deceased. Since everyone performs *kubata mavoko*, the close relatives of the dead cannot be easily identified.

RESTING DAYS

Among the Karanga of Nyajena, soon after burial, the head of the family or village may announce the resting period that is known as *mahakurimwi*, which literally means, not working in the fields. Mbiti, writing about other African peoples, postulates that this stoppage of work is a sign of respect for the dead person.[11] Among Shona people, this suspension of work starts right from the moment the occurrence of death is announced until about a week after the burial. If the deceased were a chief, a prolonged time of *mahakurimwi* may be observed. However, *mahakurimwi* may be shortened or postponed depending on the time of the year at which death occurs. For instance, if Chief Nyajena were to die during the beginning of the rain season, when planting and sowing of seeds should be done while the soil is still moist, *mahakurimwi* may be postponed to a later month or even the next Winter to enable people to plough and sow their crops on time. It seems that in the past, the sacred rest mostly concerned working in the field. However, among some Shona groups, other normal activities are suspended until all funeral rites have been performed. The forbidden activities may include weddings and other family celebrations. According to Mbiti, among other African ethnical groups, even normal activities such as washing bodies and clothes, and milking cows may be neglected for some days.

11. Mbiti, *Introduction to African Religion*, 121.

In Nyajena, the village head, as the official and traditional ritual leader of the community, after having consulted the bereaved family, announces the mourning days, which should be understood as resting days for all the villagers. People may continue to do other types of work such as building or washing clothes, but they are not supposed to work in the fields. These sacred days are more visible during the rainy season, when people normally work on the fields, because during *mahakurimwi*, they have to stop working in the fields. Since all the people in the rural areas depend on subsistence farming for livelihood, abstaining from working on the fields for a week is a big sacrifice.

Among the Karanga and other Shona peoples, this ritual symbolizes several things. First, it is observed in solidarity with the bereaved family. It symbolizes the villagers' accompaniment of the bereaved family's painful journey of grief. Although the deceased belongs to a particular family, her death affects the whole village. Hence, all villagers should be given an opportunity to accompany the bereaved in mourning the deceased, and resolving grief. Since the bereaved family cannot go back to the field immediately after burying their family member, other villagers show their solidarity by staying at home as well.

Second, the Karanga believe that the land, and its fertility and fruitfulness belong to the ancestors. When a person dies, the ancestors have the responsibility to welcome the deceased into the ancestral world. So, during the first few days after burial, it is believed that ancestors are busy giving orientation to the new member of the fold. Therefore, people should not work in the fields when the ancestors, the owners of the land, who induce its fertility, are resting. Therefore, the sacred rest is not only in honor of the deceased, but also the established ancestors of both the grieving family and the community, who are the rightful owners of the land. In addition to honoring ancestors, the Shona believe that although ancestors are ubiquitous, they mainly live in the atmosphere and under the soil. That is why they are referred to as *vari kumhepo* or *ivhu*. Because ancestors would be busy receiving the deceased, tilling the soil may open doors through which evil spirits may attack the newly deceased.

Third, *mahakurimwi* gives the undertakers an opportunity to rest after the hard work of burying their relative. Much energy is spent on digging the grave, crying, singing, and dancing. Some of the mourners would have traveled long distances to attend the funeral. Sometimes, mourners do not sleep well, particularly men, who are supposed to sleep outdoors. After burial, there is also a need for some time to debrief and reframe the future without the departed relative. By the time the villagers are allowed to return to work in the fields, everyone would have regained and renewed her or his strength.

Fourth, death makes not only a home, but the whole village, "dark." This darkness should be understood as defilement, and is caused by the bodily fluids that may come out of the corpse, and the unavailability of ancestors because they will be busy elsewhere. If one insists on going to the field during the stipulated mourning period, her crops may be defiled, and may not produce a good harvest. Also, the transgressor may get into a freak accident because working in the fields during the mourning days upsets the ancestors, who may punish the transgressor. Even if the ancestors do not punish the transgressor, it just does not feel good to be against the norms of the land. More so, it is a sign of disrespect, not only to the dead, but also to other villagers. In some places, violators may be made to pay a fine to the ancestors through the village head. It should be noted that the fine is not paid to the bereaved family but to the village head because he is the chief ritual practitioner and custodian of the ancestral land and traditions.

This ritual also shows the genius of the Shona people, and their utmost consideration for the welfare of both the invisible and visible communities. Western cultures also encourage employers to allow off days to their bereaved employees. This off time allows them to bury their dead, rest, grieve, and also to visit the burial place thereafter. Except for people who are buried in urban cemeteries, the ritual of *mahakurimwi* is still practiced in the rural areas. As shall be explored later in this chapter, urban people do not rely on farming for livelihood, so the ritual does not have any farming significance for them. Even if they wanted to observe the resting days, their employers may not understand or respect the ritual. However, most employers allow their employees some days off to go and give their last respect to their dead. These off days are given to close relatives only, unlike *mahakurimwi*, which are observed by the whole neighborhood, which is a sign of African togetherness.

DIVINER CONSULTATION

This ritual is known as *gata or mashopeshope*, among the Karanga of Nyajena. *Gata* is one of the most important and common post-burial rituals among the Shona peoples. *Gata* refers to the consultation of a diviner to find out the cause of death. Ordinarily, *gata* should be performed about three weeks after burial or even earlier. Rayner points out that in olden times, *gata* was performed at least one week, but not more than a month after death.[12] However, in situations where it was not performed during the expected time, it could be done at any other time before *magadziro*. This time range is still the same among most Shona peoples.

The Karanga of Nyajena call this ritual, *mashopeshope* or *kurasha mushamhu*, and is performed a few days or even weeks before *doro remvura*. If the ritual is not performed before *doro remvura*, it should be done a few days before the *magadziro* ritual. Gelfand, reporting about the Karanga of Nyajena, asserts that the consultation should be performed before another ritual called *doro remvura* (ritual of the water) that is performed about three weeks after the burial.[13] Usually, the findings of *gata* are revealed to the family at the *doro remvura* ritual because it gives them an opportunity to gather again as a family. Gelfand, says it is convenient for the Karanga of Nyajena to take advantage of this gathering instead of calling for another one for the purpose of revealing the cause of death.[14]

Mashopeshope comes from the Shona word, "*kushopera*" which means to consult a diviner. In Nyajena, the relatives of the deceased consult a diviner concerning five things in relationship with *magadziro* and the welfare of the departed relative. First, to establish how the *magadziro* ritual should be performed. This advice is crucial because if the procedure is not followed meticulously, the deceased may reject the ritual. Second, to be guided by the diviner in choosing the ritual leader for the *magadziro*. Usually, the diviner appoints the oldest family member or the one who is considered the family's default ritual leader. Third, to find out if the deceased is happy about the proceedings. Fourth, to have the cause of the death revealed if this was not done soon after burial, before *doro remvura*. Finally, to establish if the spirit of the deceased is still clean, and has not been defiled by evil spirits or witches. In the past, the delegation would take a piece of cloth belonging to the deceased, and would give it to the diviner so that he could tell them the cause of their relative's death. This taking of a piece of cloth belonging to the deceased to a diviner is also reported by Gelfand to have been practiced by other Shona groups in the past. In fact, Gelfand argues that the word *gata* derives from the

---

12. Rayner, 66.
13. Gelfand, *An African's Religion, The Spirit of Nyajena the case of the Karanga*, 82.
14. Gelfand, *An African's Religion, The Spirit of Nyajena the case of the Karanga*, 82.

item or piece of cloth that the delegation gives to the diviner before the divination starts.[15]

Among other Shona ethnicities, the sole purpose of *gata* is to find out the cause of the death of the deceased. When a person dies, "there is always suspicion of foul play as a result of witchcraft."[16] Although the Shona believe that death could be caused by natural forces, they can only rule out foul play after consulting a diviner. In some cases, *gata* is performed to confirm the suspicions that the relatives already have concerning the cause of death. Most people would have consulted diviners when the deceased was still sick and would have been told the causes of the ill-health. Although most *gata* delegates already have an idea as to what would have caused the death of their relative, they remain open to new, and sometimes surprising information concerning the cause.

The delegation, which consists of close relatives such as brothers, sons-in-law, and the village head, is sent by the family to do this business. They are expected to go to a specialist diviner who lives far away from the home of the deceased to avoid those who would have been influenced by rumor and gossip. The consulted diviner is expected to name the members of the delegation and to reveal the sex of the deceased as proof of his prowess. If he fails to do that, the delegation may consider his findings unreliable, and they may proceed to look for another diviner. In fact, the delegates are encouraged to consult more than one diviner so that they can compare their findings.

As the delegation visits the diviner or a couple of them, they have their expectations concerning the cause of death as informed by their cosmology. Bourdillon observes that the Shona believe that there are usually three causes of death.[17] First, if the deceased would have lived a long life, and if there is no reason to think otherwise, the suspected causes of death are usually natural. These causes include old age and God. If the deceased would have lived a long life, and no other nefarious involvement detected, the diviner is likely to tell the delegation that the cause of death is old age (*kukwegura*). The death of an old person may also be referred to as having been caused by God (*rufu gwaMwari*). In other words, the diviner is telling them that death was inevitable, and no human or spiritual force would have been involved. If death is caused by either old age or

15. Gelfand, *Shona Religion, with Special Reference to the Makorekore*, 83.
16. Mwendayi, 212.
17. Bourdillon, *The Shona Peoples*, 206–207.

God, the relatives are not very much aggrieved because of its occurrence, for they believe that God has a reason for it. Mbiti points out that among some African peoples, those dying as a result of being struck by lightning may also be thought of as having died because of God.[18] However, for most Shona people, lightning is usually thought of as being caused by witchcraft.

The second cause of death according to Bourdillon is human, particularly witchcraft.[19] Witchcraft is thought to be the most common cause of death among many Shona peoples, as has been explored earlier on. The third cause of death is spiritual. Most Africans believe that their world is replete with spirits. Some of these spirits are good, and others are evil. Although some scholars such as Mbiti have argued that there is no evidence that the good spirits such as the living-dead cause death, it is believed that they can be deadly unless they are appeased. Generally, it is the evil spirits that may cause death, and these include alien spirits seeking recognition, and nature spirits known as *zvidhoma*. *Ngozi* (avenging spirit) is also believed to cause sickness and death. A *ngozi* can be either bad or good, depending on the side one is standing. The victims are likely to see *ngozi* as evil, while the relatives of the *ngozi* are likely to see it as a good spirit seeking justice.

Once the *gata* delegation is satisfied with its findings, it comes back home with the feedback, which at first may only be shared with close relatives until a public gathering is convened by the leader of the family. Among the Karanga of Nyajena, the much-awaited results of the *gata* may not be announced until the *doro remvura*, which is performed about three weeks after burial. However, this information may be passed on at any convenient time, before the *magadziro* ceremony, if it has not been done already. The gravity of the causes of death and the family's exposure to further harm from the same cause are likely to determine the swiftness with which the delegation may call for a meeting to convey the information.

If the delegation finds out that the death was caused by any of the good spirits, some ritual action must be taken to appease the angry spirit because if not propitiated immediately, it may strike again. If the death was caused by an avenging spirit, its placation is a matter of urgency. As has been discussed earlier on, the most effective and lasting solution to a

---

18. Mbiti, *African Religions and Philosophy*, 2nd Edition, 151.
19. Bourdillon, 206–207.

ngozi is to pay reparations. As a matter of fact, some Shona groups may try to exorcize the avenging spirit, but it does not work out sometimes. If the spirit which would have caused the death is an evil alien spirit, it may be exorcized. If the death were caused by witches, the family may confront the witches with the help of the village head, who in some cases, would have been one of the delegates sent to consult a diviner. In the past, among some Shona groups, one of the witch's goats was slaughtered, and the witch was expelled from the village. If the witch were not expelled, the family of the departed would use medicinal pegs and charms to protect its members and homes from further harm by the same witch.

The underlining belief concerning diviner consultation is the belief that death does not just happen. There should be a cause, which must be identified and published. This identification and publicity of the cause of death are intended to achieve a few things. If the death has been caused by a witch, he may be confronted or even expelled from the village. The family of the deceased may also employ medicines to protect the family members and their homes from further attacks by the same witch. If death has been caused by an angry good spirit, the appropriate propitiatory rituals may be performed. If death has been caused by an avenging spirit, the family of the deceased may pay compensation to the relatives of the avenging spirit. If death has been caused by old age or other Godly causes, the family of the deceased may do nothing. So, the consultation of a diviner almost always leads the family of the departed to propitiatory, compensatory, or protective action. A family that does not know the cause of the death of one of its members becomes vulnerable to further attacks by the same cause.

DISTRIBUTION OF PERSONAL BELONGINGS

The Karanga of Nyajena call this ritual, *kugova nhumbi dzemufi*. This distribution of the deceased's personal belongings such as clothes, kitchen utensils, and other small things is done a day or a few weeks or months after the burial. Most Shona families prefer doing it on the day after the burial because of two factors. First, the clothes and other objects belonging to the deceased are defiled by her death, and therefore, should not be handled or used until an appropriate ritual to cleanse the clothes and other small objects has been performed. The promptness of performing this ritual is intended to prevent members of the family from being defiled by the clothes or items belonging to the deceased. The sooner the ritual is held, the safer, the family of the deceased is. Second, the presence of most stakeholders during the funeral prompts the family to perform this ritual at this time. It is convenient to perform it at this time because it would be difficult to gather all the family members at some other time after the burial.

The process of the distribution is simple. If the deceased is a woman, her own people take charge of the ritual proceedings. If the departed is a man, his nephew may be chosen as the ritual practitioner to distribute the belongings. If the deceased has left a written or verbal will, the ritual leader stands guided by it, even though, he can divert a little bit in pursuit of justice. Sometimes, the dying person may give instructions that are unreasonable because of the anguish and fear caused by the prospect of dying. Some dying persons may say things that they would not have said if they were not dying. Hence, if the verbal or written will of the deceased seems to have been caused by anger or fear, the family may adjust it accordingly. If there is no written or verbal will, the estate distributer may use his discretion, of course, in consultation with the close family members of the departed.

If the deceased is a married woman, her personal belongings should be treated with special care, lest her spirit is upset, and may become an avenging spirit. Ordinarily, her own family of origin should distribute her personal belongings. For instance, all her kitchen utensils, clothes, and bedroom furniture should be taken by her own relatives. If she had cows which are offspring of the beast of motherhood, or any other livestock purchased out of her personal work such as potting, they too should be inherited by her own relatives. In the past, if she had a traditional container used to store body lotion, it was supposed to be handed over to her own people. All the underclothes and sacred waist beads should also be handed over to the deceased woman's relatives. Be that as it may, her own people are expected to think of their son-in-law and the children of the deceased as they distribute the estate because this ritual should not be used to impoverish the son-in-law and the remaining children, but to fulfill the ritual obligation.

On the day of the distribution of small personal belongings, all the clothes and other personal belongings to be distributed are piled on a reed mat outside of the round kitchen, where all the relatives are sitting on reed mats, animal hides, or stools. The ritual leader then sprinkles the belongings to be distributed with sacred water made from *muzeze* (*peltophorum africanum sond*) and ordinary water. Some families are reported to use some herb called *dambamachira* or *chifumuro*, which is normally used to protect children from illnesses and attacks by witches and evil spirits. The leaves of *muzeze* are then used to sprinkle the medicated water on the property to be distributed, and on the people. In some families, the ritual leader and all the family members should briefly touch or handle all the things to be distributed after dipping their hands into the sacred water. Hence, the ritual is also called *kubata nhumbi* (handling clothes). It is believed that if these personal belongings are touched by any person before this ritual, the person who would have come into contact with them will be struck by leprosy (*maperembudzi*) or some skin disease called *zvisasa* (ring worm).

After all the personal belongings have been handled, they are then distributed to the qualifying family members, both present and absent. There are basically three rules to be observed during this ritual. First, the beneficiaries should not choose what they want to inherit unless they have been given that opportunity by the ritual practitioner. Second, no one should refuse to take whatever is offered to him. If the recipient does not want to keep whatever is given to him, he should accept it firstly, and then offer it to any of family members present. However, everyone should accept a symbolic utensil such as a spoon, or fork to affirm that she is part of the group, and that her refusal to accept more expensive things is not out of spite and malice for the deceased. Third, whatever is received during this distribution, particularly clothes, should not be mended or sewn. Once they are torn, they should be disposed of reverently by burning them.

There are reasons for this taboo. Just like their original owner's remains in the grave, which should decompose, the clothes too should be allowed to wear out naturally. Also, patches sewn to the inherited clothes may make the spirit of the deceased vulnerable to evil spirits that may accompany it into the family at *magadziro*. In addition to that, sewing the inherited clothes is believed to bring the bad habits to the one who would have sewn the clothes. For instance, if the deceased were a witch, the witchcraft can mysteriously pass on to the one who would have sewn the inherited clothes. Moreover, the inherited clothes should not be inherited twice in a row. What this means is that once the clothes are inherited the first time, their life span should not be prolonged. The inheritor must allow them to tear off naturally so that they can be disposed of in his or her lifetime. If the clothes were to be sewn, this would prolong their life span, and are likely to be redistributed when the current inheritor dies. In other words, the inherited clothes should not outlive the first inheritor. The clothes are prevented from outliving the original inheritor to make sure that an undeserving and unqualified person does not end up inheriting the same clothes. If an undeserving person inherits the clothes of the deceased unknowingly, it can offend the spirit of the deceased.

However, the Karanga of Nyajena perform a ritual that would allow those who inherit the clothes to be able to sew them without dire consequences. During the *kubata nhumbi* ritual, the ritual leader tears apart one of the clothes belonging to the deceased, and sews it again. He should also take a plate and a pot belonging to the deceased and make holes through them. Alternatively, the holes can be made on the burial day, and the pot is placed in the grave. This is known as *kurapira*. Once this ritual is performed, the people who inherit the clothes or kitchen utensils can mend them without offending the spirit or inheriting negative behaviors of the deceased. Even though small items should not be repaired if broken, large properties like vehicles, wheelbarrows, scotch carts, bicycles, and grinding mills should be repaired.

There have been reports of massive abuses of this ritual, if the departed is a married woman. Some relatives of the deceased married woman are reported to have taken everything belonging to their deceased relative, ignoring the fact that the woman would have left children who may need to use some of the clothes and kitchen utensils. The same has also been reported of the greedy relatives of a deceased husband, who sometimes want to take the belongings of their relative without thinking of the widow and children of the departed. Nowadays, it has become more commendable for the relatives of the deceased to have the interest of the children at heart during the distribution of the deceased woman's personal belongings. It is also true that some relatives of the deceased leave everything for the children of the dead.

Some of my informants reported an interesting phenomenon that they said was becoming popular among some families in Nyajena, whereby the inheritors are first asked to claim back whatever piece of clothing they would have bought for their deceased parent, particularly if the deceased is a man. Once they get back their clothing contributions to the dead parent, they may redistribute them among other family members present. Although this is not the norm, it is intended to shame those children who do not care for their parents. It is also used for didactive purposes to educate people of like minds who would be present.

The rituals surrounding the distribution of personal belongings have several meanings. They make clear the Karanga belief that death brings darkness into the family. Death makes people who come into contact with the corpse unclean, hence the need for ritual cleansing. It defiles even the clothes and other items that belong to the deceased. Therefore, both the people and the personal belongings of the deceased need to be cleansed to prevent the relatives from contracting diseases associated with the dead, such as leprosy and ringworm. The participants were not quite certain if leprosy was prevalent in Nyajena in the past, but they mentioned some names of people who suffered from the disease. This unavailability of statistics of lepers in Nyajena was compounded by the establishment of leper colonies in Zimbabwe, such as Mutemwa Leprosy and Care Center, established in the 1930s, where all people suffering from the disease were rehabilitated until death. But the fact that the people of Nyajena perform rituals to prevent people from getting the diseases shows that it was common, and that people could prevent family members from contracting the disease.

In addition to that, the rituals symbolize the solidarity and togetherness of the family members. Just like they would have offered gifts when the deceased was born, they again get a gift from his belongings after his death. It is a sign that everything belongs to everyone. They come together to share the sorrow, gifts, food, and belongings. Furthermore, in the case of a married woman's death, the way her personal belongings are distributed shows that even after having been married for many years, and having given birth to children with her husband, she still belongs to her family of origin. Even her own children are not related to her, for she remains a stranger in her marital home. Hence, everything that belongs to her may be inherited by her own people. However, some of the participants told me that the relatives of the deceased woman should always leave some of her personal belongings for her children, and in some cases, for her own sister or niece who may be offered to the widower as a replacement wife. Even though this arrangement is encouraged, some of the participants reported of incidences where the relatives of the deceased women took away all her personal belongings. In some way, it serves to counteract the misinformation which was peddled by early Western writers that the bridewealth paid for a woman was her purchase price. She is never purchased, for she continues to be a member of her family of origin.

Finally, the distribution of personal belongings shows that no single family member should try to enrich himself out of someone's death. Everything should be shared in death as it was in life. When the deceased becomes an ancestor, he will care for all the family members even though the ancestor may choose only one host through whom to communicate its wishes. The ancestral host does not enjoy more protection than other family members.

THROWING THE PEBBLE

Not all the relatives manage to attend the funeral of their deceased family members. Some people arrive at the burial place soon after the burial, and others may not arrive to pay their last respects until several weeks or even months later. Most of the people who are absent during the burial of their relatives would have had one of the elderly relatives throwing the soil into the grave on their behalf. But as soon as the absentee arrives home to perform the ritual of *kubata mavoko*, she should also perform the ritual of *kukanda chibwe*, which means throwing a stone or pebble onto the grave.

In Nyajena, this ritual is performed early in the morning before sunrise. The family member who was absent from the funeral is accompanied to the grave by another family member, particularly a close relative of the deceased. If there is more than one person performing the ritual, all can visit the grave together. As they come closer to the grave, the absentee mourner picks up a pebble. If there is more than one absentee, each of them picks up her own pebble. At the grave, the absentee places or throws the pebble on top of the grave, or closer to the headstone while introducing herself. "My name is Chipo, your granddaughter." The phrase, "have a safe journey," can also be used as the introduction. Alternatively, the pebble may be thrown at any part of the grave, hence the phrase, *kukanda chibwe* (throwing of the pebble or stone). Elsewhere, particularly in Western cultures, family members who would have been absent during the burial of a relative are expected to bring flowers to the grave of the deceased as a sign of their concern and respect.

The ritual of *kukanda chibwe* has several meanings to the Karanga of Nyajena. First, it is a sign of the familial or communal spirit of togetherness. It shows that even if one could not attend the funeral and would have failed to assist others in the burial process, he is making his manual contribution now. The pebble is a symbol of the absentee's expected manual contribution in the burial of a deceased family member. Once the pebble has been placed or thrown on the grave, the relative is seen as having assisted others in burying the deceased. In addition to that, digging and constructing a grave is like building a house for the dead. The pebble that is placed on the grave by the family member who was absent during the burial, is the material contribution to the construction of the new home of the departed. This contribution and participation are signs of family unity.

Second, most African peoples believe that it takes a village to raise a child or build a home. In raising up a child, stakeholders include the significant others, the extended family, peers, teachers, and communal elders. The pebble that is placed on the grave signifies the communal assistance in raising a child or building of the home for the dead. The buried departed is like a baby in its mother's womb, and every family member is expected to assist in any way possible in the upbringing of that child.

Third, a pebble represents eternity and durability. It is a sign that the dead has now entered a new mode of living in which she has become durable. She cannot die again. She has become as strong as the pebble being placed on top of other stones, which were piled on the day of burial. It is the symbolic strength of a pebble that signifies the qualitative strength of the ancestor as compared to its living relatives. It also signifies the attainment of eternal spiritual life by the deceased. As long as there is a family member who remembers the deceased, she continues to be an active ancestor. Even when the spirit drifts into the nameless spiritual realm, it continues to live albeit without a name, and rituals performed in its honor.

Last, if this ritual is not performed, the spirit of the dead may be upset because of the neglect by the absent family member. Failure to attend a relative's funeral is considered to be as bad as neglecting one's living relatives. The mandatory attendance of relatives' funerals gives an assurance that everyone will have some people to bury her. One has to assist in the burial of her relatives. However, if one fails to do that, the *kukanda chibwe* rituals pacifies the spirit of the departed. Comparatively, the necessity of attending a relative's funeral is upheld in most cultures of the world.

MAKING OF THE ANCESTOR

The biggest and most significant post-burial ritual is *magadziro* (making of an ancestor), or *kurova guva* (beating the grave), or *kuchenura mudzimu* (cleansing the ancestor). It is performed at least six months or a year after the burial of the departed depending on the Shona ethnic group involved. Chitakure alleges that this longer waiting period is intended to allow the corpse to decompose before it can be allowed to come back home as an ancestor.[20] He claims that if the ritual is performed before the corpse decomposes, the ancestor may come back home in his physical body, and this would scare the family members. In addition, they would mistake the ancestor for a bad spirit known as *goritoto* (ghost), which some people claim to have a human body.

While the ritual should be performed at least six months or a year after the burial of the dead, circumstances may compel its early or late performance. An early celebration may be done for fear of the witches. If the relatives of the deceased fear that the witches may tamper with the spirit of the dead before it becomes an ancestor, they may fast-track its initiation into ancestorhood. In Nyajena, the late celebration may be caused by several issues. One of the reasons is that if the spirit does not demand the ritual, the family may delay its performance. Some spirits demand the ritual by causing one of the family members to become sick, or just allowing a misfortune to happen to one of the relatives. A diviner consulted about the sickness is likely to advise the family to perform *magadziro* for the uninitiated spirit. In some circumstances, the late celebration of *magadziro* may be caused by the poverty of the family members who are directly responsible for preparing the ceremony. The successful celebration of the ritual demands the slaughter of two sacrificial animals (a cow or bull and goat), and the provision of gains for the beer, and food for the participants. In bygone times, the performance of the ritual could be delayed if there was no one willing to inherit the widows. Normally, those who were eager to inherit the widows would not delay its celebration since it was at or immediately after this ceremony that the widows could be inherited. Furthermore, the widows themselves would put pressure on the responsible family members to perform the ritual so that they (widows) would be free to remarry.

Magadziro signifies several things among the Shona. First, the ritual is performed to overcome the anxiety caused by death, and to settle the

---

20. Chitakure, *African Traditional Religion Encounters Christianity*, 85.

tension between the spirit of the dead and the members of the family. This tension may be caused by the stringent requirement to perform death rituals perfectly. Second, the *magadziro* is intended to cool the spirit, which after death would have been wandering about. It is generally believed that the ancestral spirits pass through very hot places in their adventures. Third, it is intended to initiate the spirit into the ancestral world, and to bring it back home and incorporate it as a spiritual and invisible member of the family.

This ritual is important because at this point, the spirit of the dead has no fixed abode and is believed to wander about. Death makes the spirit some kind of a vagabond, and this wandering about is believed to be tedious, and consequently displeases the spirit. The spirit yearns to be brought back home to become an active, invisible, and spiritual member of the family. Unfortunately, it should wait for the performance of *magadziro* for it to be able to come back home. As a result, the spirit of the deceased member completely depends on its living family members to be incorporated into the family as an ancestor. Without their willingness to perform the ritual, the spirit continues to grieve. The same ritual is also crucial for the family of the deceased because death defiles the home. So, the ritual is intended to purify the home and its inhabitants. Although the ritual may be delayed, most Shona people believe that relatives of the deceased should try all within their power to perform it within the stipulated time.

Magadziro is not performed for every departed person, for there are qualifications to be met and disqualifications to be avoided. Only married people are allowed to become the "living-dead" after their death. Those people who die as babies, youths, or unmarried adults, cannot become ancestors. Since *magadziro* makes ancestors, the unmarried deceased have no *magadziro* performed for them. It should be noted that in Africa, marriage implies begetting children. Therefore, even though marriage is a prerequisite to becoming an ancestor, it is far more accurate to say that the bearing of children, even outside a formal marriage, is a prerequisite. If a married couple fails to have children because of one reason or another, their families have to find ways of assisting the couple to have children. It is the children who have the obligation to perform the *magadziro* ritual. Also, the people who die of certain diseases such as leprosy, tuberculosis, and epilepsy may not have this ritual performed for them to prevent them from becoming ancestors. It is believed that if they are allowed to become ancestors, they may pass on the disease to one of their family members. Moreover, Bullock notes that *magadziro* is not allowed to be performed in November for the reasons he does not elaborate.[21]

Like at most Shona rituals, a lot of beer is brewed for the *magadziro* ritual. Bullock describes how the ritual was performed in Mashonaland, in the past.[22] Relatives and friends of the deceased would start arriving for the ritual a couple of days before the day of the ritual. On the day of the ritual, very early in the morning, the ceremonial leader would lead a group of the departed's family members to the grave, leaving all other participants at home. In the past, some groups would take a goat to the grave. Nowadays, most Shona groups take some beer in a sacred clay container called *pfuko* to the grave. As the delegation proceeds to the grave, they sing, ululate, and dance. Upon their arrival at the grave, they break the fence surrounding it and may slaughter a goat, if they have brought one. The ceremonial leader deeps the branch of *muzeze* tree into the mixture of blood and medicines, and sprinkles it on the grave. Some beer is also poured on the grave. The ritual practitioner then invites the spirit of the deceased to accompany them back home. In the past, before the delegates left the grave, they would scatter the entrails of the goat, and pour the beer on the grave, and then head back home amid much jubilation.

Gelfand's narrative of the same ritual shares commonalities with the one given by Bullock.[23] For Gelfand, it is the son-in-law who acts as the ritual leader of the delegation that goes to the grave early in the morning. He collects the branch of wattle tree (*muzeze*), which he places in a pot of water. As they approach the grave, the son-in-law should turn his back to the grave, moving backward and sprinkling water on the way, while facing the procession. When he is about to reach the grave, he faces it, and may sweep the grave, and remove one of the stones from the grave. Beer is then poured into the hole where the stone has been removed. After some beer has been consumed by the delegates, the stone is placed back to its original position, and a prayer of invitation to the ancestor is said before the procession departs for home.

Elsewhere, Gelfand reporting about the Karanga of Nyajena's performance of *magadziro*, postulates that the *muzukuru* (nephew) is the spokesman during the ritual. After the ancestor has been brought back

---

21. Bullock, *The Mashona (The Natives of Southern Rhodesia)*, 273.
22. Bullock, *Mashona Laws and Customs*, 53–54).
23. Gelfand, *Shona Rituals with Special reference to the Chaminuka Cult*, 190.

home, a goat and a cow or ox, depending on the gender of the deceased, are slaughtered.[24] The cow or ox brings the spirit of the dead into the home. Some *sadza* (thick porridge) is prepared using *zviyo* (*rapoko*). When both the sacred meat and *sadza* are ready, all the close family members gather near the threshold, and a prayer is offered. Once the prayer is done, the sacred practitioner may distribute the *sadza* and meat to the people. Once the people have finished eating the sacred meal, beer is poured on the ground as *museredzero* (wash down). The remaining sacred beer is given to the people. As soon as the cow or ox is killed, the *muzukuru* makes the *rukanda* (bangle) from the right hoof of the animal, which is supposed to come off in a complete circle and is fitted into the right wrist of the *nevanji* (firstborn).

Rayner reports that once the procession reaches the grave, and the ritual practitioner has poured some beer on it, the spirit of the deceased is persuaded to climb a nearby tree.[25] Once the delegates are convinced that the spirit of the deceased has climbed up the tree, a small branch of that tree is cut and is immediately covered by a cloth to prevent the spirit from escaping. Amid jubilation and great celebration, the branch on which the ancestor is riding is dragged back home. The delegation is met by those who would have remained at home amid much singing, ululation, and dancing.

MAGADZIRO AMONG THE KARANGA OF NYAJENA

Although the praxis of *magadziro* is almost similar among different Shona ethnicities, it is interesting to explore the ritual as it is performed among the contemporary Karanga of Nyajena. It should be noted that, there is no uniformity in the performance of the ritual among the Karanga of Nyajena. However, there are constants and commonalities in the praxis and significance of the ritual. This narrative is an outcome of the observation of *magadziro* that I did in one of the Nyajena villages. It should be noted that the significance given to the *magadziro* ritual by different Shona ethnicities are basically similar.

On the day of the ritual, a delegation of close family members, comprising both women and men, wake up at dawn, take a clay pot of beer (*pfuko*), and go to the grave where the deceased was buried. If the ritual

24. Gelfand, *An African's Religion, The Spirit of Nyajena the case of the Karanga*, 85.
25. Rayner, 67.

is being performed for a woman, this rite is done on the eve of the ritual because in the past, women were married (*kutiziswa*) in the evening. The delegation is on a special mission; to bring the spirit of the deceased home as an ancestor. Upon arrival at the grave, the team may sit or kneel around the grave, offer the beer and ground tobacco, popularly known by the Karanga as *bute*, to the spirit of the dead by pouring a little onto the grave, and then each of the delegates takes a sip of beer from the container, and a pinch of *bute* from the hand of the leader. The ritual practitioner then cuts a sizeable branch of *combretum mole flora* (*mupembere*) tree, which is then pulled around the grave, or used to sweep the grave while instructing the spirit of the deceased to ride on it. The branch on which the spirit is riding is then pulled back home amid much jubilation, whistling, and ululation. The one pulling the branch should never look backwards (*kucheuka*) to the grave because the ancestor may escape and run back to the grave. The team is met by the crowd at home, which also joins in the jubilation. The delegation enters the round kitchen and hangs the *mupembere* branch on which the spirit of the deceased is riding, inside the roof of the hut. The branch stays there until another ritual is performed to remove and dispose of it. There is more joyful dancing and singing. The spirit of the deceased is then offered more beer and ground tobacco as a sign of welcome. At this juncture, the spirit is not yet an ancestor, and no one knows for sure if the spirit has accepted the ritual, or if it has indeed come home.

Then all the people move out of the hut in which the spirit is supposed to be, and the *mhutsashungu* or *mbudzi ye*shungu (goat of anger/appeasement), is brought to the threshold of the hut by the nephew (*muzukuru*). This goat is slaughtered for a person who would have died with some unresolved anger, which could be true of most dying persons. Even if the dead never showed any kind of anger in his last moments, the consulted diviner may recommend the sacrifice of the goat. Most families, wanting to be on the safe side, volunteer to sacrifice the goat just in case, the spirit of the deceased has been offended by something that they may not be aware of.

If the deceased is a woman, a female goat, which would have given birth (*nhunzvi*) is sacrificed. A male goat (*gweme*) is sacrificed for a man. The *muzukuru* sits inside the hut, while holding the goat by the front leg, making it stand on the threshold. Relatives, starting with the oldest, stand on a line, pouring beer on the back of the goat while introducing themselves. The pouring of beer is also performed for the absent family members if the goat does not shake its body for any of the relatives present. It is believed that if the goat shakes its body after the beer has been poured on its back, the ancestor has accepted the ritual, and has indeed come home. The shaking of the goat is accompanied by much more jubilation. However, in the sad scenario of the goat refusing to shake its back, it is interpreted to mean that the spirit of the deceased has rejected the ritual, and a delegation must consult a diviner to find out the cause of the ancestor's anger and rejection of the ritual.

The sacrificial goat is then slaughtered, and all its meat is roasted, and when ready, it is consumed without salt. None of my informants seemed to know why salt should not be used. But, just looking at the characteristics of salt such as giving taste to food, and by so doing changing the original taste and flavor of the food, its use may be tabooed because it may change the mind of the ancestor. At this point, the ancestor is not yet fully initiated, and the relatives do not want it to change its mind by going back to the grave. All the remains of the sacrificial goat that include the head, legs, hide, and bones are burnt in fire lit just outside the sacred hut. Some families may burn in the same fire, the *mupembere* branch, which would have been used to bring home the ancestor. However, other families perform a special ritual later to dispose of the branch by putting it in a termite hole or burying it in the cattle kraal. Burying the branch in the cattle kraal is more significant because the ancestral beast (bull) would live in the same kraal, in which it can fertilize the family cattle. This burial or burning of the sacred branch is done to prevent witches from stealing it, and turning the ancestor into an evil spirit.

As soon as the sacrificial goat is consumed, the beast of *magadziro* is slaughtered. For a woman, a cow is sacrificed, and for a man, a bull, or sheep (*gondohwe*) is sacrificed. In Nyajena, a single beast may be used for *magadziro* of two related persons, for instance, brothers or sisters, but never a husband and wife. Once the beast is skinned, the ritual leader cuts the sacrificial meat from different parts of the beast, such as right fore-leg (*bandauko*), heart (*mhumba*), liver (*chiropa*), hind leg (*chidzva*), *guru* (stomach), small and large intestines (*vura*), lungs (*mapapu*), ribs (*mbabvu*), back (*musana*), gwatata, chest (*chityu*), and neck (*mutsipa*). The legs and head are not used. These pieces of meat are cooked in a clay pot, without salt. *Sadza* from *rapoko* is also prepared by women who have reached menopause. When both the sacrificial meat and *sadza* are ready, they are brought to the threshold and consecrated amid much clapping of hands (*gwatara*) and ululation (*mhururu*). The ritual leader, using his own hand, then offers a morsel of *sadza* and a piece of meat to each of the close family members who are gathered in a semi-circle, facing the threshold. Once this ritual is performed, more beer and food may be given to the people. The beer is allocated to people according to their villages. *Vazukuru*, who are considered ritual practitioners throughout *magadziro* are expected to steal some of the beer as a token of gratitude for their role. The stolen beer, that should be shared with friends, should be consumed in the nearby bush or behind the house of the deceased. When performing this ritual, *vazukuru* are called *mapere* (hyenas). The celebration can go on until the evening, when neighbors are supposed to return to their homes.

It should be noted that the *magadziro* ritual praxis, as practiced by the people of Nyajena, is almost uniform. However, slight differences were reported in the significance given to some specific rites within the ritual. It is interesting that the ancestor is asked to ride on the branch of a tree as if he is in the physical form. As a spirit, an ancestor can just fly home. However, whether it flies home or rides on the sacred branch, the branch's placement inside the kitchen roof symbolizes the arrival and presence of the ancestor. The round kitchen is a multiple purpose place. It is in the kitchen where food is prepared and consumed. It is also the sitting and dining room. It is in the kitchen where children are born. And it is where most traditional rituals take place.

The pouring of the sacred beer on the back of the goat, which is done to ascertain the cooperation and acceptance of the ritual by the ancestor shows that the Karanga do not take anything for granted. There has to be a physical signal that the deceased has indeed become an ancestor. If the goat shakes its body, the deceased has indeed become an ancestor. If the goat refuses to shake its body, then the deceased is not happy with the proceedings, and a remedy has to be sought. This ritual is the heart of *magadziro*, which checks the quality and efficacy of the ritual. It also compels people to perform *magadziro* meticulously because if not, the ancestor would reject the ritual, and the grains and beasts put to waste. The ritual has to be done right.

The sacred meal symbolizes the presence of the ancestor, and his affinity to every family member who partakes in the meal. It shows the communion between the newly initiated ancestor, all other family ancestors, and the living members of the family. There should be order in the consumption of this meal. Like how life is passed on from older generations to new ones, the sacred practitioners distribute the sacred meal to all relatives in attendance. The meal can also be seen as a symbolic eating of the flesh of the deceased. This symbolic consumption of the flesh of the newly made ancestor symbolizes the communion between the ancestor and the family, and also the inseparable bond between family members. This ritual resembles the Christian Holy Communion popularly known as *chirairo* by the Karanga of Nyajena.

THE SACRED BANGLE

The distribution of the estate, making of the sacred bangle, and inheritance of widows are technically part of *magadziro*, which are performed on the second morning of the ritual. Among the Karanga of Nyajena, if the newly initiated ancestor is a male, who had a son, a sacred bangle called *rukanda* is extracted from the right foreleg of the sacrificial beast slaughtered for the ritual. *Rukanda* is a diminutive noun, which comes from the noun *ganda,* meaning skin. The *rukanda* should be cut off in a complete circle to resemble a bangle, by the nephew. When it is completely removed from the sacrificial beast's leg, it is then slid onto the left wrist of the eldest son of the deceased.

According to Gelfand, in the past, some families fitted the *rukanda* onto the right wrist.[26] Also, some families extract it from the beast's left foreleg. As has already been alluded to, the left-hand side is significant since it is the side on which men usually lay in bed during conjugal intimacy. For the Karanga males, the left-hand side is full of potency, vitality, and positive energy. *Rukanda* is only prepared for male ancestors, and fitted into the wrist of a son, or grandson, if no son is available. This bangle signifies the inheritor's newly acquired authority derived from his father's name and estate, which would been given, or would be inherited soon afterwards. Since the bangle is cut around the leg of the beast close to the hoof in a continuous cut, it also signifies the family unity, which the newly appointed head of the family is supposed to uphold and foster. It reminds him that the authority he wields belongs to the deceased father, and should not be abused. Furthermore, the *rukanda* symbolizes that the ancestor would inspire the bearer in taking care of the family. It is an assurance of the ever presence of the ancestor. It also shows the intimate relationship that exists between the one wearing it, and the ancestor. All

---

26. Gelfand, *An African's Religion, The Spirit of Nyajena the case of the Karanga*, 85.

other family members should render to him the respect that was due to the deceased, for he is now the embodiment of his authority.

The sacred bangle would be removed by the nephew who would have made it in the first place, after at least a year, unless extenuating circumstances demand that it be removed earlier or later than a year. If the original maker of *rukanda* is no longer available, any other suitable *muzukuru* should carry out the ritual. *Muzukuru*, who is the sacred practitioner in this ritual is paid a cow for his duties. This cow may also cater for the cost of his *masukavuta* (washing the weapons) duties as discussed in the following section. The removal of *rukanda* and the *mupembere* branch left inside the kitchen hut roof on the day of *magadziro* may be done on the same day, by the *muzukuru*. Upon removal, it can be buried in the field closest to the homestead or in the cattle kraal. Alternatively, it can be thrown into a termite hole. If buried in the cattle kraal, it would decompose, and be used as part of manure to fertilize the crops of the family. Either way, its disposal renews the interconnectedness between the ancestors of the family, the newly appointed family head, and other members of the family.

INHERITANCE OF NAME AND ESTATE

The inheritance (*nhaka*) and the *magadziro* ceremonies are usually celebrated concurrently, or one immediately after the other. The *nhaka* ritual is performed on the morning following the *magadziro*. What is inherited is the name of the deceased, his estate, and wives, if he were a married man. If the departed is a woman, her name, personal property, and husband may be inherited in almost the same manner, but by her own people. Holleman notes that among the Hera of Chivhu, if the deceased is a married woman, the husband of the deceased has the obligation to identify all the estate of his dead wife, and this should be shown to her father or guardian.[27] Although the husband and his family are entitled to some property of the departed woman, and half of the grains in the granary, "it is left to the discretion of the woman's relatives how much of this property they will leave with the husband."[28] Holleman further asserts that if the deceased woman's relatives want to leave one of the beasts

---

27. Holleman, *Shona Customary Law*, 355.
28. Ibid.355.

with the widower, they may have to consult a diviner to find out if the spirit would be happy about it.[29]

The name of the male deceased may only be inherited by his oldest son, but the position of the head of the family may be inherited by any other qualifying relative. Whoever is inheriting the name, would be required to sit down on the reed mate, while other family members sit closer by. The ritual leader utters a few words of prayer after which the person sitting on the reed mat is declared the inheritor of the name of the deceased. Among some Shona groups, his head may be washed and anointed with oil. The family members present may offer gifts to the name inheritor as they would have done when he was named after him birth. There is also singing and dancing to celebrate the acquisition of the name by the inheritor. In some cases, the name of the deceased would have been given to one of his sons, not necessarily the oldest, or one of his grandsons. In that case, the same name is given to the oldest son. If the deceased is a woman, her name can be inherited by her oldest granddaughter, or by her niece (brother's daughter). The female name inheritor does not become the head of the family.

It should be noted that the name inheritor, unless he already has the name of the deceased as his official name, does not need to officially change his name to that of the deceased. If there is a younger brother or cousin using the same name, he continues to use it. People may not call the name inheritor by the inherited name, yet everyone knows that he would have inherited the name. Hence, the inherited name is valued because of its significance rather than practicality. The giving of the ancestor's name to his oldest son serves to assure the family that the deceased has indeed come back home, and continues to live and exercise his authority through his son. He becomes a symbolic presence of the invisible ancestor. However, it should be mentioned here, that the ancestor will not be obliged to use the name inheritor as its medium, for it may choose any other close family member including women. In addition to that, the ancestor may demand a sacrificial bull that is given its name, and is used for breeding purposes. Therefore, the name of the ancestor may be used by four different entities, namely, the sacrificial bull, the ancestral spirit medium, the son or grandson who would have been given the name at birth, and the name inheritor. In some cases, the name inheritor, the son

29. Ibid., 355.

given the name at birth, and the ancestral spirit medium could be the same person.

In addition to the name of the deceased, the oldest son, even if he belongs to a junior wife, inherits the estate of his father. The property that he inherits should also cater for the needs of his brothers, particularly assisting them in paying their bridewealth. If the deceased owed anything to anyone, the inheritor takes full responsibility for the repayment of the debts left unsettled. Of course, he does not need to use his own wealth to repay the deceased's debts, for he is expected to use some of the deceased's wealth. If the debt is so significant that the estate is not sufficient to offset it, the family head can use some of the bridewealth obtained from any of his sisters. Where there is no other means of offsetting the debt incurred by the deceased, the new family head can use his own wealth to repay it, since he will be recompensed in one way or the other.

In cases where the eldest son of the dead is still too young to take charge of the inherited property, one of the brothers of the deceased may be asked to hold it for him. This family headship is only temporary, and should be passed on to the new family head as soon as he becomes an adult. In cases where the widow is inherited by one of the brothers of the deceased, he becomes the new family head. Even though the name of the deceased is given to his oldest son, he may not be conferred with the family headship because the widow inheritor becomes the de facto family head. However, in matters involving the immediate family of the deceased and his estate, for instance bridewealth negotiations, cattle, and houses, the widow inheritor should consult with the name inheritor and the inherited widows.

Among some Shona groups, if there is no living relative on the male side, the son of the deceased's eldest sister (*muzukuru*) may be chosen as the heir. This heirship is not for his enrichment, but for the good of the family of the deceased. In fact, *muzukuru* is also qualified to inherit the widows. It is important to mention that, if the wife inheritor is already married, and has his own family, he is expected to continue living in his own home, and occasionally visiting the inherited widow in the home left by her deceased husband. That is why it is important to have the oldest son become the day-to-day head of the deceased's family since he is the man on the ground.

THE INHERITANCE OF WIDOWS

The most elaborate of the inheritance rituals concerns the inheritance of the widows of the departed. Gelfand presents a detailed explanation of how the Karanga of Nyajena celebrates this aspect of the *nhaka* ritual.[30] On the day following the *magadziro*, the *muzukuru* takes the *vuta* (weapons) belonging to the deceased, which he would have washed in a river and placed in the granary before the ritual. Usually more than one weapon is cleansed, particularly if there is more than one widow. The cleansed weapons would have been placed in a *dura* (granary) on the day of burial to avoid their defilement. *Vuta* can be an axe, bow and arrow, gun, or spear belonging to the late husband that is placed across the doorway of the round kitchen. The weapon should be at least half a meter in length. Hence, a knife does not qualify although it is considered one of the weapons of the deceased. The *muzukuru*, who officiates at this ritual is compensated for the *masukavuta* (cleansing the weapons) duty.

When all the family members present have gathered outside the sacred kitchen, the weapon is then placed on a reed mat on which about three people are seated. The widow or widows are then asked to jump over the weapon as proof that they would have been faithful to their deceased husband from the time of his death until this ceremony. Gelfand states that among some Shona groups, this jumping over the weapon is done for three times, back and forth.[31] It is believed that if a widow, who would have committed adultery during this period, disregards the taboo by jumping over the weapon, her private organs may be diseased, or she may fall on top of the weapon.

If the widow has committed adultery, her father or guardian is required to pay a fine. In such a case, the used *vuta* becomes defiled, and should be discarded and replaced by a fresh one to enable other wives to perform the same ritual of *kudarika vuta* (jumping the weapons). The *vuta* is handed over to the inheritor who upon receiving it, agrees to inherit the widow. If any bridewealth is outstanding, the heir has to pay up the arrears. Also, in the event of a divorce between the new husband and the inherited widow, the heir may claim back some of the bridewealth from the father or guardian of the woman.

---

30. Gelfand, *An African's Religion, The Spirit of Nyajena the case of the Karanga*, 84–87.

31. Gelfand, *Shona Rituals with Special reference to the Chaminuka Cult*, 191.

Some Shona groups that were observed by Bullock give the widow some water or beer, which she pours on the head of the chosen inheritor, who would be sitting on the reed mat, with an unstrung bow of the deceased.[32] The widow also gives some water to the elected inheritor to drink, and the chosen man is allowed to refuse the offer if he does not want to inherit the woman. In that case, he is supposed to utter, "*jira iguru*," which literally means, the blanket is too big. He also washes off the mixture of water and beer that would have been poured on his head. Some Shona groups call this washing off of the mixture, *kushamba nhaka*. The rejected widow may try her luck with other qualified contenders.

The rejection of the widow is embarrassing, particularly to her family. It should be counteracted before the ceremony. Among the Karanga of Nyajena, it is believed that the widow does not just choose any of the available candidates randomly. Ordinarily, the widow would have done her homework, and identifed a likeable man who is interested in inheriting her. Or the interested heir would have approached and proposed to the widow before the ceremony. In a few cases, they would have already started being intimate. Although this premature intimacy is against the norms of widow inheritance, it is not as scandalous as when the man is not related to the deceased. Hence, there are no surprises in this ritual. If the widow and the heir would have started being intimate before this ritual, the widow is expected not to jump the weapons, but does not shoulder the blame alone, for she is likely to publicly reveal the violator's name. In this case, both are allowed to go ahead and formalize their relation in this ceremony, and may be asked to pay a small fine for defiling the deceased (*kupisira guva*).

Among other Shona ethnic groups, the widow is handed the knobkerrie of the deceased husband, which she is supposed to hand over to the relative of the deceased husband by whom she would like to be inherited. If she does not want to be inherited, she should put it down on the reed mat. The knobkerrie is handed to her three times, and each time, she puts it down on the mat. After the knobkerrie has been handed to her for the fourth time, she should give it to the grandson of the deceased to show that she does not want to be inherited as a wife, but only as a dependent.

An older woman, who is no longer interested in conjugal interactions, may select one of her own sons to inherit her. Ordinarily, the son should be the oldest. This son would be required to take care of his

---

32. Bullock, *Mashona Laws and Customs*, 54–55.

mother economically. In any case, the son will be the family head who should take care of his mother and siblings. If one of the younger widows refuses to elect an inheritor among those qualified, she is free to go and remarry elsewhere, but she has to leave the home of the deceased husband. If she has not given birth to a sufficient number of children, her father or guardian may be asked to return part of the bridewealth.

If the deceased were polygynous, and some of his wives are still young, they can be inherited by the deceased's sons from any of his senior wives. The candidates for this type of *nhaka* are usually older and unmarried sons. Married sons are also qualified, although preference is given to unmarried sons of the deceased. When this happens, it complicates relationships in the new family, particularly if the deceased had children with the inherited widow. In the Shona culture, the widow's children with her original husband would refer to the heir as their brother. But the inherited widow's children with the heir would be the heir's sons and daughters. Unlike the son who is chosen for *nhaka* by his biological mother, this type of *nhaka* is both conjugal and economical. The son who would have inherited his father's junior wife is saved from paying bridewealth for a wife since his father would have already paid the bridewealth. If the bridewealth were not fully paid, the inheriting son will be responsible for the payment of the bridewealth arrears only. The other sons who do not get the *nhaka* women may be paired with their sisters to obtain the bridewealth that would be paid upon their sisters' marriages. This phenomenon is called *chipanda* among the Karanga of Nyajena. The sons would in turn use their sisters' bridewealth to pay for their own bridewealth.

If the deceased is a married woman, who has died prematurely before providing her husband with a sufficient number of children, the father-in-law or guardian of the dead woman may be obliged to give the widower another woman, particularly, a sister, cousin, or niece of the deceased woman.[33] This only happens if a substantial amount of bridewealth was received, and the family of the deceased woman has no means to pay back some of it. Also, a new woman can be offered to take care of the children if the deceased would have left young children. In some cases, some sisters of the deceased may volunteer to marry the widower in order to take care of the children, and the widower's conjugal needs. The woman who inherits her sister's or aunt's husband is called

---

33. Chitakure, *The Pursuit of the Sacred*, 45.

chimutsamapfihwa, which means the one who revives the cooking. Chitakure notes that *mapfihwa* (the stones that balance a pot when cooking) are used both literally and symbolically.[34] Literally, they refer to the cooking of food that the new woman would do for the family. Symbolically, the cooking refers to the sexual activities that would be revived by the heir to the husband. Either way, the cooking produces and sustains life. The inherited man has to pay a nominal bridewealth for the *chimutsamapfihwa*. There is no jumping of the weapon for the widower.

Among some other Shona groups in the north, a few months after inheriting a widow, the new husband is obliged to perform the *sendekavuta* ritual. *Sendekavuta* is a compound word from two Shona words, *sendeka*, which means to put something in a standing position against a wall, tree, or stone, and *vuta*, which means weapon. This ritual, which is part of the woman inheritance, is intended to make it public to the people who may not have been present at the inheritance ritual that he indeed has inherited his deceased relative's widow. Beer is brewed and friends and relatives are invited for the celebration. This celebration is not a wedding feast because the widow inheritor is performing conjugal duties on behalf of his departed relative.

However, this new union cannot be formally registered unless the widow and her deceased husband were married according to the customary law that allows polygyny. It was easier in the past since all marriages were unregistered customary marriages. Nowadays, if the man intending to inherit a widow is already married according to an exclusive type of marriage, his official wife may deny him permission to inherit the widow. Even if the formal wife permits it, the new marriage with the widow would be unlawful civilly. To counteract such a challenge, the inherited woman may never be declared the inheritor's lawful wife, although he is expected to fulfill her conjugal and economic needs.

At this ceremony, the goat, which is known as *sendekavuta* is slaughtered and eaten by the guests. There is also a lot of dancing and singing. The performance of this ritual puts an end to post-death rituals. Of course, there will be other rituals to be offered from time to time in remembrance of the particular ancestor, but are not closely linked to his death and burial. Usually, such periodical rituals are referred to as *doro renyota* (beer to quench the ancestral thirst).

---

34. Ibid., 45.

The ritual of *kugara/kugagwa nhaka* is very significant among the Shona people. It is intended to provide a breadwinner and husband for the widow, who in most cases, in the past, was not gainfully employed, and had young children who needed support. It was not intended for the satisfaction of the inheritor's sexual greed, although this intimacy came as a byproduct of the other responsibilities shouldered. Hence, among the Shona, a man could inherit a widow with the intentions to only care for her economic, and not sexual needs. Certainly, sexual intimacy acted as an attractive incentive for wife inheritors.

In addition to that, the ritual would provide the widow with someone to care for her emotional and conjugal needs. This provision was important because, in some cases, it would be difficult for a widow to find a stranger to marry her. Among some Shona ethical groups, marrying a widow or single mother was sometimes frowned upon. One of the reasons for that was the value placed on virginity. However, since the choice of a wife rested on the man, he was free to choose a woman to marry. If the woman were a widow or single mother, his relatives and other villagers would initially laugh at him, but would soon forget about it because the value of a woman is not in her past life or virginity, but the present and how well she performs the role of the mother of the family.

Furthermore, the children that result from the new union belong to the departed, which affirms the Shona's belief in the continuation of life in the hereafter, albeit in the spiritual form. The inheritance of the widow is a sign that the departed family member is still an active and concerned member of the family. The children of the deceased would be taken care of by the new father, who in the general sense of the word, would have been a "father" (*babamunini*) to them even before the death of their biological father. If the inherited is a man, the new wife who is already considered a wife to him, takes over from her deceased sister or aunt. She is not a stranger, and is expected to treat the children fairly and justly, as her own.

It should be noted, as shall be explored in the subsequent section, that the widow inheritance ritual has become unpopular. One of its integral parts, *kudarika vuta*, has been criticized for being gender insensitive, for it is performed by widows only. Although this criticism is significant, it should be noted that the Shona society is patriarchal. So, the patriarchal biases, though unpalatable, are expected, and even tolerated. Perhaps, the Karanga wanted to guard against inheriting widows who were already pregnant with someone else's child since there were no pregnancy tests that would detect early pregnancies. Although men are not required to perform the ritual, they are also expected to remain celibate if possible.

THE SACRED BULL

A male ancestor may request a bull known by the Karanga of Nyajena as *bhuru remusha*, which becomes the secondary ancestral host, if the ancestor already has a human host. Usually, one of the family members is already a medium of the ancestral spirit. The ancestor may communicate the need to have a sacred bull dedicated to it using various communication methods. It can communicate it to the most senior member of the family in a dream. Also, the ancestor in need of a bull may communicate to the family through its medium during spiritual possession. In addition to that, the family may consult a diviner after encountering a misfortune, where they are told of the ancestor's need for a sacred bull.

Once the family of the deceased becomes aware of this need, all the family members are notified. The oldest son of the deceased is expected to provide the beast. If the oldest son does not have a beast, any of the sons can provide one. If all the sons do not have a bull, some monetary contributions can be made. One of the bridewealth bull from one of the daughters of the deceased can be used for this purpose. It should be noted that the bull should be a yearling or stirk. Its color is usually black, or black and white, although red bulls are also consecrated. The consecration is done using finger millet (*rukweza*) beer that is poured on the back of the bull.

The bull's main responsibility is to fertilize the family and communal herd. To be able to fulfill this ritual, the bull should be the undisputable conqueror of other ancestral bulls. It should be able to fight other contenders, and once it defeats them, should be able to defend its title. Even, if the bull is not strong enough to fight and defeat other bulls, it is not deprived of its role of fertilizing the family and communal herd. However, the weaker bulls can enjoy this right in the absence of the strongest bull, which always guards the communal cows jealously. Hence, it should be exempted from manual labor of any kind. It should be treated and respected as if it were a human being. The bull is given the name of the ancestor, and it symbolizes three things. First, it symbolizes the power of the ancestors. This power is experienced when it bellows and fights other bulls of the neighborhood. Second, the bull is a symbol of ancestral potency and fecundity. It mates and fertilizes the communal herd just like the ancestors fertilize the land. Moreover, its dung or manure is also used to fertilize the soil for farming or gardening purposes. In addition, it is a sign that the ancestor is ever present to protect the family. Of course, the bull may wonder about, particularly during Winter, but it should stay with the family herd during the rainy season.

The sacred bull must not be slaughtered unless the ancestor demands it. If it becomes too old, or sick, the family members should gather again as they did at its consecration. Beer should be brewed. The bull should be deconsecrated by removing the ancestor from it, and placing it on a replacement bull, if available. If the bull is slaughtered without being deconsecrated first, its flesh will be considered the flesh of the deceased. Once the bull has been deconsecrated, it can be slaughtered, and the meat should be distributed among all family members present and absent. If there are spirit mediums in the family, during the slaughter of the sacred bull, they may, under ancestral possession, drink some of the blood of the animal. They do this on behalf of other ancestors. However, other family members present should restrain them from drinking too much blood, which can be detrimental to their health.

CULTURAL CHANGES

Many Karanga post-burial rituals have changed or have been abandoned completely. One interesting change concerns the *doro remvura* ritual. The Karanga of Nyajena now refer to this ritual as *masukafoshoro*, which is clearly a Shona compound word from *kusuka*, which means cleaning, and *foshoro*, meaning shovel. Since shovels are not indigenous to Zimbabwe, this term is a recent one, which might have been coined in post-independent Zimbabwe. The term literally means the cleaning of the shovels, which would have been used in burying the deceased. This cleaning can mean the ritual purification or ordinary cleaning of the tools. As if the change of name is not strange enough, now several Shona ethnical groups have replaced *masukafoshoro* by a Christian ritual called *manyaradzo*. This *manyaradzo* is performed about the same time *masukafoshoro* is supposed to be held. The Christian ritual is intended to give fellow Christians an opportunity to offer their condolences and empathize with the bereaved family, and to celebrate the life of the departed. What is surprising is that, in some cases, *manyaradzo* is performed even if the deceased were not a professed Christian. The reason given is that the one who is being empathized with is not the deceased but the bereaved, who may be a Christian.

Usually, *manyaradzo* involves a church service, which is celebrated under the leadership of the pastor, where participants sing, dance, and pray. Sometimes, food is prepared, and shared, and soft drinks are offered to the participants. Beer may not be brewed for the ritual depending on the congregational doctrines of the Christians involved. The Christian *manyaradzo* ritual is likely to exclude the gravediggers unless they are Christians themselves. So, the conception of purifying both the gravediggers and the tools used during the burial is lost. The notion of quenching the thirst of the gravediggers and ancestors is also lost. In fact, sometimes, the ancestors are openly lambasted at such Christian gatherings. Also, the aspect of revealing the cause of death to the people, if not yet known, is excluded because most Christians understand death as the will of God. Hence, both the ancestors and the gravediggers are left out in a ritual that is supposed to be performed to thank them. This sidelining of ancestors and gravediggers at *manyaradzo* is likely to offend ancestors. It is reasonable to argue that there is nothing wrong with *masukafoshoro* even for Christians, particularly where it is intended to thank the gravediggers for their manual labor during the burial of the deceased because showing gratitude is one of the Christian virtues. Therefore, thanking the gravediggers in one way or the other should be encouraged even by the Christians. The replacement of *masukafoshoro* with *manyaradzo* does not do justice to the gravediggers, ancestors, and perhaps, the tools, which also need to be cleansed ritually.

Resting days (*mahakurimwi*) is another ritual that has changed. The shift of the Shona people's economy from being mainly agrarian to industrialization saw many people migrating to urban areas in search of jobs. Hence, *mahakurimwi* ritual is only performed for the people who are buried in the rural areas, whose families rely on subsistence farming for livelihood. Since some family members have to go back to towns soon after the burial of the departed family member, they do not take part in *mahakurimwi*. So, some of the Shona mourners are governed by two different traditions, with reference to their attendance of funerals that take place in rural areas. On the one hand, the town relatives who attend rural area funerals are expected to observe the sacred rest, like the rest of the family. On the other hand, they may have no time for such a sacred rest because they should report back to their jobs back in town. Of course, some of them may have sufficient leave days to observe *mahakurimwi*. Rural people are different, for they own their time, and may use it as they see fit. They belong to the *kairos* or ancestral time, which is measured by the amount of work that needs to be done. Ancestral time can never be wasted. Therefore, the *kairos* people can afford not to work on the fields for a few days, and will never complain of having lost time. It is their time, and they control how they want to use it. Whatever they decide to use their time for is important. For the *kairos* people, the time was made for them, not the other way round.

The urban dwellers reckon time according to the Western system that is upheld by their employers. They use the *chronos* time, which refers to graduated time, which can be wasted if not utilized efficiently. For their employers, time is money. Urban dwellers must go back to town where their labor is needed as soon as possible, and it is understandable that they may have no time for *mahakurimwi* because the time system that governs their activities is different. They have to go back to work so that time and profits may not be lost. Also, in urban areas, only the people closely related to the deceased are given off time on compassion reasons. Some employers understand close family relatives to be one's parents, siblings, and children. The extended family is ignored. Moreover, the people who are not related to the deceased, even if they are neighbors of the bereaved may not be given off days by their employers to attend the burial. There is a clash of time reckoning.

In some rural areas, it is reported that the ritual of *mahakurimwi* is no longer observed as strictly as it used to be. Unlike the past, nowadays, the ritual can be shortened if the death happens during the rainy season, when people have to work in the fields. This leniency has been brought about by two issues being faced by rural subsistence farmers. First, the rainfall patterns have significantly changed. The rains come too late, and have become increasingly unreliable. The farmers have to make use of the moisture as soon as the rain stops. Now, if death occurs during the time of planting, the people may not afford to stay away from their fields longer because they cannot waste the sowing opportunity. It looks like there is a shift from the *kairos* to the *chronos* time reckoning. For most Karanga people, time can now be wasted.

Nowadays, *Mashopeshope* or *gata* is rarely performed because of three reasons. First, if the ill person dies in a hospital or at home, after having been discharged from a hospital, the relatives are likely to have been told of the cause of death by medical practitioners at the hospital.

Most of the Western causes of sickness and death are biological. People may die of malaria, HIV/AIDS, accidents, cancer, diabetes, heart attack, among many others. Once people are told of these causes, they are not likely to consult a diviner.

Second, the performance of *mashopeshope* has been outlawed by many Christian churches. Consulting a diviner is considered a sin, which believers should avoid. Sometimes, during the burial, the mourners are reminded by their pastors not to consult diviners. Many believers accept the message of their pastors, and are in most cases, convinced of the cause of death explained to them by Western medical practitioners. However, it should be noted that the explanation given by Western medical practitioners may be considered incomplete by some bereaved families. Yes, people may understand that their relative would have died of malaria, which is caused by the type of mosquitoes called anopheles. But there is no satisfactory explanation as to why the mosquito would have chosen to bite that particular person, and not any other. The other question that is not answered by Western explanations of the causes of malaria is why the victim happened to be at that place where the killer mosquito was hunting. But the traditional diviner has an explanation for that. A diviner may find out that the ancestors were offended, and would have then withheld their protection from the victim, who became vulnerable to attacks from dangerous mosquitoes. It could be that there is an avenging spirit tormenting the family in search of compensation. Also, the death could have been a result of witches sending their invisible children to beat up the victim. Traditional medical practitioners go beyond the physical and obvious.

Third, the Witchcraft Suppression act of 1896, which has been amended for several times, contributes to the shunning of the ritual of consulting a diviner to learn the cause of death. The Act made it illegal to name any person as a witch or even to claim to have the ability to identify witches. Hence, it has become almost futile to consult a diviner because he is not likely to name the witch who would have caused the death of the deceased for fear of being arrested. For some people, it is a waste of money to consult a traditional healer because the cause of the death is already known. Even if the diviner is courageous enough to name the culprit, the relatives may not be able to confront the witch because of the fear of violating the Witchcraft Suppression Act. Some people have been reported to law enforcement agents for accusing others of witchcraft. Although none of the reported people was prosecuted, the reprimand that some of them received at the police station was strong enough to prevent others from committing the same crime.

Although some Karanga families may perform the ritual a few days before *magadziro*, the consultation may be merely ceremonial because they already know what would have killed their relative. It was also reported that some families now consult the African Independent Churches "prophets" instead of traditional medical practitioners. Turner has defined African Independent Churches as those churches that were "founded in Africa by Africans and primarily for Africans."[35] Although this shift is a notable cultural change, at least, the "prophets" provide the same service that the traditional diviners provided. What is unfair is for the Christian "prophets" to demonize the diviners, as if the services that they provide are different from diviners' services.

The ritual of *kubata mavoko* is still valued by most Shona groups. However, some factors such as migrations to urban areas, resettlement far away from the traditional home, and going into the diaspora make it almost impossible for most family members to live in the same locality. When death occurs, it is likely that the relatives are scattered all over the world. Hence, the relatives who fail to attend the burial may perform the ritual of *kubata mavoko* through phones or social media. This way of performing the ritual of *kubata mavoko* has its strengths and weaknesses. On the positive side, it is faster and cheaper since one does not need to travel to perform the ritual. At the stroke of a key, one can give his condolences to the bereaved wherever they may be provided they have phone signals or internet.

However, the speed of modern means of communication becomes its own undoing. Sometimes, online mourners mistakenly replace the ritual of announcing death by *kubata mavoko*. There is always a danger of performing *kubata mavoko* before the relatives of the deceased have been officially notified of the death of their family member. If this happens, they are likely to be shocked because of their unpreparedness to receive such devastating news. People must find out if the person to whom they want to extend their condolences has been notified of the death. In some cases, this has not been done properly. In addition to that, talking on the phone cannot replace being with the grieving person, crying with her, and sharing her grief. Sometimes, the accompaniment of grieving people

---

35. Turner, *History of an African Independent Church*, 92

does not include talking, but just sitting with them in utter silence, which cannot be done using social media or a telephone call.

The rituals of *kukanda chibwe* has significantly changed as well. Since many Shona people are being buried in urban cemeteries, stones are no longer used to cover their graves. Each town has its own regulations and ordinances concerning the burial of the deceased. In some cases, stones are no longer used even in rural areas if the relatives of the departed intend to use bricks and cement to build the grave. This development can be a result of the shortage of stones in some rural areas. The construction or plastering of the grave may be done several months or even years after the burial. In such cases, only soil is used to cover the grave. Eventually, perhaps after many months, the grave mount is covered with bricks, and the walls are then plastered. Although cement graves look smarter, the relatives who are absent during the burial cannot perform the *kukanda chibwe* ritual since this would make the grave dirty. Even if they wanted to do so, the pebbles may not be available in urban cemeteries. Moreover, the placing of pebbles on graves may be against town council ordinances.

However, the latecomer mourners can still introduce themselves at urban cemetery graves as they would do at rural graves. Some of the participants in this study shared that some families now prefer to place flowers on the grave instead of pebbles. Of course, there is nothing wrong with the offering of flowers to the deceased by placing them on top of the grave provided both the buried and the living share a common understanding of the significance of flowers. Unfortunately, some rural people would rather have stones placed on their graves than flowers. This does not mean that they do not value flowers; they do, but pebbles are more symbolic in their worldview than flowers. After all, flowers wither, but stones are durable, which is a symbol of the longevity of the spiritual life the deceased would have attained. Moreover, flowers are seldomly offered to rural parents when they are still alive. Therefore, the same parents may not begin to appreciate flowers after death. Flowers may be very significant to the family members offering them to their deceased relative, but they may not be understood as manual labor that the giver would not have contributed during the burial.

The other challenge about plastered graves concerns the wellbeing of the spirit of the deceased. Although spirits are not bound by space and time, a plastered grave does not look very liberating. The concrete plaster may prevent the ancestor from leaving the grave since it is completely sealed with cement. No one wants to be trapped underground for all eternity. The plastered walls are a sign of imprisonment. The walls may prevent the percolation of water into the grave, and this may delay the decomposition of the body. Since the deceased does not need the body to become an ancestor, the sooner the body decomposes, the faster the deceased may become an ancestor. The use of stones allows the spirit of the deceased to get out of the grave relatively easily. A plastered grave may aggravate the family ancestors who may punish their living family members.

Notable changes to the ritual of the distribution of personal belongings such as clothes and small utensils (*kubata nhumbi* or *kugova nhumbi*) have taken place. Among the Karanga of Nyajena, the ritual has two names, which are closely related. *Kubata nhumbi* refers to how the ritual practitioner handles or touches the clothes and utensils after having dipped his hands in medicinal water. *Kugova nhumbi* refers to the distribution of the clothes. The things to be distributed have to be handled with medicinal water first. More people, particularly Christians, now sprinkle the belongings of the deceased with holy water, which would have been blessed by their priest, pastor, or any other authorized church leader. Hence, in some cases, *muzeze* and *chifumuro* water have been replaced by the Christian holy water. Be that as it may, the rules of distribution are still the same.

A question has arisen concerning the efficacy of the Christian holy water. Is this holy water as effective as the *muzeze* and *chifumuro* sacred water? When asked if the two sacred waters can be used interchangeably or concurrently, some of my informants felt that the onus was upon particular families to decide what to do. The challenge that some families have encountered concerns disagreements arising out of the disparity of cult within families. Among family members, some people may not consider the traditional sacred water as effective as the Christian holy water, and the other way round. However, looking at it from a postcolonial theory perspective, if the Shona peoples would like to keep their cultural identity and integrity, they should stick to their own sacred water. There is no integrity in roping in the Christian holy water into a Shona religious ritual. The bringing in of Christian symbols is tantamount to the acknowledgement of the inferiority of the Shona sacred water. This view does not intend to denigrate the efficacy of Christian symbols or rituals, but to avoid unnecessary and unhelpful syncretism.

It has also been reported that, at this ritual, some widows may present just a few items and personal belongings of the deceased husband, and hide the rest to prevent them from being distributed. This dishonesty in the distribution of personal belongings is intended to save some clothes for the children of the deceased, which can be considered thoughtful of the widow. However, this way of doing things may be a result of selfishness, which does not recognize that the deceased would have been assisted by his brothers and sisters to become the man he would have become. It takes a village to raise an African kid. Denying the people who would have assisted in raising the dead man a little share in his property is failure to appreciate the contribution of the society in the raising of children. This behavior has been interpreted to be a result of greed, individualism, and selfishness, which some postcolonial theorists allege were planted into Africans by some Christian missionaries who preached a heaven where one could go alone without a family. The same missionaries and other colonialists also discouraged African communalism by preaching an exclusive private ownership of land and goods.

To justify the withholding of some personal belongings of the deceased, some widows are believed to do it in the pretext of preventing greedy family members from taking the deceased's personal belongings at the expense of his children. In the past, the acceptance of any of the personal belongings of the dead was tantamount to the acceptance of the responsibility to take care of his children. Nowadays, some relatives may accept or even demand some of the personal belongings of the deceased without willing to assist in raising the children of the dead in any way. If one accepts a share in the belongings of the deceased, one should also accept a share in the care of the widow and children of the departed relative. That is why, at this ritual, some families may also distribute responsibilities over the remaining children for the purpose of their education and care. Each close relative may be assigned a child of the deceased to care for, particularly in the payment of school fees. However, it should be borne in mind that all relatives, even those who have not inherited anything from the deceased's personal belongings, should assist in the care of the children of the deceased whenever there is a need.

Perhaps, the ritual, which has been neglected by most Shona ethnicities is *magadziro*. In this study, it was evident that this ritual is pending for many qualified deceased Shona people. In most of these cases, there are no signs that the ritual is likely to be performed any time soon. There are several reasons for the delay or even abandonment of this ritual in Nyajena. Many Karanga people have become Christians, and are not allowed by their church doctrines to perform *magadziro*. According to

Creary, the ritual of *kurova guva (magadziro)* was "initially banned by Catholic missionaries shortly after their arrival in Southern Rhodesia in the early 1890s," and was condemned by subsequent commissions as the worship of ancestors and violation of the first commandment.[36] Christians expect their deceased to go to heaven, not to come back into the family as ancestors. What is surprising is that some Christians, such as Roman Catholics, believe in saints whose job is almost similar to that of ancestors.

In some cases, the deceased would have instructed his relatives not to perform the ritual because of his Christian beliefs. There are several reports of Shona Christians who have instructed their relatives not to perform the ritual. These people say that they want to go to heaven, and *magadziro* may prevent them from attaining eternity. Some of them would have abandoned traditional ways of doing things long ago. So, some families have to honor the wishes of the deceased, as expressed before their final demise. The challenge posed by such instructions is that no one knows with certainty what happens after death. If the Christian heaven exists, such deceased persons would be happy. However, if such deceased persons fail to enter the Christian heaven, they are likely to haunt their families for not initiating them into ancestorhood. Also, the Christian heaven may be established in the future as the bible says, and in the meanwhile, the deceased may want to come back home while waiting to enter heaven. In addition to that, ancestors are known to be unpredictable. What one rejects when alive may change as soon as one dies. As a result, those Shona people who instruct their families against performing *magadziro*, may change their minds in the hereafter, and punish their relatives for ignoring them.

There are Shona people who have abandoned the performance of *magadziro* not because they are Christians, but because they are disciples of Western culture as advocated by colonialists and missionaries. These colonialists and missionaries demonized African cultures in order to impose their own. African names, rituals, deities, and way of life were condemned as primitive and ugly. Consequently, any African abandoning the African way of doing things is considered civilized, educated, and modernized. This brainwashing of some Africans may result in some Africans hating their cultural identity. Some Africans also join in the condemnation of African culture by Westerners. They have become

---

36. Creary, *Domesticating a Religious Import*, 222, 224.

their own enemies. Hence, some Shona people think that neglecting the performance of *magadziro* and other life-giving rituals is a sign of being civilized. The neglect makes them more acceptable to the Western world and Christianity. However, this condemnation of African cultures by the missionaries and colonialists was intended to strip Africans of their cultural identity and integrity, without which a people ceases to be. A people without a cultural identity and integrity can be manipulated and toyed with. Such a people lack any cultural pride and cohesion. Perhaps the Shona people should be reminded that they can learn from and respect other cultures, while holding on to theirs, and that African cultures are not inferior to any other culture; they are just different. They should be convinced that no culture is perfect because every culture has blessings and weaknesses.

Some Shona people would like to perform *magadziro,* but they lack the funds to acquire the required sacrificial beast and grains for the sacrificial beer. The economic quagmire in which Zimbabwe has been since the year 2000 has made life very difficult for many Zimbabweans. Many ordinary people struggle to make ends meet. They use everything that they get to care for the living not for the dead. The dead should wait until the economy improves. Hence, given a conducive environment, people are likely to perform the ritual for their deceased family members. This way of looking at things stems from the lack of an understanding that the dead are still part of the family, and that their spiritual welfare is a responsibility of their living family members. They depend on their living family members for *magadziro*, which initiates them into a new and everlasting life as ancestors, and later, as nameless spirits. Ancestors would have played their part of giving life to their children as progenitors, and they expect their offspring to honor their part by assisting them to become the "living dead."

Furthermore, some people are ignorant of the importance and significance of this ritual. They do not understand why it should be performed. Some Shona people do not understand that the dying process does not end with the burial of the corpse, but with the initiation of the departed into ancestorhood. They do not know and appreciate that the living family members play an important role in this process. No one becomes an ancestor unless the *magadziro* ritual has been performed. The children of the departed hold the key to the performance of this ritual. They should be willing to do it, but for them to be willing to perform it, they should value it. Without the knowledge and appreciation of the value of the ritual, nobody is likely to care much about it. What this means is that the uncleansed dead are still waiting for the relatives to assist them to complete the dying or living process to enable them to attain everlasting life. This lack of knowledge may not be blamed on the young generations alone, but the whole education system. The knowledge of Shona rituals is mostly acquired through praxis. One should be present when these rituals are performed in order to appreciate them and attain some knowledge of their performance. But modern life does not allow a constant attendance of traditional rituals because the introduction of industrialization forced the youth to migrate to urban areas or even to other countries. There should be a system to inculcate traditional values in the younger generations.

Moreover, some families have been overwhelmed by the HIV/AIDS pandemic, which, in some cases, wiped all adult family members, leaving no one to perform *magadziro*. For some lucky families that still have someone who can perform the ritual, the number of the departed in need of initiation is overwhelming. To worsen the issue, it is believed that the most senior dead member of the family should have his or her *magadziro* earlier than the junior members. Where there is a backlog, it becomes expensive to perform the ritual for all the departed senior members of the family.

In some cases, some of the children who are supposed to perform the ritual are scattered all over the world, and may have no time to perform the ritual. There is a backlog of deceased relatives awaiting the ritual. In one of the villages where the interviews for this study were conducted, one family, which had one of the deceased promoted into ancestorhood, was planning to have four *magadziro* for the departed elders of the family. The leader of the family referenced above wanted to perform the ritual for his father who had died recently, but could not perform the ritual for him alone because his grandmother (father's mother), who had died more than twenty years ago had not been made into an ancestor. Hence, instead of performing *magadziro* for his father, he did it for his grandmother, which cleared his path to perform the ritual for his father and uncles. Eventually, he would perform *magadziro* for his deceased father.

But it is believed that there are consequences for not performing the *magadziro* ritual. For instance, inexplicable misfortunes, droughts, and family feuds faced by individuals and the community are seen as signs of the anger of the ancestors. It is believed that ancestors are angry because their deceased family members have been neglected by the living relatives.

Ancestors become enraged if *magadziro* is not performed, and they may team up to deal with the culprits. Unfortunately, the punishment, which may be meted out for this neglect does not spare the community. When drought and diseases come, they affect the whole community. Hence, people should be encouraged to honor their ancestors and offer them due sacrifices.

What is surprising is the fact that, some of the people, who have abandoned their ancestors, are said to believe in Christian saints, and Roman Catholics can be used to illustrate this point. Looking at it from postcolonial perspective, what the Shona Catholics look for in saints, they already have in ancestors. Saints are deceased people who are canonized by the Catholic Church and recognized as having lived exemplary lives that earned them a place in heaven, and a responsibility to intercede for the living members of the church. Unlike the saints, ancestors are the spirits of people who are personally known and closely related to their living family members. In fact, they are members of the family and are concerned about its welfare. Ancestors know the needs of each family member better than any other spirit. It seems absurd to believe in the existence of saints while rejecting the importance of one's own ancestors. That is tantamount to self-hatred.

The ritual of *kudarika vuta* has also significantly changed. One of the major changes concerning this ritual is that many widows now resent or even refuse to perform it. However, the refusal does not imply that the widow would have been unfaithful to her deceased husband, but is a sign of women's displeasure about the gender bias enshrined in the praxis of the ritual. Men are not required to perform the same ritual, a clear indication of the patriarchal biases that exist in most African societies. In addition to that, nowadays the dead are not initiated into ancestorhood timely, if at all. Therefore, it becomes unfair for the family of the deceased to expect the widow to remain chaste for an indefinite number of years. So, it is important to perform *magadziro* as soon as possible so that widows may not be required to be chaste for an indefinite period of time. As has been explained above, there was a reason for the Karanga to perform the ritual for women alone. Women are the mothers of any given nation; hence, their wellbeing and cultural integrity was safeguarded. However, if the deceased's male relatives would like widows to observe their part of the ritual, they should also observe their own part by performing the ritual as soon as stipulated by Shona society.

In addition to changes in *kudarika vuta* ritual, which is part of the widow inheritance ritual, there have been significant changes to the wife inheritance ritual in general. Most families have abandoned this ritual mostly because of the fear of spreading incurable contagious diseases such as HIV/AIDS. Zimbabwe has suffered a great deal due to this pandemic. Since HIV/AIDS can be spread through sexual intercourse, if the husband dies of it, it is more likely but not always that the widow is also infected. There are cases where only one partner is infected. Diseases such as HIV/AIDS makes it almost impossible to perform *kugara nhaka* ritual, particularly where conjugal relationships are included. Of course, the widow can choose her own son as her guardian. She can also choose any of the husband's authorized relatives as an exclusive economic guardian, which may not be acceptable to some heirs.

The other reason for the unpopularity of this ritual concerns the liberty and economic freedom that Shona women have experienced since Zimbabwe's attainment of independence from the British in 1980. More women are now gainfully employed, so, they can take care of their children in the event of their husbands' demise. In some cases, widow inheritance was compelled by the need to care for the widow and her children. However, this care included conjugal intimacy, perhaps as an incentive to the widow inheritor or to both. Economic independence of Shona women has allowed them to make decisions concerning their future in the event of the husband dying. In addition to that, Zimbabwe now has laws that protect women from losing the property, which they would have acquired together with their deceased spouses. It should be observed that this economic freedom and protection by laws do not forbid Shona women from participating in this ritual, but they give them an option to opt out without the danger of being driven out of their marital homes.

This development in the *kugara nhaka* has brought both blessings and challenges to widows. One of the blessings is that they are free to find a husband anywhere else. In the past, their choice was limited to the qualifying male relatives of the husband. They may also elect to remain single for the rest of their lives without any repercussions from the deceased husband's family. The downside is that widows who are not gainfully employed may find it difficult to care for their families if the husband's relatives refuse to assist. Sometimes, it is hard for a widow to find another man to marry her, which may deprive her of emotional and financial support. Mbugua, writing from a different context bemoans the lack of arrangements for the care of the widow and her children in modern African families as was the case in the past.[37] This lack of arrangement exposes the widow and her children to economic hardships. Although it is the responsibility of the remaining family members to take care of their brother's family, there is no single person pin-pointed to shoulder this responsibility unless the widow is inherited.

Another significant cultural change is in the inheritance of a married woman's estate. Holleman notes that among the Shona of Hera, the inheritance of a woman's property is left to the discretion of her own relatives.[38] The husband's only responsibility is to show the in-laws all the property that belongs to the deceased wife. In the past, it is reported that the deceased wife's relatives were entitled to half of the food and other properties, and they would leave the rest to the son-in-law and his children. However, if there were any livestock, they would be taken by the relatives of the departed wife. But things have changed. Some relatives of the deceased may take everything, leaving the son-in-law with nothing. Such acts have been condemned as a result of greed and selfishness that have overridden the Shona traditional values. However, it is true that some of the Shona rituals can be abused, but there is no practice, in any culture, that is immune to abuse. What is needed for the people whose culture has been demonized, and almost discarded, is to reclaim their cultural practices for the sake of saving their cultural identity.

The practice of the *chimutsamapfihwa* inheritance has significantly changed. Because of the HIV/AIDS pandemic, it has become dangerous to offer one's daughter to a widower. If the deceased wife would have died of an infectious disease, the inherited wife is likely to contract the same disease. In addition to that, the illegalization of marrying minors has also changed this type of marriage. Girls can no longer be forced to marry people that they do not love, and a girl may refuse to marry her deceased sister or aunt's husband. There are also men, who refuse to take the offered women, preferring to look for a wife from somewhere else. Although, the rejection of an offered *chimutsamapfihwa* is seen as an insult to the departed wife's family and ancestors, it saves young girls from getting entangled in a marital union with older men.

Another change has been introduced by unofficial online memorial ceremonies of deceased relatives that are becoming popular. This type of

---

37. Mbugua, *Funeral Rites Reformation for Any African Ethnic Community Based on the Proposed New Funeral Practices for the Agikuyu*. 104.

38. Holleman, *Shona Customary Law*, 325.

memorial is increasingly becoming popular on social media. People who would have lost a family member in the past, sometimes, continue to commemorate their birthdays or death anniversaries on Facebook. Some of them read like, "Today, my mother, who passed away three years ago, would have been seventy years old." Or "it's now ten years ever since my father died. I miss you father, and life has never been the same ever since you left us." The memorials take many different forms and shapes. These posts keep the memory of the deceased going. At least, the deceased is remembered two times every year—at her birthday and death anniversary. These gestures of love may be significant to both the living family members and the departed. It is good for the dead to be remembered. Also, this yearly commemoration of the deceased serves as a notification of the occurrence of death to friends and relatives who would have missed the sad news when death happened. Every time, these memorials are posted on social media, there is bound to be some people who offer their condolences even if the death would have happened about fifteen years back. It should be observed that some people who are not keen on reading the whole memorial post may mistake it for a death notice. Sometimes, the one who would have posted the memorial has to correct his followers by reminding them that the death is not a recent one.

Be that as it may, Shona people should know that there are rituals designed to honor their departed family members. Ancestors may not be able to access social media, but they understand the traditional rituals, which should be performed by their offspring. For instance, social media memorials cannot replace the ritual of *magadziro*, for no one can become an ancestor unless it is performed. Consequently, online memorials can be therapeutic to the one posting them, but may not be helpful to the dead. The dead are thirsty. The dead want to come home. They want to be honored in a way that gives them eternity. The Shona people, who post memorials for their dead parents on social media, but have not performed the liberating *magadziro* ritual for them, should be encouraged to honor their deceased parents by assisting them to attain everlasting life as ancestors.

Some Christians argue that *magadziro* should not be performed for Shona people who have become Christians. As Christians, they are expected to either go to heaven when they die or wait for the end time or *parousia* in their graves. The Shona ritual of *magadziro* does not prevent the deceased from going to heaven when the time comes. In fact, it allows them to have some responsibility while waiting for heaven. They should come home to inspire and intercede for their family members before God. They should be assisted to be ready for heaven by their family members. Even the Christians saints are helped by the church to become saints through the ritual of canonization. The ritual of *magadziro* does not intend to make the dead a god. In fact, it makes her more acceptable to God, by giving her another chance and another life. An ancestor does not work against God, but for God. An ancestor aspires what God aspires. It should be noted that the Shona believe that all ancestors will end up being resident in the spiritual realm. Hence, the Shona belief in ancestors and the Christian belief in heaven are compatible. While waiting for heaven, the deceased can continue to do good as an ancestor.

CONCLUSION

This chapter has explored the importance and interdependence of the relationship between the living and the deceased members of the Shona peoples. The dead and the living family members need each other. While death is so destructive and painful, it does not cut off the relationship between the departed and their living family members. On the one hand, the departed rely on their family members for proper burial rituals, which enable them to become ancestors. On the other hand, the living family members depend on their ancestors for protection, blessings, and inspiration. The eagerness with which the Karanga of Nyajena perform these rituals, confirms their unwavering belief in life after death. As attested by the reviewed scholars and participants in this study, death is a transition from this visible, physical, and limited life to a new spiritual, eternal, and invisible life as an ancestor. Although death is feared and evaded by all means necessary, most people accept its inevitability and appreciate the eternal life and unlimited powers that it gives to those who become ancestors. They say, "it takes a village to raise an African kid." Perhaps the same adage is equally true about making an ancestor—for it takes the same village to make an ancestor.

Also, post-burial rituals are crucial because without them the dying process is not complete. The Shona people who decide against performing them at all, or improperly do so, choose to upset and ostracize the invisible members of their families. According to Mbiti, the process of dying continues as long as there is someone who knew the "living dead," and would be completed "when the last person who knew him dies," and at this point, the "living-dead" loses personal immortality, and acquires collective immortality as a spirit.[39] The refusal to perform post-burial rituals, particularly, *magadziro*, is an insult to the collective wisdom of the Shona elders and ancestors. It is like choosing death for one's own family members, instead of life, and is tantamount to committing murder of one's own family members. To deprive the deceased of becoming an ancestor is to condemn him to eternal darkness. Therefore, post-burial rituals should be performed.

However, the encounter between the Shona and Western cultures has brought about changes to the performances of these rituals. Some of the changes are inevitable and desirable, but others are a result of the Shona cultures' incessant demonization by colonialists and Christian missionaries. Unfortunately, the demonization of such rituals has been accepted and internalized by some Shona ethnic groups to the extent that they perpetuate the condemnation of the rituals themselves. Yes, it is true that the Shona, perhaps just like all other African peoples, need redemption from self-hate. They need salvation from a distorted image of themselves that they have embraced. They should reaffirm their cultural identity, and run away from self-loathing. Suggestions of what they should do to reclaim their cultural identity and dignity will be dealt with in detail later.

---

39. Mbiti, *African Religions, and Philosophy*, 2nd Edition 158.

Chapter 7

Karanga Traditional Death Rituals Manual

INTRODUCTION

THIS CHAPTER PROVIDES A brief manual of selected death rituals that are carried out from the time a Karanga person dies until the *magadziro* (making of an ancestor) ceremony is performed. Even though this chapter deals with numerous death rituals, it gives primary emphasis to *magadziro*. A manual is a series of clear, concise, and progressive instructions about how to perform a certain process—in this case, it concerns the performance of some selected Karanga death rituals according to the people of Nyajena's death ritual praxis. The main purpose of this chapter is to provide readers with a step by step, pocketable, intelligible, and some practical information on how to perform selected important Karanga death rituals. All the information presented in this chapter is a logical synthesis of the field research findings done for this study. Although the praxis of rituals described here may be similar to what other scholars have observed elsewhere, this manual is composed out of the field data gathered for this study. The similarities render this manual usable by other African ethnicities if they find it applicable to their needs. However, it should be noted that this manual, like any other manual, may be of great help to people who already know something about the rituals dealt with. Novices in African traditional practices should first acquaint themselves with the details of the rituals before they can make sense out of this summarized manual.

WHAT IS A MANUAL?

According to Mason, one of the first and important things to do before writing a manual is to identify the readers, and make assumptions about their knowledge concerning the topic under scrutiny.[1] In addition to that, another significant area to consider is the audience. For Reddout, the specific names of the audience should be mentioned if it adds to the clarity of their identity.[2] In the case of this study, the people of Nyajena in particular, and other Shona or African people in general are the audience. For a manual to make sense to its readers, the readers should have some prior, general knowledge about the task at hand. In this case, the audience should know something about the Karanga death rituals.

This manual assumes that the readers have read or know something about Karanga ritual praxis, and possess a working knowledge of the performance of some of the explored death rituals. It should be mentioned that this manual synthesizes what most of the practitioners already know about the subject. The question that arises at this juncture concerns the identity of ritual practitioners in African Traditional Religion. Some scholars argue that although there are ritual specialists in African Traditional Religion, it cannot be denied that almost everyone can be classified as a ritual practitioner. These ritual practitioners may include elders, midwives, daughters-in-law, sons-in-law, nephews, healers, village heads, and so on.

Also, a good manual should include an introduction, which gives the readers a short overview. This introduction may include" four key elements," namely, a complete explanation conscientizing the readers about the reason for performing the procedure, and the results of not performing the task, a list of supplies, common mistakes that may happen, and instructions on how to fix the appearances of undesired outcomes.[3]

In addition to the above sentiments, Mason contends that, another significant step in the composition of a manual is to use clear, logical, short sentences, and simple words for the reader's easy understanding of

---

1. Mason, "How to Write Clear Instructions," 26.
2. Reddout, "Manual writing made easier," 66.
3. Mason, 28.

the instructions.⁴ The use of technical jargon should be avoided because it is likely to confuse the readers or users. When people consult a manual for information on how to perform a particular task, their main objective is not to read or master detailed processes, but to read the minimal information that enables them to perform the task at hand. In affirmation of the same point, Fitzgerald encourages the author to stay focused on the topic and to use coherent language.⁵ In other words, the steps to be performed should follow each other logically to avoid misunderstandings. Although a total avoidance of the use of technical terms can be difficult if they are the names of the process to be performed, pictorial diagrams may be used for the readers to understand what is being referred to. However, in the case of this manual on Karanga death rituals, pictorial diagrams will not be used, but every effort will be made to use clear and intelligible language.

Furthermore, Reddout encourages the use of the personal pronoun "you" throughout the manual.⁶ He claims that the pronoun "you" creates rapport between the reader and the writer by involving the reader personally. It is also believed to give more clarity to the technical ideas involved.⁷ The use of "you" is likely to convince the user or reader that the instructions were composed specifically for him or her, and for the purpose of assisting him or her to understand and perform the procedure. In addition to the use of the personal pronoun "you," Reddout recommends the use of words such as "should" to suggest an action, "must," for recommending an action, and "shall," when requiring that an action should be used.⁸ This manual will use the second person pronoun "you," and some of the suggested words, wherever applicable, and in pursuit of adding clarity to the instructions.

Last, when the instructions are finally written, Callison and Donna encourage the writer to ask other people to read the instructions to identify deficiencies and errors, which may be difficult for the writer to identify because of familiarity.⁹ Callison and Donna postulate that it

---

4 Ibid., 28.

5. Fitzgerald, "WRITE RIGHT! owners' manual project develops communication skills," 17.

6. Reddout, 66.

7. Ibid., 67–68.

8. Ibid., 66.

9. Callison and Donna, *How to write clear work instructions*, 331.

does not take an outsider a long time to identify errors in a manual.[10] Although this step should be done when the manual is already composed, it is important because it allows the writer to make necessary or recommended corrections to the manual before users can use it. Unless the mistakes are identified and corrected, the readers may not understand how to perform the required procedure smoothly.

In a nutshell, this manual has five elements, namely, the identification of the ritual, an introduction, a list of items or supplies that are needed for the ritual; the use of short, clear, and logical language, and of the personal pronoun "you" whenever necessary. This manual deals with the last rites or death rituals.

1. LAST RITES

In this manual, last rites or pre-burial rituals refer to all the rituals that are performed as soon as the ill person dies, up to the time his corpse is taken outside of his home for burial. These rites include, closing the eyes and mouth, folding the hands of the deceased, and washing and dressing of the body. Usually, these rituals are performed by the person caring for the dying person, or the closest family member who is available at the time of death. If there was no one to perform some of these rites at the time of death, the rituals can still be performed later. Consequently, it is recommended that the dying patient should never be left alone. Although this watching of the dying patient is intended to give him company, which he desperately needs at this final moment of his life, and to minimize his fears of being abandoned, it is also intended for the availability of a family member to perform these last rites. Most of the participants in this study emphasized the importance of having the dying person watched, day and night.

There are several signs that may herald the impending death of the ill person, such as the loss of sensation, motion, and reflexes, the arms and legs of the patient becoming cool because of low circulation of blood, confusion of time and place, loss of control of bowel and urine movement, restlessness, irregular breathing.[11] Once death is assumed to have occurred, the person present should check if it has actually happened by examining if the patient has ceased breathing, her heartbeat has stopped,

---

10. Ibid., 331.
11. Sankar, 150–151.

her eyelids have involuntarily opened, her eyes have become fixed at a certain spot, and her jaws have involuntarily relaxed, which forces the mouth to open slightly.[12] In the rural setup, the above symptoms may mean that someone has died. However, in most Western health caregiving institutions, appropriate and relevant technology is used to verify the occurrence of death. The following instructions are for caregivers or persons in charge of the dying person, who is being cared for at home, where modern technology may not be available. In the home environment, these rituals should be performed as soon as the occurrence of death has been ascertained.

Audience

Health caregivers, people present at the time of death, family ritual leaders.

Supplies

Water, towel, soap, dish or bucket, fire, coin, body ointment (preferably Vaseline), handkerchief, clean clothes, blanket, pillow.

    1.1 As soon as death occurs, you should check if the deceased has involuntarily lost control of bowels or bladder during the process of dying. If he has done so, you must immediately remove the soiled garments or blankets, clean the back of the deceased, and replace the wet or soiled clothes or blankets with clean ones. If this initial cleaning is not done immediately, the odor would fill the house. This initial cleaning of the deceased may not be ritualistic, but hygienic.

    1.2 You should move the body of the deceased to make it lie on its back so that you can close the deceased's mouth and eyes properly.

    1.3 You must close the deceased's eyes and mouth if they are open, and you should check them regularly for a couple of hours after the occurrence of death. If the deceased has been dead for a couple of hours, and the body is already stiff (*rigor mortis*), you should use some warm water and a towel to relax the muscles. You should then use a towel or handkerchief to tie the top of the head and the chin together until the mouth no longer opens involuntarily. If the departed's eyes are open, you should use the same wet and warm towel to relax the eyelids. You may

---

12. Ibid., 151.

place a coin on the closed eyes to keep the eyelids in place. Care should be taken not to allow the eyeballs to fall into the eye sockets.

1.4 You should fold the hands of the deceased by placing one palm on top of the other, or by stretching each hand along the sides of the body.

1.5 The people responsible for the ritual washing of the corpse should do so as soon as possible. They should use a wet towel with soap to clean the following: face, mouth, (if fluids are coming out), armpits, and private parts. The whole body may need to be cleaned with the wet towel and soap as well. Do not throw away the remaining dirty water and towel. The towel, water, and bucket used for bathing the corpse may be placed in the grave during burial. You should make sure that the towel is torn a little, and the bucket or dish has holes drilled into it before placing them into the grave.

1.6 Apply body lotion to the corpse, and comb its hair if need be.

1.7 Dress the body in clean clothes, if there are no new clothes that have been purchased for that purpose. After you dress the body, you should bring back the hands to the desired position.

1.8 Things to remember

If the caregiver is not the appropriate person to perform the last rites, she should call the closest family member of the deceased as soon as she becomes aware of the occurrence of death. If the one who is supposed to perform these rituals is afraid to do so, she should wait for the senior members of the family to arrive and request them to perform the rituals.

2. BURIAL OF BABIES AND FETUSES

Among the Karanga of Nyajena, babies that are born prematurely (stillbirths) or die before they cut their first teeth receive a special burial, which is different from the burial given to adults. The rituals surrounding the burial of such babies are crucial because if not performed properly, the spirit of the deceased baby may make its mother barren or may bring misfortunes to the entire community. You should perform the burial early in the morning when it is still cool. Only women who have gone past childbearing ages (menopause) should take part in the burial. The shallow grave must be dug along the riverbanks or swampy areas.

Audience

Senior women who have gone past childbearing ages, women, men.

Supplies

Hoe, pick, cloths or small blanket, and broken clay pot (*gambe*).

2.1 There should not be any public mourning rituals such as crying, *kubata mavoko*, or *chema*.

2.2 Relatives should be notified about the death, and if they come for the funeral, they should not talk about the death directly.

2.3 Only old men should choose a stream, river, or swampy area where they want to bury the baby. They should also assist in the digging of the shallow grave. If the grave is dug in the river, it should not be in the middle of the river, but its banks.

2.4 When the grave is complete, the older women should be notified, and they should put the baby in a cracked clay pot (*gambe*) (if it is premature), or just wrap the baby in a thin cloth or blanket (if born alive and died later).

2.5 Early in the morning, the older women should bury the baby in the shallow grave along the riverbanks.

2.6 If the deceased baby is a girl, she should be laid on her right-hand side, and if a boy, on his left-hand side (the natural sides men and women use when being intimate).

2.7 As soon as the burial is done, the women should go back home, and join the rest of the family, who are just siting and talking with each other. Even though everyone knows why they are gathered, it is forbidden to refer to the dead fetus or baby directly. This taboo is observed to let the spirit of the deceased baby know that it is not welcome back into the family.

2.8 Things to Remember

You should not mourn or perform normal burial rituals because the baby may come back again to deceive the parents. The mother should not attend the burial because she may become barren.

Women who have not reached menopause should not attend the burial but may stay at home accompanying the bereaved mother. You should never bury the baby on dry land because the spirit of the baby may become aggravated, and would come back to punish the mother or the whole community with some kind of calamity.

3. BURIAL OF AN UNMARRIED MAN OR WOMAN

When an unmarried man dies, efforts should be made to find out if he ever fathered a kid outside wedlock. If none of the family members knows of any such a kid, then the departed is considered to have died single and childless. As for a deceased woman, it is easier to find out if she ever had a kid or not. Definitely, someone would know if she ever mothered a kid. Once the lack of paternity or maternity is proved beyond any reasonable doubt, the burial proceedings should begin. Most rituals that are performed should be similar to those of a married adult. What is outlined below are the extra rituals that should be done in addition to the usual ones.

Audience

Ritual leaders, all other people.

Supplies

Rat, mortar, pestle, maize cob (*guri*), and all the supplies required when burying an adult person.

3.1 Once the corpse has been washed, you should find a rat, that would be inserted into the anus of the corpse. *Ruredzo* (slippery plant) maybe used to enable the rodent to get into the deceased's back.

3.2 If you do not find a rat, *duri* or *musi* (mortar or pestle) depending on the sex of the deceased, should be taken to the grave, and placed by the side of the corpse.

3.3 As this ritual is being performed, a prayer should be said by the ritual practitioner. The words may be uttered audibly or silently. "My son or daughter or (whatever the case might be), you have died, and you have not left any family. No children, and no wife/husband. There is no reason for you to come back home as an ancestor because you have no one to look after. There is no offspring to perform the *magadziro* ritual for you. Please, go for good. Do not come back. This is your wife or child (pointing at the *duri* (mortar), *musi* (pestle), or rat). Please, go, and never come back. We do not want you to come back."

3.4 You should not perform *magadziro* and inheritance ceremonies for such a man or woman. However, his or her personal belongings and estate should be distributed in the normal way.

3.5 Things to remember

You should note that all other rituals apart from the few described above in this section, should be similar to the ones performed when a married person dies. The Karanga fear that if an unmarried person is allowed to come back into the family home, his spirit may demand a wife or haunt other people's wives or husbands. In addition to that, since the deceased has not left any children, he has no one to perform *magadziro* for him or her.

4. MARKING THE GRAVE

This is one of the most important rituals among the Karanga of Nyajena, which should be performed by a close relative of the deceased. If a man has died, his father or brother should perform the ritual. If a woman has died, her own father or brother, or their representative should mark the grave. The ritual is performed early in the morning, in the presence of family members and gravediggers. It marks the beginning of gravedigging.

Audience

Everyone.

Supplies

Hoe, pick, shovel.

4.1 The family representative, in the company of family members should go to the place, which has been selected to bury the deceased. Families that have family cemeteries are likely to use them to bury their deceased family members.

4.2 The family leader, with the help of close family members, in the presence of gravediggers, should select the spot where the grave should be dug.

4.3 The one marking the grave should use a pick or hoe to make three or more strokes into the soil while praying. The digging is symbolic.

4.4. He or she should say, "This is the place where we are making you a new home, or this is where we are going to lay you to rest."

4.5 After this symbolic digging, the grave diggers may begin the digging of the grave.

4.6 Things to remember

This ritual should be performed by a close family member, who is authorized to perform it. In some cases, you can delegate younger family members to perform the ritual on your behalf. If a person dies and is buried in a foreign land, far away from his relatives, anyone who is related to him by totem or in any other remote way may perform the ritual. If the deceased is a woman, only members of her family of origin should perform the ritual. Her husband or children should not mark the grave unless all her family members cannot be located. In that case, her oldest child may be asked to perform the ritual.

5. BURIAL OF A WOMAN OR MAN WHO BORE CHILDREN

The Karanga burial of a person who would have been married, or who has given birth to or sired children is elaborate. The Karanga of Nyajena believe that the spirit of such a person will become an ancestor, unless it is disqualified because of certain conditions. Everything should be done with extreme caution, lest the spirit of the deceased is upset. These rituals start with taking the corpse outside the room where it was being prepared for burial.

Audience

Ritual leaders, family members, mourners.

Supplies

Coffin, bier, pick, shovels, water, stones, reed mate, brooms (*mitsvairo*), blanket.

5.1 You should tell the deceased that you are taking him to his final resting place. The following prayer may be used: "We are now taking you to your resting place."

5.2 The nephews or sons-in-law should lift the coffin or bier and place it outside of the hut, but closer to the doorway.

5.3 The leader should invite people to bid their farewell to the deceased, starting with the most senior members of the family. One at a time, they may approach the open coffin, and gaze at the face of the deceased. They are free to remain silent, bow a little, or say a few words silently.

5.4 The coffin bearers should lift up the coffin, and walk around the hut in which the corpse was kept. If the deceased is a man, you should do it in a clockwise direction, and if a woman, you should do it in an anti-clockwise direction.

5.5 Daughters-in-law should walk in front of the coffin bearers with indigenous brooms in their hands. They may sweep the spot on which the coffin would be placed during resting. The men carrying the coffin should follow the daughters-in-law, while carrying the coffin with the side where the head of the deceased is located facing the home, and the legs side facing the gravesite.

5.6 The body should be rested two times before reaching the grave, and for the third time, when the mourners reach the grave. When resting the body, the coffin bearers should place the coffin on the ground or reed mat for about two minutes, while the rest of the mourners are clapping hands and ululating, or just silent. The same should be repeated at the second stop.

5.7 After the second resting, the coffin side where the deceased's head is located should now face towards the grave. Upon reaching the grave, the coffin should be placed close to the grave.

5.8 Speeches may be given at this time. Only selected people should give short speeches.

5.9 The sons-in-law and nephews should now place the body into the grave, which is then closed with flat rocks separating the rest of the pit from the coffin compartment.

5.10 The people who have not done manual work in the preparation of the grave should pinch a little soil and throw it into the grave, while praying as follows: "I am X, your son. Have a safe journey, my father," or whatever the relationship might be. This ritual should also be done on behalf of those family members who are not present at this time. Parents can perform this ritual for their absent children.

5.11 When the grave is halfway filled with soil, the remainder of the water used to bath the corpse, and the towel and bucket or dish that would have been used in the bathing of the deceased should be placed into the grave. You should make sure that the towel is slightly torn, and the bucket or dish has holes drilled into it. If a tree bark bier (*bwanyanza*) would have been used, it also should be destroyed before throwing it into the grave. A shirt or pair of trousers of the deceased selected for this purpose should also be torn apart not more than halfway and placed into the grave at this point.

5.12 The rest of the people may quickly fill the grave with the soil using shovels. At any point during the covering of the grave with soil until it is completely done, there should be at least one person shoveling soil into the grave.

5.13 Once all the soil from the grave has been put back onto the grave, mourners should be instructed to bring stones to the grave. You should line the stones on top of the grave. You must instruct the people responsible for carrying the stones to bring one stone at a time. Women should assist in bringing the stones to the grave. If a scotch cart or wheelbarrow has been used to carry stones in large quantities from where they are available to the grave, all the stones should be offloaded at least several meters from the grave, from where the people can bring them to the grave one by one.

5.14 After the mount of the grave is completely lined with stones, the daughters-in-law should sweep the area around the grave while going backwards so that no footprints are left on the ground.

5.15 Gravediggers should wash their hands, and the remainder of the water should be sprinkled on the swept ground.

5.16 All may go home now where the village head will announce the resting days (*mahakurimwi*) if not yet announced. Also, the family may announce the date for the *masukafoshoro* or *manyaradzo*.

5.17 If the mourners have not had their meal, you should give them food at this point. You should make sure that the women who serve the food to the mourners must carry a plate of food at a time.

5.18 Things to remember.

Burial should not be done between 12 noon and 1:00 pm. It is also recommended to avoid burial about an hour before noon, just in case, noon comes before they finish. Children should not be compelled to view the body if they do not feel comfortable in doing it. In fact, in the past, the Karanga did not allow small children and pregnant women to attend the burial for fear of attacks by the evil spirits. The spouse of the deceased is not expected to give a speech. The women who serve the food at the funeral should bring one plate at a time. It should be borne in mind that mourners should carry only one article at a time during and immediately after the burial.

6. HOW TO PERFORM MAGADZIRO

This ritual is very important and should be performed for the departed who qualify or are not disqualified. One should have been married, sired, or given birth to offspring, and should not have died of any disqualifying disease such as leprosy, tuberculosis, and so on. Ordinarily, it is performed by one's children or grandchildren, at least six months after the burial. Other Shona groups perform the same ritual at least, one year after the burial. This ritual makes an ancestor by bringing his or her spirit from the grave back into the family home. In other words, *magadziro* reincorporates the deceased back into the family as its newest invisible member. No one can become an ancestor unless this ritual has been performed. Hence, senior ancestors of the family and the spirit of the uninitiated deceased are very much aggrieved if the children of the dead person deliberately refuse to perform the ritual. This ancestral anger may bring misfortunes to those who are neglecting the performance of *magadziro*, also known as *kurova guva*.

Audience

Everyone.

Supplies

Finger millet (*rapoko*, *rukweza*), big traditional clay containers (*makate*), one male or female goat (*mbudzi*) depending on the gender of the deceased, one cow or bull, depending on the gender of the deceased, water, clay pots (*hari*), axe (*demo*), drums (*ngoma*), firewood, jingles, knife, maize meal, cups, ground tobacco (*bute*).

6.1 You should notify all the family members and relatives of your intention to perform *magadziro* on time. If the departed is a woman, her family of origin must be notified, and their permission solicited for because they are the ones who would officiate at the ritual.

6.2 Contributions of grain and money may be made to the person responsible for the ritual.

6.3 A few weeks before the ritual, you and some closest family members should visit a diviner to enquire about the process of the ritual, and to have the ritual practitioner appointed.

6.4 You should encourage people to gather at the place of the ritual on the eve of the ritual.

6.5 Early in the morning, a delegate of close family members and the deceased's nephew, if the deceased is man, or grandson, if the deceased is a woman, should go to the grave of the deceased. The delegation should include women who can sing and ululate, and men who can dance, sing, play the drums, and whistle.

6.6 The delegates should take to the grave a small clay pot of beer (*pfuko*), a ground snuff container (*chibako chefodya yemhino*), and an axe (*demo*).

6.7 As the procession nears the burial place of the departed, they may sing, dance, and ululate.

6.8 Upon arrival at the grave, the nephew should cut a medium sized branch of *mupembere* tree, and bring it to the grave. The delegates should kneel around the grave, with the leader kneeling closer to the headstone.

6.9 The delegates should clap their hands reverently, and the women should ululate. You should then draw out some beer from the *pfuko* using *mukombe*, and present it to the spirit of the deceased saying the following prayer: "X, we have come to take you home. You cannot live in the bush any longer. Here is your drink to quench your thirst." You then pour some beer on the grave. Draw out some more beer, and take a sip, and then do the same for all the delegates.

6.10 Again, you should pour some ground tobacco into your left palm, and talk to the spirit of the departed. "Here, is your tobacco." You then put it on the grave. It is advisable to take a pinch of the ground tobacco, and sniff it before placing it on the grave. There should be more clapping of hands, ululating, drumming, and dancing.

6.11 The nephew should pull the *mupembere* branch around the grave in a clockwise direction if the deceased is a man, and in an anti-clockwise direction if she is a woman. As the nephew is doing this, the leader should beg the spirit of the dead to jump onto the branch for a ride home. The nephew momentarily places the branch on top of the grave. The leader should notify the deceased of the trip home. "X, ride on this branch. We are taking you home." There should be more ululating, dancing, singing, whistling, and drumming.

6.12 On the way back home, the nephew should lead the way, while pulling the branch. He should never look backwards until he enters the sacred hut (round kitchen). The procession should be done amid much jubilation, dancing, drumming, and singing. Upon arrival at home, other people should join in the celebration.

6.13 The nephew should pull the branch right into the sacred hut (round kitchen), and put it in the inside of the hut's roof where it will remain until a ritual to remove it has been performed, and the nephew paid for this job, and also for other duties such as the *rukanda* business.

6.14 The goat of emotion (*mbudzi yeshungu*) should be brought to the threshold, and the nephew should hold it by the front leg. For a woman, the grandson should hold it by the right leg, and for a man, by the left leg. The nephew should be sitting inside the sacred hut, while the goat is standing with its head inside the hut, and its whole body outside.

6.15 You should then invite the close family members who are gathered outside the hut, starting with the most senior, to pour beer on the back of the goat while introducing themselves to the ancestor. "I am X, your grandfather," or whatever the relationship might be. "If you are happy with this ritual, please, show us."

6.16 This ritual should be repeated until the goat shakes its body. This shaking is interpreted as the acceptance of the ritual by the spirit of the dead. From now on, the spirit has become an official ancestor of the family. This ritual can be performed by proxy.

6.17 The ritual may be repeated until the goat shakes its body. If it does not shake its body, it is believed that the ritual would have been rejected, and another one would be performed in the future after rectifying the issue that would have angered the ancestor.

6.18 You should slaughter the goat, and its meat should be roasted and eaten without salt. Adding salt to the sacred meal invalidates the ritual. Its head, legs, hooves, skin, and bones should be burnt in the fire.

6.19 At this point, beer may be given to the people who should be seated according to their villages.

6.20 As soon as the goat meat is all consumed, you should lead a delegation to the cattle kraal, and present the sacrificial beast to the ancestor and the people. Once this is done, the sons-in-law and nephews should slaughter it.

6.21 Once the beast has been skinned, and its parts separated, you should cut a few pieces from all organs except from the head and legs of the beast, and place them into a clay pot. This meat should be cooked without salt, and it will be the sacred meal for close family members. All the other meat should be cooked separately.

6.22 If the ancestor is a man, the nephew should use his knife to cut a skin bangle (*rukanda*) from the left leg of the front leg of the beast, while making sure that it comes out as a circle. He should slide it into the left arm of the oldest son of the ancestor. This son should be the one who would inherit the name and estate of the deceased.

6.23 The sacrificial meat, and *sadza* (thick porridge from finger millet) should be cooked by a woman who has reached menopause. When the meal is ready, you should bring both the *sadza* and meat to the threshold, and all family members should sit outside facing the doorway of the sacred hut. You should take a lump of *sadza* and a piece of meat by your right hand, and give it to the members of the family gathered. Once every member has received and consumed his or her share, the nephews may snatch away the remaining meat and run away into the nearby bush to consume it. They are considered hyenas, and are allowed to steal this meat and some beer. This is one of the ways to compensate them for their ritual duties.

6.24 You should give more beer, and food to the people at this point. Dancing and singing should continue until evening. The distant relatives and other villagers may depart at the end of the day, but close relatives should remain for more rituals on the next day.

6.25 Things to remember

Magadziro is a make-or-break ritual. Everything should be carried out meticulously. If you have any question, do not hesitate to ask any of the elders present even if they are not close members of your family. There are variations to the performance of this ritual depending on each family and the gender of the deceased. In any case, special attention should be given to what the elders of the family say.

7. INHERITANCE CEREMONIES

Among the Shona peoples, there are several post-burial rites, which deal with inheritance (*kugova* or *kugara nhaka*). These include the rites concerning the inheritance of the deceased's name (*zita*), personal belongings (*nhumbi*), wives (*vakadzi*), and estate (*pfuma*).

Audience

Family ritual leaders, nephews/grandsons, everyone.

Supplies

Reed mat (*rupasa*), money, plate, blanket or cloths, drums, water, dish, towel, deceased's weapon (axe, gun, bow and arrow, and so on).

7.1 INHERITANCE OF THE DECEASED'S NAME

This ritual is performed on the morrow of *magadziro* ceremony. It is performed for both men and women. If the ancestor is a man, his name is given to his oldest son. If the deceased is a woman, her name is given to any of her granddaughters or nieces (daughter of her brother). The son, who inherits his father's name, also assumes other responsibilities for the family.

    7.1.1 You should spread the reed mat so that the one inheriting the name sits on it. Cover him with a big cloth or blanket. Do not suffocate him. All other family members should gather around him or her.

    7.1.2 You should kneel down and talk to the ancestor. "Today, we are giving your name to your son, X. Protect him from all harm. Inspire him to do what is right. Help him to take care of his mother and the siblings." Then you pour some ground tobacco onto the soil. The family members gathered should clap hands, sing, and ululate.

    7.1.3 You should also address the one who has inherited the name. "Now you have inherited your fathers' name. You also should assume the responsibilities that your father had. Take care of your siblings and mother (if she is not inherited). Pay back his debts."

    7.1.4 You then uncover the name-inheritor, and invite the people present to offer their gifts. You should provide a plate for the monetary gifts.

    7.1.5 The people gathered should celebrate and congratulate the name-inheritor amid much pomp and fanfare.

7.1.6 Things to Remember

Sometimes, the person inheriting the name, is already named after the deceased. In such situations, this ritual is performed as if the inheritor is getting the name for the first time. There are cases where the younger son or a cousin has the name of the deceased already. In such circumstances, the name should be given to the oldest son of the deceased even if his younger brother already bears the name. This name inheritance is more about shouldering responsibilities left by the deceased father than just getting a name. In the case of a deceased woman, if one of the granddaughters or nieces already has her name, she should be the name inheritor. It should be remembered that the ritual name inheritor does not need to officially change his or her name to that of the deceased unless it is already his or her birth and official name.

7.2 INHERITANCE OF THE DECEASED'S PERSONAL BELONGING

This ritual can be carried out a couple of days or months after burial. It is important to carry out the ritual as soon as possible because the deceased's personal belongings may be defiled if they remain unpurified for a longer time. If the deceased is a married woman, her family of origin should be encouraged to perform the ritual on the day following the burial, unless if they arrange to do it on a later date. You should remember that the deceased woman's children and husband are not considered her relatives in terms of death rituals.

Audience

Ritual leaders, everyone.

Supplies

Small branch of *muzeze* tree tied into a bundle, leaves of *chifumuro*, a dish of medicated water, personal belongings of the deceased (excluding livestock), reed mat, axe, bow and arrow, gun, knobkerrie, immovable properties, wives.

7.2.1 You should gather all the close family members at the home of the departed, and explain to them the purpose of the gathering.

7.2.2 Mix the water in the dish with pounded *chifumuro* leaves.

7.2.3 Dip your hands into the medicated water, and touch the items (*kubata nhumbi*) that have been brought outside, and placed on the reed mat.

7.2.3 When you have touched each of the belongings, you should use the bundle of *muzeze* leaves to sprinkle the medicated water onto the people gathered.

7.2.4 Once the personal belongings have been handled, and the people sprinkled with the medicated water, you should distribute them among the family members of the deceased, making sure that the wishes of the departed are respected, and all the qualified family members benefitting.

7.2.5 If the deceased is a woman, her own people should take charge of the distribution of personal belongings. Traditionally, they are supposed to acquire half of her personal belongings. These include pots, plates, stoves, clothes, blankets, and so on. However, about half of them should be left for the husband and the children. All her cows, underwear, *chinu* (body ointment container), and waist beads (*chuma*), should be given to her family of origin.

7.2.6 THINGS TO REMEMBER

At this ritual, no one should refuse to take what is offered to her or him. However, the recipient may pass the item on to a more deserving family member after first accepting it. It is morally and culturally evil for the family of a deceased woman to take all the personal belongings of their relative without leaving some for the children and husband of the dead.

7.3 THE INHERITANCE OF THE WIDOWS

This ritual should be carried out a day after the *magadziro* ceremony. Until then, all the widows are supposed to remain chaste in honor of the deceased husband. It should be carried out in the morning. All family members of the deceased man, and of the widows should be invited. At this ceremony, each widow should choose a man to inherit her among the qualifying candidates, but only after having jumped the weapon (*kudarika vuta*) of the deceased. So, there are two rituals that run concurrently. The qualifying members are brothers, nephews, and sons of the dead man. The man chosen, if a brother, nephew, or son (of one of the senior wives) of the deceased man, immediately assumes the responsibility over the widow's economic and conjugal needs. He always takes care of the deceased's children, and may sire more children on behalf of the deceased relative. If the chosen man is the son of the deceased and of the widow being inherited, he assumes economic care of his mother and siblings only.

Audience

Family ritual leaders, family members.

Supplies

A dish of warm water, towel, reed mat, weapon of the deceased (axe, gun, bow and arrow).

    7.3.1 You should make all the family members gather outside, about four meters from the doorway of the round hut in which the other rituals associated with the ancestor were performed.

7.3.2 Place the weapon of the deceased husband across the doorway, about two meters from the door. This weapon should have been washed by the *muzukuru* on the previous day, and stored in a granary. This ritual is called *kusukavuta* (cleansing of the weapon).

7.3.3 You should invite the widow or widows to jump over the weapon into the hut, and again when getting out of the hut, starting with the most senior widow. You should let the widows know that whoever was unfaithful to the deceased husband from the time of the burial to this day, should not jump over the weapon, and if she does, she may fall over the weapon or get infected by some mysterious disease.

7.3.4 The widow may perform the ritual silently, or may utter the following words, "*Murume wangu, handina chakaipa chandakabata*," (My husband, I have been faithful to you).

7.3.5 There should be ululation, clapping of hands, and rejoicing for the successful jumping of the weapon. If any of the widows refuses to perform the ritual, her relatives have to pay a fine, usually, a cow, to the relatives of the departed husband.

7.3.6 As soon as *kudarika vuta* has been done, the qualifying men should sit on the reed mat in a circle with the widow kneeling inside the circle, while holding a dish of water and a towel.

7.3.7 You should instruct her to offer the water to the man who she would like to inherit her.

7.3.8 After the chosen inheritor has washed his hands, and the widow has wiped his hands with the towel in her arms, people gathered should ululate. The washing of hands signifies the acceptance of the widow.

7.3.9 The same is repeated until all the widows have performed the ritual.

7.3.10 Things to remember

Any qualifying man chosen should not refuse to wash his hands as a sign of accepting responsibilities over the widow and her children. You should let the widows know that if they no longer want a sexual relationship, they should choose their oldest sons. The chosen son would care for all the widow's needs except conjugal. But if she chooses to go this way, she should remain chaste all her life as long as she lives in the home of the deceased.

7.4 INHERITANCE OF THE ESTATE

In Nyajena, estate refers to the land, cattle, houses, businesses, and other immovable properties of the deceased. In the traditional Karanga society, the oldest son was earmarked to inherit the estate of his departed father. But this inheritance had responsibilities attached to it. For instance, he would pay off all of his deceased father's debts, and support his mother and his siblings, financially. Technically, he would act as if he were the father of the family. However, some fathers would leave a verbal or written will with details of how their estate is to be distributed. If the deceased is a woman, her family of origin must inherit most of her estate. This ritual can be performed on the same day the deceased's personal belongings are distributed.

Audience

Family ritual leaders, family members.

Supplies

Weapons of the deceased father (gun, bow and arrow, axe).

7.4.1 You should instruct the family members to gather early in the morning.

7.4.2 If there is a written will, you should produce it, after consultation with the close family members of the departed.

7.4.3 You should distribute the estate following the will or as per the agreement with the family members.

7.4.4 Technically, all the cattle should remain in the widow's home, although the eldest son is responsible for their care.

7.4.5 In situations where the father would have distributed some of his cattle to all his sons before death, the family leader should follow the wishes of the deceased. However, he should always make sure that the widow and young children will be cared for.

7.4.6 You should distribute businesses, if any, accordingly. The land remains in the hands of the widow.

7.4.7 Things to Remember

The wishes of the widow should be respected. Nowadays, the inheriting son is just symbolic because the widow inherits almost everything. You should make sure that you distribute the estate according to the modern laws of Zimbabwe. All legal documents concerning the occurrence of death, and the transfer of ownership of properties should be followed meticulously. If the deceased would have died at home, an affidavit from the village head, sometimes, signed by two witnesses should be shown to the government department in charge of the registrations of births and deaths.

CONCLUSION

It should be noted that this manual does not deal with all the death rituals of the Karanga of Nyajena, and the omission of some does not mean that such rituals are not important, but it is because of the limitedness of space and time. Also, although these rituals are common in Nyajena, each family may have a slightly different variation of the ritual. However, despite these slight variations, the crux of the rituals is similar. For instance, the prayers are not standardized because they are not in written form. Hence, this manual should be used with prudence, and in consultation with the ritual practitioners of the family in question. Where this manual and the wisdom of the elders of the community differ, please, follow the direction of the elders. Be that as it may, this manual gives an important framework within which to perform the explored rituals. It can safely be used as a resource, where the ritual leaders are not certain as to the procedure to be followed.

Chapter 8

THE WAY FORWARD

INTRODUCTION

THIS CHAPTER HAS THREE sections. The first section gives a synopsis of chapters 1–7. The second section offers recommendations concerning how and why the Karanga of Nyajena, Shona peoples, and Africans should reclaim and affirm their cultural identity, particularly their traditional death rituals. The third section suggests a postcolonial theory, a philosophical framework that students of African religions can use in their research of African religious and cultural identities. However, the chapter acknowledges that some of the Karanga death rituals have been transformed because of their encounter with other cultures. In such cases, the chapter encourages the Karanga of Nyajena to be prudent in choosing whether to go back to their traditional rituals or to stick with the hybrid rituals while using either to their own advantage. Whatever they choose to do, it is imperative that they should know the praxis and significance of their traditional and modern death rituals, and should record them for posterity.

THE OVERALL PICTURE

This study was about death rituals as they are performed by the Karanga of Nyajena. However, since the Karanga of Nyajena are an ethnicity within the larger Shona ethnical group, who are also African, most of the explored rituals are also practiced by most Shona and African peoples. In most instances, what has been said about the Karanga of Nyajena, may be equally true about other Shona or African ethnicities. However, it should be admitted that there are also many ethnical variations concerning both the praxis and significance of some of the death rituals across Africa. Mbiti rightly emphasizes that point when he writes, "Each African people has its own heritage. Some aspects of our cultures are fairly similar over large areas of our continent. There are also many differences, which add to the variety of African culture in general."[1]

The Karanga death rituals that were explored in chapters 3–7 were classified into three major themes, namely, pre-burial rituals, burial rituals, and post-burial rituals. Pre-burial rituals included all the rituals performed when a person is terminally ill, until she dies. Burial rituals refer to all the rituals that are performed before and during the actual burial of the deceased, up to the time the mourners leave the grave after burial. Post-burial rituals explored the rituals, which are performed intermittently after burial, and may continue to be performed for several years after burial. But, since most natural deaths are preceded by some kind of illness, or are attributed to certain mysterious or spiritual forces, this study briefly explored the causes of sickness and death among the Karanga of Nyajena, and of course, other Shona peoples. Of all the different causes of sickness and death among the Shona peoples, it was noted that the most dreaded are witchcraft and the avenging spirit (*ngozi*).

The study whose outcome resulted in this book had three fundamental objectives. First, it sought to describe the death rituals as they were or are performed by the Karanga of Nyajena both in the past and present. The second objective was to explore the significances of these rituals, then and now. The third objective was to identify the changes that may have happened to these rituals, for the purpose of affirming the positive transformations, and pointing out, and in some cases, challenging unhelpful changes. The overall goal of the study, which can also be seen as the fourth objective of the study, was to produce a brief manual on Karanga death rituals as they are practiced by the Karanga of Nyajena. The manual was intended to guide the people who would want to bury their dead in the traditional way but may fully rely on oral tradition because of the unavailability of written guidelines. Of course, there is nothing

---

1. Mbiti, *Introduction to African Religion*, 2nd Edition, 8.

wrong with oral tradition as a source of history. In fact, some historians of religion emphatically support the use of oral traditions in indigenous religions. Smith has pointed out that the spoken word is more versatile and flexible than the written word, for it aids the human memory.[2] However, Bourdillon begs to differ when he asserts that orality has its own challenges such as being recounted only to serve a specific purpose, its exposure to manipulation to suit a certain purpose, and its "telescopic tendency."[3] Hence, the writing of a manual, though not intended to replace orality but to complement it, may be of great help to aid the people's memory or even preserve the integrity of their death rituals in the face of cultural changes brought about by acculturation and other agents of cultural dynamism.

The investigation utilized qualitative research designs, particularly ethnography, in the collection and interpretation of the relevant research data, in pursuit of the objectives, which have been mentioned above. Ethnography was the research design of choice for this study despite some foreseen time constraints that would limit the utilization of some of its aspects such as participant observation. Interviews were mainly used to gather the necessary data. In addition to interviews, participant observation was also employed, although a limited number of rituals could be observed due to time limitations. However, this limitation did not negatively affect the quality and validity of the study because the people interviewed were practitioners in Karanga Traditional religious practices, and the data, which they provided were representative of the death rituals performed by the Karanga of Nyajena. Furthermore, ethnically, I belong to the people whose death rituals were studied, and I had participated in, and observed many of the rituals under investigation, prior to this study. Even though I tried to avoid being influenced by the ritual knowledge acquired prior to the fieldwork for this report, that information made it easier for me to analyze and understand what the interviewees said or did.

Postcolonial theory provided the theoretical or philosophical worldview or assumptions through which death rituals among the Karanga of Nyajena were explored in this study. According to Hall, postcolonial refers to a "descriptive," and "not evaluative process," of detachment from the multi-faceted and inescapable "colonial syndrome," which affects all

2. Smith, *The World's Religions*, 368.
3. Bourdillon, *The Shona Peoples*, 4–5.

the people of former colonized countries.[4] It admits that the colonial created a new hybrid culture that continues to live in its "aftereffects."[5] In other words, colonialists demonized African cultures, and tried to replace them with Western cultures, to the extent that, even long after the political decolonization of Africa, many Africans are still suffering from the aftermath of that dehumanization and subjugation, and are struggling to reclaim and reaffirm their cultural identities as Africans. In this study, postcolonial theory was used to explore the Karanga death rituals to identify how they were practiced in the past, their significance then and now, and the changes that have occurred in their performance. These inevitable changes were ushered by their encounter with the cultures of the colonialists, and of course, the cultural dynamism found in every society. This work encourages the Karanga to reclaim, reaffirm, and practice their death rituals.

RECOMMENDATIONS

Human beings are not born with a culture, even though they are born within a culture. Hence, culture is a learned behavior, which children acquire as they grow up through the process of enculturation or socialization. In the early stages of children's development, most of the culture is imparted upon them by the significant others, and later, by peers and teachers. Since culture is an acquired trait, it can be forgotten if not practiced, or distorted if abused. It is also equally true that culture is dynamic, as the United States Conference of Catholic Bishops (USCCB) observed; "Indeed, it would be a mistake to regard any culture as fixed and immutable. All cultures are in constant processes of change as their members seek new ways to address individual and group needs and as they encounter new situations and other cultures."[6] To a certain extent, cultural change is a positive development, which may benefit the people who uphold that culture. However, cultural change becomes undesirable when instigated by another culture, which claims superiority over the receiving culture. More so, imposed cultural change becomes detrimental to a people's cultural identity and integrity, and therefore, unacceptable,

---

4. Hall, "When was 'the Post-Colonial'? Thinking at the Limit," 246.
5. Ibid., 248.
6. USCCB, *Welcoming the Stranger Among us*, 28.

particularly when it is achieved through the demonization of those cultures erroneously considered inferior.

The Karanga in particular, and Africans in general, while learning from others, as they have been doing for decades, have their own death rituals, which they should observe for the sake of maintaining cultural identity and integrity. Their rituals may be different from other people's rituals, but that does not mean that they are culturally inferior to others. It is a fact that Africans had their own death rituals before the arrival of colonialists, which were replete with meaning and efficacy, and helped them make sense of human finitude, and the life in the hereafter.

Although it is true that culture is dynamic, that dynamism should not be at the expense of a people's identity. If Africans want to change their death rituals, it should not be a result of being demonized or belittled by Western cultures. It should be a result of their desire to do so. Below, are suggestions about how those Karanga, Shona, and Africans who have deliberately or unconsciously lost their cultural or religious identity, can retrace their footsteps back to who they are. The suggestions are also intended to strengthen those Africans who still hold on to some or all of their death rituals by providing them with more information and a manual that they can use to refresh their memories.

Equality of all Cultures

It should be emphasized that all cultures are equal though different. Since all cultures are equal, every culture deserves to be preserved and respected by its adherents. According to Law, a culture is neither good nor bad, but different, and the people who fail to grasp this point suffer from ethnocentricity, which he defines as a belief that one's cultural way of doing things is the only right one.[7] Ethnocentrism, though not intrinsically evil, creates a cultural superiority complex, which is likely to blind the one suffering from it from seeing the beauty in other cultures. All human beings start at ethnocentrism, where all their evaluations of other people's experiences are based on their own cultures. However, as people become more exposed to people of other cultures, they should begin to learn that their own culture is one of the many that exist, and is not superior to other cultures. The colonialists who came to Africa, empowered by Western imperialism and superiority complex, failed to understand

---

7. Law, *The Wolf Shall Dwell with the Lamb*, 4.

that fact. Hence, during the colonization of Africa, this superiority complex caused colonialists to condemn most African cultural practices and beliefs, and engendered relentless attempts and brutal measures to replace them with Western cultures. This attitude affected Africans psychologically. The USCCB insightfully writes, "The truth that we must face is straight forward. When one culture meets another, lack of awareness and understanding often leads to grossly distorted value judgments and prejudice," which may fuel attitudes of superiority in the people belonging to the imperialistic culture, and inferiority in the oppressed people.[8]

In this globalized world, unless each ethnicity stands its ground in affirming and preserving the integrity of its culture, some cultural aspects of that ethnical group are going to be demeaned or even lost. Each ethnic group should be proud of its religious or cultural practices and beliefs. Although culture is dynamic, every culture should maintain some cultural constants, which should be passed on to future generations. A people that loses its culture, also loses its cultural identity. Without a cultural identity, humanity becomes alienated from the source of its vitality. Hence, it is important for African traditional leaders, and those members of the communities that still have the knowhow of performing traditional death rituals to preserve and pass them on to the next generations.

African leaders should try to reignite cultural pride in Africans so that they may realize that there is nothing wrong with their cultural worldview. The acquisition of African cultural identity may lead to African pride, and confidence, and perhaps developmental creativity. This African pride and confidence will encourage Africans to invent their own technology and to pursue their own educational endeavors, instead of imitating the West in everything. It should be noted that the acquisition of cultural pride and confidence comes from a strong conviction that all cultures are equal, although different, and that, no culture is superior or inferior to any other.

Death Rituals are Crucial.

Death rituals, though they may differ from one culture to another, are crucial for the people who perform them, and are equally important. There is no culture that possesses superior death rituals, for all rituals serve the purpose for which they were formulated. They initiate the

---

8. USCCB, *Open Wide your Hearts*, 9.

deceased into the ancestral or spiritual world, and also help the surviving family members cope with grief. Every ethnical group should know how to perform its own rituals flawlessly so that the deceased members of the family are not deprived of the fullness of life in the invisible world.

Although the Karanga of Nyajena still practice some of their traditional death rituals, particularly pre-burial and burial rituals, there is a general neglect of the post-burial rituals. For instance, most people have stopped performing the *magadziro* ceremony, which is intended to reincorporate the spirit of the deceased back into the family. Failure to incorporate the deceased back into the family is tantamount to depriving them of their right to a complete process of dying and living. Unless the *magadziro* ritual is performed, the wandering spirit of the deceased cannot be admitted into the union of family spirits. Hence, the failure to perform *magadziro* is tantamount to the excommunication and ostracization of the deceased family member. It is an abuse of the power the living members of a family do have. A deprivation of this kind aggravates all ancestors, and there are serious repercussions for that because ancestors cannot allow that neglect go unpunished.

Karanga Death Rituals have Changed.

It is true that many Karanga death rituals have changed because of acculturation, and this changing face of rituals is likely to continue. Some of these changes are positive, while others are negative. Gittins equates acculturation (encounter between two or more cultures) to blood transfusion, which can be life "enhancing—or death dealing," for there is always a potential or danger of either of the cultures being overpowered and trashed.[9] Once a culture is overpowered by the other, like what happened to most African cultures due to colonialism, its rituals are likely to be condemned and discarded. The acceptance of that condemnation by the colonized leads to cultural self-depreciation, which some people are likely to internalize. A person who suffers from cultural self-depreciation tries by all means to run away from her own culture by imitating the other culture. Sometimes, such people become frustrated when they experience a repulsion by the cultures that they have adopted at the expense of their own.

9. Gittins, 59.

The Karanga need to be encouraged to embrace the positive and inevitable ritual changes that were brought about by their encounter with other religions and cultures of the world. However, any negative change that is aimed at belittling and demeaning some Karanga death rituals should be shunned, for it robs them of their cultural heritage and identity as a people. The Karanga should know how death rituals were performed in the past, their significance, and the changes that have occurred. They say, "knowledge is power." The knowledge of the traditional death rituals will enable them to choose how they want to honor their deceased members of the family. This choice between modern and traditional rituals can only be possible if the Karanga have both versions of the rituals—the old and the new. On the one hand, they should embrace the positive changes, and on the other hand, they should guard against negative foreign cultural influences that rob them of their cultural identity and integrity.

Let Them Write Down Their Rituals

Although oral traditions have their own advantages as has been mentioned above, they also have serious setbacks. The surest way to preserve the Karanga death rituals for posterity is to write them down. That which has been written down though it becomes rigid, cannot be altered or even forgotten. Both the praxis and significance of Karanga death rituals should be recorded and archived lest the next generations forget them. It is true that the flexibility, which these rituals have enjoyed up to now will be lost through writing, but it is better that way.

One of the objectives of the study that culminated in the writing of this work was to compose a death ritual manual for the Karanga of Nyajena. Even though the manual that was produced is not exhaustive, it remains a significant foundation on which other researchers may build. If all the Shona ethnicities were to write down their death rituals, people would have a compendium of such rituals from which those who choose to bury their dead according to their own rituals can draw. It is true that some of the rituals have been distorted, but it is never too late to do something about it. Whatever can be salvaged from what still exists, should be embraced, and magnified.

Encouraging Dying at Home

The social reality that most ill Karanga people seek treatment at modern hospitals cannot be denied or even discouraged because many times, patients are cured of their illnesses there. However, for every patient, a time comes when the Western healthcare system fails to cure his illness, and the patient is discharged from hospital to receive palliative care at home. To be discharged from hospital means that the Western healthcare system would have done everything in its power to restore the patient's health back to its normal position to no avail, and now suggests that the best option available for the patient is to receive pain management at home, while waiting for the "moment of truth"—death. The relatives of the dying person should be encouraged to accept that moment of truth, by taking their relative home, and rendering him the best care they can at home. That way they may be able to deal with his final moments and death wishes from a cultural point of view.

At home, the relatives of the dying person can perform the Karanga death rituals without being discouraged by the Western healthcare workers. Also, at home one dies surrounded by his family members, if available. In addition to that, dying at home reduces transport costs of ferrying the corpse from the hospital to the rural home, if the burial is to take place there. If the deceased would be buried in an urban cemetery, his urban home, if he has any, is also a good place to die at. Furthermore, dying at home ensures early burial, thereby preventing the patient from being embalmed. As has been discussed in preceding chapters, despite the many advantages of embalmment, there are also disadvantages. One of the disadvantages of embalmment is that it interferes with the natural way of body decomposition, which in turn may affect one's ancestorhood. One of the reasons for performing the *magadziro* ceremony, at least six months after one's burial is to allow the body to decompose so that the ancestor does not come back home with a human body. If that happens, he would be more of a ghost than an ancestor. Now, with embalmment, the body may go for years before decomposition, which may interfere with the deceased's becoming an ancestor. Embalmment can be avoided if there is an early burial of the deceased lest the body decomposes before burial. Early burial is possible if the person dies closer to the burial place. People with terminal illnesses should be allowed or even encouraged to die at home as long as there are people to care for them, and medication to manage their pain.

Gathering for Burial Early

The Karanga should encourage the close family members of the dying person, if death is anticipated, to gather at the home of the patient or be in the vicinity before the onset of death. This early gathering of family members will allow people to be present when their beloved one dies. Some Karanga of Nyajena believe that some dying people may delay dying if the family member that they love most has not yet visited them. The pre-death gathering of family members may facilitate a quick dying process of the sick person.

However, for the relatives to be able to gather before the demise of their ill family member, there should be people who can sense the proximity of death so that they can alert others. Since some of the relatives work in places far away from home, the family may not be able to wait for them to attend the funeral since the body would become bad unless it is embalmed. This long waiting can only be prevented if all the close family members gather at the home of the dying person just before his demise. The timely gathering of relatives just before death can only be possible if some of the caregivers at home can sense the impending death. Therefore, there is a need to train people concerning the signs of the coming of death, and how to care for the terminally ill.

Educating the Youth about Death Rituals

If the Karanga death rituals are to survive acculturation, the elders should pass the ritual praxis on to the younger generations. There should be a deliberate move by the ritual practitioners and family leaders to educate the youth. Even though some schools in Zimbabwe include culture and religious studies in their curriculum, not enough is done. Until recently, the only religious tradition that was studied in Zimbabwean schools in detail was Christianity, not African Traditional Religion, which shows the cultural self-depreciation, which was championed by colonialists, from which Zimbabweans have failed to free themselves ever since they attained their independence from Britain in 1980.

Ritual leaders should complement the efforts of the schools by encouraging the youth to visit dying relatives, and attending burials. The youths that attend burials should be encouraged to ask questions or even be offered unsolicited for information about the proceedings. It would be helpful if the ritual leader or master of ceremony would explain the significance and importance of the rituals being carried out to the audience. For example, when the time to bring the stones to the grave comes, the leader may say, "Now it's time for some of us to go and fetch the rocks that we will use to seal the grave mount. We must use these rocks to prevent wild animals and witches from digging up the grave. When you carry the stones, please, make sure to carry only one at a time. There are repercussions for carrying two rocks at the same time. First, if the spirit of the deceased is angered and decide to come back home to punish us, two persons would die at the same time. Second, if the deceased's spirit is defiled and decide to turn against us, it may bring another spirit to fight us. Now instead of facing the wrath of only one spirit, we would face the anger of two."

Explaining the praxis and significance of every death ritual would educate the youth about the ritual process and the meaning. If the ritual leader has forgotten the meaning or significance of a particular ritual, he may ask any of the elders gathered to explain it to the gathering. These young people would then pass the knowledge to their own children, and as a result, everyone would have the knowledge of what to do, how to do it, and why doing it. This would be practical education as opposed to theoretical learning gained at school.

A POSTCOLONIAL THEORY: RADICAL ETHNIFICATION

Globalization has taken the world by storm. Every day, there are thousands of people on the move, looking for greener pastures, wealth, peace, and sometimes, justice. As people relocate to new places, they carry their cultural baggage with them. Inevitably the culture of the immigrants meets the cultures of the natives, or dominant cultures, in a process called acculturation. Depending on the power and influence of the newcomers, this acculturation may lead to cultural assimilation, integration, or colonialism. The encounter between Europeans and Africans during colonialism led to the cultural subordination of the African people, and demonization of their cultures. Consequently, they were colonized economically, politically, and culturally. For instance, African food, medical practices, philosophy, religion, morality, houses, wisdom, and so on were savaged and demonized. The cultural subjugation of the African people, to a certain extent, led to the loss of the African cultural identity. In an attempt by Africans to assimilate to the culture of the colonists, many started thinking of their culture as inferior to the European culture, and tried hard to look, eat, speak, think, worship, dress, and laugh like Europeans. To be civilized was to become Western.

There is nothing wrong in learning from others, but something is wrong when a whole ethnicity runs away from its cultural identity to unreservedly embrace another people's culture. Africans must realize that Europe's dealings with Africa have not been only disrespectful, but also abusive. For Africans to attain their respectful place in the global community, they have to think, look, behave, and worship like Africans. They need a process of radical ethnification, a term which is defined by Schreiter as "the process of rediscovering a forgotten identity based on one's cultural ties."[10] In the same spirit, ethnification can be defined as a process by which a people retraces its footsteps backwards to locate and save the baby that was thrown away with the bath water. It is a process of going back into the cultural antiquity to unearth the culture at the verge of extinction, in order to revitalize it. This process has six stages, namely, rediscovery of the various African cultural heritages, denunciation of cultural assimilation, reaffirmation of African cultural identities, reeducation of Africans, and the reidentification by the Africans.

Rediscovery of the Various African Cultural Heritages.

This process refers to the reconstruction of the African cultures as far back as memory and historical archives can allow us. This should be done as soon as possible before all the guardians of the African cultural practices are gone. The researcher should try to find out how certain rituals were practiced, unearth their original significance, and assess what might have changed. This process also calls for a partial disidentification with Western cultures in order to achieve an objective pursuit of the original and unadulterated African cultural heritages. This cultural disidentification calls for a mental rejection of Western cultures that undermine African cultural practices. This disassociation may lead to the disenslavement of the African mentality by European cultures, and the affirmation that there is nothing wrong with African cultures.

---

10. See Schreiter, *The New Catholicity*, 23–24.

Denunciation of Cultural Assimilation

Cultural assimilation refers to a process by which a people tries to abandon its culture in order to adopt the culture of the other, which is seen as more appropriate and superior. This process can systematically be imposed by the people of the so-called superior culture, or can be accepted willingly by the people of the so-called inferior culture. During the colonization of Africa, Europeans, at first imposed their cultures upon Africans by the use of guns and the establishment of their own laws, which had to be upheld, or else the lawbreaker would go to jail. For instance, they established taxes that had to be paid in their own currencies, and Africans had to work on European farms and mines in order to get money for taxes. They introduced Western education, and those Africans who were willing or could afford to be initiated would get better jobs, and earn more money, and acquire more Western goods.

As if that was not bad enough, they confiscated Africans lands, and pushed Africans to infertile soils to impoverish them. In addition, they brought in Christian preachers, who constantly denounced African culture as an evil that had to be abandoned and completely eradicated. The Africans who refused to receive Western education were committed to unrewarding manual labor. Likewise, those Africans who refused to convert to Christianity were anathematized and threatened with eternal damnation and suffering in hell. Hence, Africans were mentally forced to leave their cultural ways in order to appear civilized here on earth, and to receive eternal life in the hereafter. Consequently, most Africans tried to bury their Africanness in order to be accepted and rewarded by Europeans. Fortunately, or unfortunately, they could not change the color of their skin and hair texture despite desperate attempts by some to bleach it or tame their kinky hair. The idea was that, if only they could look, eat, sing, appear, laugh, and live like Westerners, they would be completely accepted as equals. But this blind assimilation backfired, for it did not lead to an acceptance of Africans by Westerners as equals, but to the dehumanization of African peoples as a people without an identity. Africans should be encouraged to denounce this blind assimilation in favor of cultural integration, a process by which they can retain their cultural identity while accepting helpful cultural dynamism caused by their encounter with Westerners.

Reaffirmation of the African Cultures

The stage of reaffirmation of the African cultures is about revisioning, maintaining, and emphasizing the value of African cultures. This celebration of African cultures does not render other cultures of the world less important. What it does is to affirm and confirm that all cultures are equal, although different. When the Westerners arrived in Africa, there was nothing wrong or ugly or primitive with African culture, it was only different. Africans should not be ashamed of practicing their own culture because it is as valid and important as any other cultures of the world. This stage calls for a deliberate reaffirmation of the African indigenous food, dresses, rituals, medical practices, song and dance, hair style, and skin color. Africans should learn from others while continuing to develop and refine their own ways. They should denounce the cultural stagnation or even abandonment of indigenous cultures by Africans, in pursuit of Western cultures.

Africa lags behind in terms of medical research as observed in 2020 during the Covid-19 pandemic. Certainly, Africa has to play its part rather than looking up to the West for medicines and vaccines. There were medicines and healthcare practices in Africa before the arrival of Western medicines, and Africans should hunt down those medicines, study them, reaffirm them, and continue to work on them. Be that as it may, Africans can only develop their own medicines, economies, philosophy, and politics, if they cease to demonize them, and embrace the little that they still have. The reaffirmation of African cultures will raise the African self-esteem, curiosity, creativity, and excellence, which were brought to their lowest point by their demonization by Westerners.

It should be reaffirmed that Africans are beautiful, intelligent, and a people with a unique cultural identity. It should be shouted from the hilltops that African traditional religions are as valid as any other religions, and are capable of bringing salvation to their adherents. It should be reiterated that African medicines, philosophy, educational systems, and values are not inferior to any other. It must be inculcated in every African child that there is nothing wrong in being black and having kinky hair. And that it is not primitive and a sign of savagery to sing African songs, eat African food, worship in an African way, and perceive reality from an African perspective.

Reeducation of the Africans

The reeducation of African peoples about their own cultures should be done in all places of formal and informal learning. Right from primary education, students should be introduced to African culture by developing appropriate curricula. African children should be caught young before they are mentally colonized by the oppressive systems put in place by colonists. African cultures should be taught in schools and colleges as individual subjects. State universities should compel students to take at least three African cultural courses in order to graduate irrespective of the degree program they are pursuing. Governments should encourage the formation of school clubs and associations that promote African cultures.

Researchers should carry out more research and propose innovative ways of instilling pride and patriotism in African children. They should also produce educational material that promote African identity and integrity. African governments should also play their part in the reeducation of Africans about their culture. They should promote and fund radio programs on culture. Aggressive religious evangelization targeted on African cultural practices should be discouraged. In some cases, the abuse of the African way of life has been championed by Christian missionaries and their surrogates, and continues to happen in many African countries. Every religion should preach love, peace, justice, equality, human dignity, and not hate and intolerance. Africans have suffered a great deal because of the demonization of their cultures by preachers of other religions.

For this reeducation endeavor to succeed, it should also start at home. The parents who would like to promote the cultural education of their children should be supported by the African governments. Researchers should also assist by composing manuals of how to practice certain African rituals. If radical ethnification is to be successful, it should start at home where the primary enculturation of children takes place, and reaffirmed at school where systematic education is imparted to children.

Reidentification

Reidentification is the last stage in the process of radical ethnification, and it calls for a reclaim of one's cultural identity and integrity. It is both a denunciation of the accepted and appropriated Western cultural superiority by Africans, and a relentless pursuit of the African cultural identity. It is a realization that Africans are Africans, and should live and think like Africans. Of course, they should learn from others, but not at the expense of losing their identity. They should reclaim their battered cultural identity, embrace it, and cherish it.

Cultural reidentification is a celebration of our diverse cultures, and the acknowledgement that there is nothing wrong with being African. It involves taking pride in African indigenous languages, names, food, wisdom, values, and rituals. It is the refusal to have African cultures downplayed by people of other cultures or by brainwashed Africans. It calls for reclaiming African totems, and relearning how to recite them. It invites Africans to go back to their rituals by relearning how to perform them, and to understand their significance. It acknowledges that African cultures are not perfect, just like all other cultures, but are as important as any other cultures. It encourages Africans to be proud of being Africans, and share their African heritage with the rest of the world. Yes, Africans have an identity that cannot be wished away by softening their kinky hair, bleaching their skins, speaking Western languages, eating Western food, governing countries according to Western principles, and denigrating African ancestors and deities.

A WORD OF CAUTION

It should be noted that culture is dynamic, but cultural transformation should come out of a people's needs and own volition, not through imposition by other people. Imposed cultural dynamism is not only unnatural, but also dehumanizing. Africans should accept change that does not dehumanize them by taking away their cultural identity. In the pursuit of this radical ethnification, people should avoid hate rhetoric against other cultures because it only leads to a defeat of the purpose of this process. The goal of radical ethnification is to consider all cultures as different, but equal. However, as Schreiter observed, ethnification "involves memory, and memory is necessarily selective and creative, since any group involved in ethnification by definition lives in changed social circumstances."[11] The other challenge is that ethnification can result in "hybridization" because once acculturation takes place there is bound

---

11. See Schreiter, Robert J. The New Catholicity, 24.

to be changes in the cultures involved, and cultural purity may not be achievable.[12]

In addition, the process of cultural rediscovery is not an easy task. First, some cultural aspects would have been long forgotten, and are beyond retrieval. Second, the people involved in the process of rediscovering cultural practices would have been culturally changed as well. They may want to go back to the original, but they may not have a taste for that original. For them, the original is the hybrid culture that they have experienced. There is nothing wrong with having a hybrid culture as long as it has strong traces of the African cultures. After all, every culture is a hybrid of diverse cultures.

Furthermore, it is not easy to just denounce cultural assimilation because people would have been assimilated already. There are Western cultural aspects, which have been internalized by Africans that they cannot be easily discarded in favor of African practices. These cultural aspects have become part of the African cultures, and trying to run away from them may disfigure Africans. The process of radical ethnification acknowledges this, but does not shy away from pursuing and reaffirming the traditional African cultures.

Moreover, introducing curricula in schools and colleges that reflect African cultures may seem easy to do, but in practice, it is not. In many African countries, missionaries and other Christian organizations built schools and hospitals which are partly still under their governance. They decide what should be studied at such schools, and they may not support the study of African cultures and religions. In addition, some government ministers in charge of education may not think that African cultures are important because of decades of being brainwashed by the colonial education system. Such leaders cannot be trusted to champion the African cause.

Therefore, it should be admitted that it is difficult to restore a pure African cultural identity because it may not be desirable, or even practical for many Africans. The objective of radical ethnification is to come up with something that will increase the Africans' cultural self-esteem and awareness in the hope that one day, they may retrace their footsteps to their cultural identity as far back as they can go. Perhaps the result will be a hybrid culture, which honors both, but maintaining that Africans are Africans.

---

12. Ibid, 24.

CONCLUSION

It cannot be denied that the Karanga of Nyajena in particular, and most African peoples in general, have lost some of their traditional death rituals because of their encounter with abusive and overpowering Western cultures. However, there still exist people who know the praxis, even though some of them have forgotten the significance of some of their traditional death rituals. There are also Africans who have lost their cultural identity, and sometimes, openly denounce their own culture. However, there are many death rituals that the Karanga people still remember, and even practice. Each community is blessed with a member or more, who are the custodians of the undying memories of the Karanga death rituals. Before all these ritual practitioners are gone, whatever information that they do have should be written down and preserved. It is not too late for the Karanga of Nyajena or any other African ethnicity to go back to their traditions and gather up the pieces. Africans should reclaim their cultural identity and integrity so that they can be counted among the cultures of the world.

Glossary of Foreign Words

Amasvina: derogatory term used for Shona peoples

Ashaika: literally, he or she has disappeared (he or she has died)

Atisiya : literally, he or she has left us (he or she has died)

Atungamira: literally, he or she has gone before us (he or she has died)

Azorora: literally, he or she has rested (he or she has died)

Bandauko: foreleg of an animal

Bembera: threatening to reveal the name of the witch at a village meeting

Bvuri: shadow

Bwanyanza: bier made of two poles and tree bark

Chema: death token or gift

Chibako: ground tobacco container

Chibwe: a pebble

Chidzva: hind leg of an animal, or thigh

Chifumuro: a herb used to treat a variety of diseases, and also to ward off evil spirits

Chimutsamapfihwa: young sister or niece of a deceased married woman given to the deceased's husband as a wife

Chiremba: traditional or Western medical practitioner or healer

Chiropa: liver

Chirungu: modernity (Westernization)

Chityu: brisket

Chizhuzhu: confeti tree used to expose witches or witchcraft

Demo: axe

Divisi: witchcraft used to increase one's agricultural produce using mysterious means

Doro remvura: ritual that is performed a few weeks after burial at which beer is given to the undertakers to quench their thirst, and to thank them for their manual contribution during the burial

Dota kudota: ashes to ashes

Duri nemusi: mortar and pestle used to pound grains to remove chaff

Dzivaguru: a praise name given to God by the Shona, which acknowledges his responsibility of providing rain

Fodya yemhino: ground tobacco, which is sniffed

Gambe: a big piece of a broken clay pot used to roast peanuts or to bury premature babies

Gata/mashopeshope: the consultation of a diviner particularly to find out the cause of a relative's death, and how the *magadziro* should be performed

Goritoto: ghost

Gumbwa: consultation of a diviner by all the adults of a village to identify a witch who would have bewitched a sick villager

Guru: tripe, or lining of an animal's stomach

Guruva kuguruva: dust to dust

Gwatata: pancreas

Hakata: bones or wooden objects used by diviners to explain things

Hakuchina: literally, he or she is no more, (he or she has died)

Hari: clay pot

GLOSSARY OF FOREIGN WORDS

Hazvieri: small bush whose lives are used to purify people and objects

Ivhu: soil (ancestor)

Jira guru: large blanket or piece of cloth

Karanga: one of the ethnicities of the Shona people of Zimbabwe whose traditional rural home is Masvingo province

Katanda botso: a shaming ritual performed by the perpetrator to appease the spirit of his deceased mother who would have died aggrieved

Kubata mavoko: a ritual in which mourners greet the family of the deceased to commiserate with them for their loss

Kubata nhumbi: a ritual to purify the personal belongings of the deceased before they are distributed to the qualifying relatives

Kubwereketa: Karanga word that means to talk

Kuchenura: to purify or cleanse

Kucheuka: to look back

Kufa: to die

Kugara nhaka: to inherit the property or wife of the deceased

Kugeza: to wash or bath

Kugezesa mufi: to wash the corpse

Kugova fuma: to distribute the deceased's estate

Kugova nhaka: see *kugova fuma*

Kugova nhumbi: to distribute the deceased's personal belongings

Kuwungudza: to wail as a sign of deep grief

Kukanda chibwe: to place a pebble on top of a grave while introducing oneself to the deceased

Kukwegura: growing old

Kupeta: to fold, particularly the legs and arms of the corpse

Kupfekedza mufi: to clothe the deceased

GLOSSARY OF FOREIGN WORDS

Kupisa: to burn/hot

Kuradzika chitunha: to lay down the body in the grave

Kurindira: to wait on or watch the dying person

Kurova guva: a ritual performed at least six months after the burial of the dead person to bring his spirit back into his home as an ancestor (also called *magadziro*)

Kusengudza: relocating the dying person

Kushamba: to wash

Kutama: to resettle

Kutara guva: to mark the grave. It is also known as *kutema ruhau*

Kutarira: to look at

Kutema: to cut

Kutiziswa: a type of Shona marriage whereby the girl elopes with the boyfriend

Kutsvaira pabwiro: to sweep around the grave

Kuviga gavamwedzi: to bury a premature baby

Kuvona: to see

Kuwana: to get married

Kuzivisa: to notify

Kuzorodza mufi: to rest the deceased during the procession to the grave

Kuzovona mugwere: a visit to the sick person, which is expected of all relatives

Mafuta eshato: python fat/oil

Magadziro: a ritual performed at least six months after the burial of the dead person to bring him back into his home as an ancestor. It is the same as *kurova guva*

Mahakurimwi: mandatory rest in honor of the deceased, usual for less than a week

Makate: huge clay containers used to process and store beer

Mamhepo: evil spirits

Manenji/mashura: misfortunes that may happen to a family member who has not been notified of the death of a close relative

Manyaradzo: a Christian ritual to commiserate the death of a person

Mapapu: lungs

Maperembudzi: leprosy

Mashavi: alien spirits that seek recognition among unrelated people

Masukafoshoro: a ritual to cleanse the tools of the gravediggers, and also to thank them for their job. It is also called *doro remvura*

Masukavuta: a ritual where the nephew of the deceased washes or cleanses one of the weapons of the deceased to prepare for the jumping of the weapon ritual. In the past, the weapon was mostly a bow and arrow

Matombo: stones or rocks

Mavhitori: derogatory term used for the Karanga people derived from the colonial name of the present-day town called Masvingo—Fort Victoria.

Mazango: medicinal waistband used to ward off evil spirits and a variety of misfortunes

Mbabvu: ribs

Mbanda: Karanga indigenous "incense" used to drive away evil spirits or to purify the air

Mbudzi: goat

Mhondi: murderer

Mhondoro: clan ancestral spirit (ancestral spirit of a chief), usually symbolized by a lion

Mhumba: heart

Mhururu: ululation or rhythmic sound made by the rapid movement of the tongue in and out of the mouth

Mhutsashungu: a goat sacrificed to appease an ancestor who would have died aggrieved

Moyo: heart, or totem of the Vajena and several other Shona clans

Muchakata: Parinari curatellifolia. An indigenous sacred fruit tree. (Also called *muhacha*)

Mudzimu: ancestor

Mukadzi ane mimba: a pregnant woman

Mukombe: a container made from wood or gourd, which is used to fetch water or beer

Mukwambo: son-in-law

Munhu: person

Mupembere: Velvet leaved Combretum whose branch is used to bring back the ancestor from the grave

Muposo: type of witchcraft placed in the way of the victim

Muroyi: witch

Murume: man

Musana: a person or animal's back

Museredzero: wash down

Mushozhowa: Pseudolachnostylis maprouneifolia (small tree used for rituals)

Musikavanhu: Shona praise name for God depicting his creation of humanity

Musvisvinwa: a bush used to purify the air

Mutarara: Gardenia thunbergia (a tree that is believed to drive away evil spirits and people)

Mutimwi: medicinal waistband made of a piece of cloth and herbs

Mutsago: pillow

Mutsipa: neck

Muvonde: fig tree

Muzeze: an indigenous tree whose leaves are used to sprinkle sacred water

Muzukuru: nephew/niece or grandson/granddaughter

Mveva: fruit of a sausage tree

Mwari: God

N'anga: traditional medical practitioner

Nevanji/dangwe: male first born of a chief/male first born

Ngozi: avenging spirit

Nhaka: inheritance

Nhungamiri: a goat or cow/ox slaughtered for the mourners

Nhunzvi: a female goat that has given birth to kids

Njodzi: hazard or death

Norwa: male goat

Pfuko: small to medium clay container used to store beer

Rufu: death

Rugumudzambwa: herb used for purification

Kutema ruhau: marking the grave

Rukanda: ritual bangle extracted from the foreleg of the sacrificial bull, and worn on the wrist of the oldest son like a bangle

Rukweza: rapoko (small red grain used for food and brewing beer)

Rupasa: reed mat

Ruredzo: (*decerocaryum zanguebarium*) a vine like, slippery wild plant

Sadunhu: headman

Sadza: staple food for Zimbabweans made from maize meal and boiled water. Also known as *ugali* or *nzima*, by other African peoples

Sahwira: best friend

Sendekavuta: a ritual where the man who would have inherited the deceased's wife makes it public

Shona: one of the main composite ethnicities found in Zimbabwe

Tsikamutanda: itinerant diviner who specializes in identifying and exorcizing witches

Vadzimu: ancestors

Vajena: the people of Nyajena (members of the aristocracy)

Vakwambo: sons-in-law. Also known as *vakwasha*

Vanhu: people

Varoora: daughters-in-law

Vazukuru: nephews/nieces or grandchildren

Vura: intestines

Vuroyi: witchcraft

Vuta nemuseve: bow and arrow

Wafa wanaka: idiom, which means the dead has become good

Zita: name

Zvidhoma/zvitupwani: evil spirits that may appear in the form of small children and are used by witches to beat up their victims

Zvisasa: ringworm

Zviyo: rapoko

Bibliography

Aiken, Lewis R. *Dying, Death, and Bereavement*. Needham Heights, MA: Ally and Bacon, 1994.

Akrong, Abraham. "A Phenomenology of Witchcraft in Ghana." In *Imagining Evil: Witchcraft Beliefs and Accusations in Contemporary Africa*, edited by Gerry ter Haar, 53-66. Trenton, New Jersey: Africa World, 2007.

Anderson, Allan. *Zion and Pentecost: The Spirituality and Experience of Pentecostal and Zionist/Apostolic Churches in South Africa*. Pretoria: University of South Africa, 2000.

Aschwanden, Hebert. *Symbols of Life: An Analysis of the Consciousness of the Karanga*. Gweru: Mambo, 1987.

Backer, Barbara A., et al. *Death and Dying: Understanding and Care*. 2nd ed. Albany, New York: Delmar, 1994.

Bailey, Carol A. *A Guide to Field Research*. Thousand Oaks, California: Pine Forge, 1996.

Bendann, Effie. *Death Customs: An Analytical Study of Burial Rites*. New York: Alfred A. Knopf, 1930.

Bennett, Jennet M and Bennett, Milton J. "Developing Intercultural Sensitivity: An Integrative Approach to Global and Domestic Diversity." In *Handbook of Intercultural Training*, edited by Milton Bennett et al., 147-165. 3rd ed. Thousand Oaks, California: SAGE, 2004.

Berg, Bruce L and Lune, Howard. *Qualitative Research Methods for Social Sciences*. Indianapolis, Indiana: Pearson, 2012.

Bhebe, Ngwabi. *Christianity and Traditional Religion in Western Zimbabwe 1859-1923*. London: Longman, 1979.

Bogdan, Robert C. and Biklen, Sari Knopp. *Qualitative Research for Education: An Introduction to Theories and Methods*. 5th ed. Boston: Pearson, 2011.

Bourdillon, Michael F. C. "Anthropological Approaches to The Study of African Religion." In *The Study of Religion in Africa: Past, Present and Prospects*, edited by Jan G. Platvoet eds., et al., 139-154, Cambridge: Roots and Branches, 1996.

———. *The Shona Peoples*. Rev. ed. Gweru: Mambo, 1987.

———. *Religion and Society: A Text for Africa*. Gweru: Mambo, 1990.

———. "Witchcraft and Society." In *African Spirituality: Forms, Meanings, and Expressions*, edited by Jacob K Olupona, 176-197. New York: Crossroad, 2000.

Brodd, Jeffrey, et al. *Invitation to World Religions*. 2nd ed. New York: Oxford University Press, 2016.

Bucher, Hubert, *Spirits and Power: An Analysis of Shona Cosmology*. London: Oxford University Press, 1980.
Bullock, Charles. *The Mashona (The Indigenous Natives of S. Rhodesia)*. Cape Town: Negro Universities Press, 1928.
———. *Mashona Laws and Customs*. Salisbury (Harare): Argus, 1913.
Callison, George; Nash, Donna M. *How to write clear work instructions,* 1999. Quality Congress. ASQ's ...Annual Quality Congress Proceedings, 331. Retrieved from http://uiwtx.idm.oclc.org/login?url=https://search.proquest.com/docview/21439 1899?accountid=7139. Date Accessed: November 28, 2019.
Césaire, Aimé. *Discourse on Colonialism*. Translated by Joan Pinkham. New York: Monthly Review, 1972.
Chapman, Erie. *Radical Loving Care: Building the Healing Hospital in America*. Nashville, Tennessee: Erie Chapman Foundation, 2015.
Chavhunduka, Gordon L. *Traditional Medicine in Modern Zimbabwe*. Harare: University of Zimbabwe Press, 1994.
Chigwedere, Aeneas S. *From Mutapa to Rhodes 1000 to 1890 A. D.* London: Macmillan, 1980.
Chitakure, John. *African Traditional Religion Encounters Christianity: The Resilience of a Demonized Religion*. Eugene, OR: Pickwick, 2017.
———. *The Pursuit of the Sacred: An Introduction to Religious Studies*. Eugene, OR: Wipf & Stock, 2016.
———. *Shona Women in Zimbabwe—A Purchased People*. Eugene, OR: Wipf & Stock, 2016.
Choron, Jacques. *Death and Modern Man*. New York: The Macmillan, 1964.
Corbin, Juliet and Strauss, Anselm. *Basics of Qualitative Research: Techniques and Procedures of Developing Grounded Theory*. 3rd ed. Thousand Oaks, California: SAGE, 2008.
Corr, Charles A, et al. *Death and Dying, Life and Living*. 2nd ed. Pacific Grove, CA: Brooks/Cole, 1997.
Crawford, J. R. *Witchcraft and Sorcery in Rhodesia*. London: Oxford University Press, 1967.
Creary, Nicholas M. *Domesticating a Religious Import: The Jesuits and the Inculturation of the Catholic Church in Zimbabwe, 1879-1980*. New York: Fordham University Press, 2011.
Creswell, John W. *Qualitative Inquiry and Research Design: Choosing Among Five Traditions*. Thousand Oaks, California: Sage, 1998.
———. *Research Design: Qualitative, Quantitative, and Mixed Methods Approaches*. Thousand Oaks, California: SAGE, 2009.
Creswell, John W. and Creswell J. David. *Research Design*. 5th ed. Thousand Oaks, California: SAGE, 2018.
Creswell, John W. and Poth, Cheryl N. *Qualitative Inquiry and Research Design: Choosing among Five Approaches*. 4th ed. Thousand Oaks, California: SAGE, 2018.
Cunningham, Lawrence S., et al. *The Sacred Quest: An Introduction to the Study of Religion*. 2nd ed. Englewood Cliffs, New Jersey: Prentice Hall, 1995.
Daneel, M. L. *The God of the Matopo Hills: An Essay on the Mwari Cult in Rhodesia*. Leiden: Mouton, 1970.
———. *Old and New in Southern Shona Independent Churches. Volume I: Background and Rise of the Major Movements*. Leiden: Mouton, 1971.

DeWalt, Kathleen Musante and DeWalt, Billie R. *Participant Observation: A Guide for Fieldworkers*. Walnut Creek, California: Altamira, 2002.

Doumbia, Adama and Doumbia, Naomi. *The Ways of the Elders: West African Spirituality and Tradition*. Saint Paul, Minnesota: Llewellyn, 2004.

Duda, Deborah. *A Guide to Dying at Home*. Santa Fe, New Mexico: Muir, 1982.

Elsener, J and Kollbrunner, F. *Traditional and Christianized Rites of Accommodating the Spirit of the Dead: The History of a Case of Inculturation in Zimbabwe*. Harare: Imbisa, No.6., 2001.

Esposito, John L, et al. *World Religions*. New York: Oxford University Press, 2002.

Evans-Pritchard, E. E. *Nuer Religion*. Oxford: The Clarendon, 1956.

———. *Witchcraft, Oracles, and Magic Among the Zande*. New York: Oxford University Press, 1976.

Fanon, Frantz. *Black Skin, White Masks*. Translated by Richard Philcox. New York: Grove, 1952.

———. *The Wretched of the Earth*. Translated by Richard Philcox, New York: Grove, 1965.

Fisher, Robert B. *West African Religious Traditions: Focus on the Akan of Ghana*. Maryknoll, New York: Orbis, 1998.

Fitzgerald, Mike. "WRITE RIGHT! owners' manual project develops communication skills."66,1418.Retrievedfrom.http://uiwtx.idm.oclc.org/login?url=https://search.proquest.com/docview/218543431?accountid=7139, 2007. Date Accessed: November 28, 2019.

Freud, Sigmund. *Totem and Taboo*. Translated by A. A. Brill. New York: Dover, 1998.

Gelfand, Michael. *Shona Religion, with Special Reference to the Makorekore*. Cape Town: Juta, 1962.

———. *An African's Religion, The Spirit of Nyajena the case of the Karanga*. Cape Town: Juta, 1966.

———. *The Genuine Shona: Survival Values of an African Culture*. Gweru Mambo, 1973.

———. *Shona Rituals with Special reference to the Chaminuka Cult*. Cape Town: Juta, 1959.

———. *Shona Religion, with Special Reference to the Makorekore*. Cape Town: Juta, 1962.

———. *An African's Religion: The Spirit of Nyajena; Case History of a Karanga People*. Johannesburg: Juta, 1966.

———. *The African Witch with Particular Reference to Witchcraft Beliefs and Practice among the Shona of Rhodesia*. London: E and S Livingstone, 1967.

Gennep, Arnold van. *The Rites of Passage*. Translated by Monica B. Vizedom and Gabrielle L. Caffee. Chicago: The University of Chicago Press, 1960.

Gittins, Anthony. *Living Mission Interculturally: Faith, Culture, and The Renewal of Praxis*. Collegeville, Minnesota: Order of Saint Benedict, 2015.

Goody, Jack. *Death, Property, and Ancestors: A Study of Mortuary Customs among the LoDagaa of West Africa*. Stanford, California: Stanford University Press, 1962.

Göttsche, Dirk. "Post-imperialism, postcolonialism and beyond: Towards a periodization of cultural discourse about colonial legacies." In Journal of European Studies Vol. 47(2), 111–128. University of Nottingham, 2017. sagepub.co.uk/journalsPermissions.nav. DOI: 10.1177/0047244117700070 journals.sagepub.com/home/jes. Date Accessed: July 4, 2019.

Gundani, Paul. "The Roman Catholic Church and The *Kurova Guva* Ritual in Zimbabwe." In *Zambezia* (1994) XXI (ii), 123–146. Zimbabwe, 1994.

———. "The Roman Catholic Church and the *Kurova Guva* Ritual in Zimbabwe." In *Rites of Passage in Contemporary Africa: Interaction between Christian and African Traditional Religions*, edited by John Leland Cox, 198–222. Cardiff: Cardiff Academic Press, 1998.

Haar, Gerrie ter. "Ghanaian Witchcraft Beliefs: A View from the Netherlands," In *Imagining Evil: Witchcraft Beliefs and Accusations in Contemporary Africa*, edited by Gerrie ter Haar, 93–112. Trenton, New Jersey: Africa World, 2016.

Hall, Edward T. *The Silent Language*. New York: Anchor, 1990.

Hall, Stuart. "When was 'the Post-Colonial'? Thinking at the Limit." In *The Post-Colonial Question: Common Skies, Divided Horizons*, edited by Curti, Lidia and Iain chambers, 246-260. New York: Routledge, 1996.

Hall, T. William., et al. *Religion: An Introduction*. San Francisco: Harper and Row, 1986.

Hiddleston, Jane. *Understanding Postcolonialism*, Stocksfield, UK: Acumen, 2013.

Holleman, J. F. *Shona Customary Law: With Reference to Kinship, Marriage, the Family and Estate*. London: Oxford University Press, 1952.

Idowu, Bolaji E. *African Traditional Religion: A Definition*. Maryknoll: Orbis, 1975.

Ikenga-Metuh, Emefie. *Comparative Studies of African Traditional Religions*. South Onitsha: IMICO, 1987.

Imasogie, O. *African Traditional Religion*. Ibadan: University Press, 1985.

Janesick, Valerie J. "The Dance of Qualitative Research Design: Metaphor, Methodology, and Meaning." In *Strategies of Qualitative Inquiry* edited by Denzin, Norman K and Yvonna S. Lincoln, 35–55. Thousand Oaks, California: SAGE, 1998.

Jorgensen, D. L. *Participant Observation: A Methodology for Human Studies*. London: SAGE, 1989.

Kalton, Graham. *Introduction to Survey Sampling*. Newbury Park, California: Sage, 1983.

Kalu, Ogbu U. "Ancestral Spirituality and Society in Africa." In *African Spirituality: Forms, Meanings, and Expressions*, edited by Jacob K. Olupona, 54–84. New York: The Crossroad, 2000.

Kayode, J. O. *Understanding African Traditional Religion*. Ile-Ife: University of Ife Press, 1984.

Kim, Van Nam. *Multicultural Theology and New Evangelization*. New York: University Press of America, 2014.

Kübler-Ross, Elisabeth. *Death: The Final Stage of Growth*. Translated by J. B. Carman. Englewood Cliffs, New Jersey: Prentice-Hall, 1975.

Kumar, Malreddy Pa Van. "Postcolonialism: interdisciplinary or interdiscursive?" In *Third World Quarterly*, Vol., 32, No. 4, 653–672, published by Taylor & Francis, Ltd, 2011.

Kuper, Adam. Wives for Cattle: *Bridewealth and Marriage in Southern Africa*. London: Routledge and Kegan Paul, 1982.

Kuper, Hilda, et al. *The Shona and Ndebele of Southern Rhodesia*. London: International African Institute, 1954.

Law, Eric H. F. *The Wolf Shall Dwell with the Lamb: A Spirituality for Leadership in a Multicultural Community*. St. Louis, Missouri: Chalice, 1993.

———. *The Bush was Blazing but Not Consumed: Developing a Multicultural Community Through Dialogue and Liturgy*. St. Louis, Missouri: Chalice Press, 1996.

Lawton, Julia. *The Dying Process: Patients' Experiences of Palliative Care*. New York: Routledge, 2000.

Leeuw, Gerardus van der. *Religion in Essence and Manifestation*, Vol. 1. Translated by J. E. Turner. London: George Allen and Unwin, 1967.

Lynes, David A. "Postcolonialism." In Encyclopedia of Case Study Research, edited by A. J. Mills, Albert J., et al. 688–694. Thousand Oaks, CA: SAGE Publications, Inc, 2012. DOI: https://dx.doi.org/10.4135/9781412957397. Date Accessed: July 1, 2019.

Magesa, Laurent. *African Religion: The Moral Traditions of Abundant Life*. Maryknoll, New York: Orbis, 1997.

Maldonado-Torres, Nelson. "On the Coloniality of Being." In Cultural Studies Vol. 21 Nos. 2-3, 240-270, March/May 2007. http//www.tandf.co.uk/journals. Date Accessed: July 5, 2019.

Mason, B. "How to Write Clear Instructions." *RN*, vol. 59, no. 11, 26–28, Nov. 1996. EBSCOhost, uiwtx.idm.oclc.org/login? Date Accessed: August 20, 2019.

Mayer, Robert G. *Embalming: History, Theory, and Practice*. 4th ed. New York: McGraw-Hill, 2006.

Mbiti, John S. *Introduction to African Religion*. Johannesburg: Heinemann Publishers, 1975.

———. *African Religions, and Philosophy*. 2nd ed. Oxford: Heinemann, 1990.

Mbugua, Johnson N. *Funeral Rites Reformation for Any African Ethnic Community Based On the Proposed New Funeral Practices for the Agikuyu*. Eugene, OR: Resource, 2016.

Memmi, Albert. *The Colonizer and the Colonized*. Boston, Massachusetts: Beacon, 1965.

Merriam Sharan B. "Introduction to Qualitative Research," 3–17, In *Qualitative Research in Practice: Examples for Discussion and Analysis*, edited by Sharan B Merriam and Associates. San Francisco: Wiley and Sons, 2002.

Merriam, Sharan B. and Tisdell, Elizabeth J. *Qualitative Research: A Guide to Design and Implementation*. 4th ed. San Francisco, CA: John Wiley & Sons, 2016.

Mishra, Vijay. "Postcolonialism 2010–2014". In The Journal of Commonwealth Literature. Vol., 50(3), 369–390, 2015. sagepub.co.uk/journalsPermissions.nay. Date Accessed: July 15, 2019.

Mishra, Vijay and Bob Hodge. "What Was Postcolonialism?" In New Literary History, Vol. 36, No. 3, *Critical and Historical Essays*, published by The Johns Hopkins University Press, 375-402, Summer, 2005, Stable URL: https://www.jstor.org/stable/20057902. Date Accessed: July 1st, 2019.

Mlambo, Alois S. *History of Zimbabwe*. New York: Cambridge University Press, 2014.

Muchemwa, Berry. *Death and Burial Among the Shona*. Harare: Pastoral Center, 2002.

Mwandayi, Canisius. *Death and After-life in the Eyes of the Shona: Dialogue with Shona Customs in the Quest for Authentic Inculturation*. Bamberg: University of Bamberg Press, 2011.

Ndlovu-Gatsheni, Sabelo J. *Empire, Global Coloniality and African Subjectivity*. New York, NY: Berghahn, 2013.

Olupona, Jacob K. "Spiritual Beings as Agents of Illness." In *African Spirituality: Forms, Meanings and Expressions*, edited by Jacob K. Olupona, 152–175. New York: The Crossroad, 2000.

Opoku, Kofi Asare. *West African Traditional Religion*. Accra: FEP International, 1978.

O'Rourke, Kevin D. *Medical Ethics: Sources of Catholic Teachings*. 3rd ed. Washington D.C, Georgetown University Press, 1999.

Osterhammel, Jürgen. *Colonialism: A Theoretical Overview*. Translated by Shelley L. Frisch. Princeton: Markus Wiener, 1997.

P'Bitek, Okot. *African Religions in Western Scholarship*. Dar Es Salam: East African Literature Bureau, 1979.

———. *Decolonizing African Religions: A Short History of African Religions in Western Scholarship*. New York: Diasporic Africa, 2011.

Parrinder, Geoffrey. *Witchcraft: European and African*. London: Faber and Faber, 1963.

———. *African Traditional Religion*. Westport, Connecticut: Greenwood, 1970.

Pine, Vanderlyn R. "Dying, Death, and Social Behavior," In *Anticipatory Grief*, edited by Bernard Schoenberg, 34–47. New York: Columbia University Press, 1974.

Praagh, James van. *Healing Grief: Reclaiming Life after any Loss*. New York: Penguin Putnam, 2000.

Quarcoopome, T. N. O. *West African Traditional Religion*. Ibadan: African Universities Press, 1987.

Rayner, William. *The Tribe and Its Successors: An Account of African Traditional Life and European Settlement in Southern Rhodesia*. New York: Frederick A. Praeger, 1962.

Reddout, Donna J. "Manual writing made easier. Training and Development Journal," 41(4),66,1987. http://uiwtx.idm.oclc.org/login?url=https://search.proquest.com/docview/227010817?accountid=7139. Date Accessed: August 15, 2019.

Rodlach, Alexander. *Witches, Westerners, and HIV*. Walnut Creek, CA: Left Coast, 2006.

Rubin, Herbert J and Irene S Rubin, *Qualitative Interviewing: The Art of Hearing Data*. 2nd ed. Thousand Oaks, California: Sage, 2005.

Said, Edward W. *Orientalism*. London: Vintage, 1979.

Sankar, Andre. *Dying at Home: A Family Guide for Caregiving*. Baltimore, Maryland: The John Hopkins University Press, 1991.

Schreiter, Robert J. *Constructing Local Theologies*. Maryknoll, New York: Orbis, 1985.

Schreiter, Robert J. *The New Catholicity: Theology Between the Global and the Local*. Maryknoll, New York: Orbis, 1997.

Shoko, Tabona. *Karanga Indigenous Religion in Zimbabwe: Health and Well-Being*. Hampshire, England: Ashgate, 2007.

———. "Teaching African Traditional Religion at the University of Zimbabwe." In *African Traditions in the Study of Religion in Africa*, edited by Ezra Chitando et al., 53–65. Surrey, England: Ashgate, 2012.

Shorter, Aylward. *Toward A Theology of Inculturation*. London: Geoffrey Chapman, 1988.

———. *African Culture and Christian Church: An Introduction to Social and Pastoral Anthropology*. London: Geoffrey Chapman, 1973.

Silverman, David. *Doing Qualitative Research: A Handbook*. Thousand Oaks, California: SAGE, 2000.

Singleton, Royce A., Jr., et al. *Approaches to Social Research*. 2nd ed. New York: Oxford University Press, 1993.

Smith, Huston, *The World's Religions*. New York, NY: Harper One, 1991.

Smith, Wilfred Cantwell. *The Meaning and The End of Religion*. New York, NY: Macmillan, 1963.

Snape, Dawn and Liz Spencer. "The Foundations of Qualitative Research," In *Qualitative Research Practice: A Guide for Social Science Students and Researchers*, edited by Ritchie, Jan and Jane Lewis, 1–23. Thousand Oaks, California: SAGE, 2003.

Spivak, Gayatri Chakravorty. "Can the Subaltern Speak?: Speculations on Widow-Sacrifice." In *Wedge*, 7/8, Winter/Spring, 120–130, 1985.

Spradely, James P. *Participant Observation*. Long Grove, Illinois: Weaverland, 1980 (reissued 2016).

Strauss, Anselm and Juliet Corbin, *Basics of Qualitative Research: Grounded Theory Procedures and Technique*. Newbury Park, California: SAGE, 1990.

Taylor, Steven J and Robert Bogdan. *Introduction to Qualitative Research Methods: The Search for Meanings*. New York: Wiley and Sons, 1984.

Thomas, Douglas. *African Traditional Religion in the Modern World*. Jefferson, North Carolina: McFarland and Company, 2005.

Thomas, Morgan Thomas. *Eleven Years in Central South Africa*. London: Snow, 1872.

Thorpe, S. A. *African Traditional Religions: An Introduction*. Pretoria: University of South Africa, 1992.

Tichagwa, Kundai. "Local histories and present realities' Towards a socio-political history of the Nyajena area with particular reference to power dynamics.c1800-2008." MA Dissertation submitted to the University of Zimbabwe, Harare, 2006.

Turner, T. W. *History of an African Independent Church - Volume I: The Church of the Lord (Aladura)*. New York: Clarendon, 1967.

USCCB. *Open Wide your Hearts: The Enduring Call to Love; A Pastoral Letter Against Racism*. Washington D. C: USCCB, 2018.

———. *Welcoming the Stranger Among us: Unity in Diversity*. Washington D. C: USCCB, 2000.

———. *Building Intercultural Competence for Ministers Bilingual*. Washington D.C: USCCB, 2014.

ilson, Monica. *Rituals of Kinship among the Nyakyusa*. London: Oxford University Press, 1957.

Witchcraft Suppression Act, Chapter 9:19: Ord. 14/1899, Acts 18/1989 (s. 11)., 22/2001.

Young, Robert J. C. *Postcolonialism: A Very Short Introduction*. New York, NY: Oxford University Press, 2003.

Index

acculturation, 6, 12, 28, 39, 138, 145, 241, 245, 248–49, 254
African ethnicities, 4, 30, 76, 105–6, 110, 118, 135, 216, 240
African spirituality, 26, 70
African Traditional Religion, 7, 13–14, 18, 23–25, 79–80, 217, 248, 252
Aiken, Lewis, 143
Akrong, Abraham, 76, 81
ancestors, 1, 9, 14–15, 18, 26–27, 56, 60, 63, 65, 68–73, 83–84, 90, 92–93, 97, 104, 109, 111–13, 117, 120–22, 128, 133, 137–38, 149, 153, 155, 160–62, 164, 166, 170–71, 183, 188–90, 198, 200, 202, 205, 207, 208–10, 212–15, 228, 245, 254, 264
ancestral rituals, 71, 160
Anderson, Allan, 50, 69
Aschwanden, Herbert, 61, 65, 97, 110, 117, 121, 126, 132
ashaika, 109, 257
atisiya, 109, 257
Atungamira, 109, 257
azorora, 109, 257

Backer, Barbara, 92, 141
bandauko, 187, 257
bembera, 9, 87, 94–95, 98, 257
Bhebe, Ngwabi, 60
body viewing, 9, 101, 116
Bogdan, Robert, 35, 37

Bourdillon, Michael, 19–20, 25, 36, 39, 65–67, 75–79, 81, 108, 115, 117, 121, 164, 173–74
Brodd, Jaffrey, 12, 15
Bucher, Hubert, 72–73, 82
Bullock, Charles, 92, 97, 103, 118, 120–21, 124–25, 128, 130, 136, 137, 164, 184, 194
burial by proxy, 10, 101, 135–38
burial rites, 3, 9, 72, 101, 152, 232
burial, x, 1–3, 7, 9–10, 15, 36, 56, 71–73, 82, 87, 93, 99, 101–2, 105, 108–9, 112–17, 119, 122–28, 130, 131–38, 144–45, 149, 151–53, 155–57, 160, 162–67, 171–72, 175–76, 178, 180–82, 187, 193, 196, 200–4, 208, 214, 219, 221–23, 225, 228–29, 232, 236, 240, 245, 247–48, 258, 260
bvuri, 131–33, 257
bwanyanza, 103, 116–17, 154, 227, 257

calendrical rituals, 16
Callison, George, 218
Césaire, Aimé, 44–45
Chapman, Erie, 142–43
Chavhunduka, Gordon, 61, 71, 75, 77, 124
chema, 115–16, 151, 157–58, 222, 257
chibako, 229, 257
chibwe, 127, 153, 167, 180–81, 204, 257, 259
chidhoma, 64
chidzva, 187, 257

chifumuro, 171, 205, 234, 257
Chigwedere, Aeneas, 73
childbearing women, 110
chimutsamapfihwa, 196, 212, 257
Chitakure, John, 26, 36, 80, 105, 110, 113, 128, 182, 196
chizhuzhu, 123, 258
Choron, Jacques, 4
Christian, 1, 2, 7, 13–15, 43, 83–84, 98, 115, 156, 189, 199–200, 202–3, 205, 206–7, 210, 213–15, 251, 253, 255
Christianity, 7, 29, 45, 51, 56, 60, 96, 98, 112, 156, 208, 248, 251
cleansing, 10, 124–25, 128, 161, 163–166, 179, 182, 193, 236
coffin, 103–4, 116–17, 119, 122, 149, 153–155, 161, 226
colonial, 20, 46–47, 49, 51, 54, 98, 145, 242, 255, 261
colonialism, 3, 5, 6, 41–49, 51, 54–55, 245, 249
colonialists, 7, 29, 44, 54, 206, 207–8, 215, 242–44, 248
colonists, 46, 119, 249, 253
colonization, 28, 41, 44– 45, 47, 49, 51, 98, 129, 139, 145, 244, 251
commiserating with the bereaved, 10, 115, 127, 161, 166
Corbin, Juliet, 33–34, 37
Corpse, 1–2, 9, 90, 93, 97, 101, 103–5, 109–15, 117–19, 121, 124–25, 128, 130–32, 141, 145, 147–50, 152, 154, 156, 158, 162, 165–69, 171, 179, 182, 202, 219, 221, 223, 225–27, 247, 259
Corr, Charles, 18, 141, 144–45, 148–49
Crawford, J. R, 64, 66, 68, 79, 94
Creary, Nicholas, 207
Creswell, John, 31–32, 34–35, 37, 40
crisis rituals, 16
cultural anthropologists, 27, 32
cultural change, 3, 5–6, 8, 11, 27–29, 58–59, 83, 85, 88, 98–99, 101, 111, 138, 144, 150, 156–57, 159, 199, 203, 212, 241–42

cultural dynamism, vi, 6, 28, 241–42, 251, 254
cultural identity, vi, 3, 5–6, 10, 15, 26, 29, 31, 47, 121, 159, 205, 207–8, 212, 215, 239, 242–44, 246, 249–56
culture, vi, ix, 4, 6–8, 10–12, 18, 27–30, 32–36, 40–41, 45–46, 48–51, 53, 55–77, 86, 117, 138, 153, 156, 159, 163, 171, 180–81, 195, 207–8, 212, 215, 239–40, 242–46, 248–56
Cunningham, Lawrence, 11, 13

Daneel, M. L, 60, 66–67, 72–73
daughters-in-law, 117, 125, 133, 217, 226–27, 264
death euphemism, 109
death rituals manual, 3, 56, 215
death token, 9, 101, 115, 151, 157, 257
death, announcing, 9, 101, 107, 109, 150-52, 203
death, confirming, 97
death, fear of, 4, 88
death, natural, 63, 240
death, spiritual causes, 58, 63
deathbed, 1, 102
DeWalt, Billie, 32
disease, 156, 162, 167, 177, 179, 183, 210–12, 228, 236, 257
diviner, 10, 59, 62, 63, 65–69, 74, 77–78, 81–86, 94–98, 100, 136, 143, 161, 171–73, 175, 182, 186–87, 191, 198, 202–3, 229, 258, 264
doro remvura, 163–64, 166, 172, 174, 199, 258, 261
Doumbia, Adama, 90, 111, 118, 125, 138
Duda, Deborah, 139–40

embalming, 148–50
Esposito, John, 12
Evans-Pritchard, E. E, 75, 105, 114

Fanon, F, 45–46, 50–51
fetuses, 127, 156, 221
Fisher, Robert, 89

Fitzgerald, Mike, 218
Freud, Sigmund, 21
funeral rites, 2, 90, 169

gambe, 111, 126, 222, 258
Gata, 62, 81, 165, 171–74, 258
Gelfand, Michael, 8, 21–22, 60, 65–66, 70–73, 76–77, 82, 107, 115, 117–18, 120, 123, 126, 128–29, 137, 164, 172, 184, 189, 193
Gennep, Arnold van, 16–17, 38–39, 90
Gittins, Anthony, 6, 12, 30, 245
God, 9, 14, 22, 24, 27–28, 43, 51, 56, 60–63, 65, 83–84, 153, 155, 173–74, 200, 214, 258, 262–63
Godly, 58, 60, 62–63, 83, 175
gods, 14, 42
Goody, Jack, 88, 102, 107, 110
Göttsche, Dirk, 49
grave, digging (of), 112–14, 122, 127, 134, 155, 164–65, 170, 181, 222, 224–25
grave, marking (of), 112, 145, 152, 157, 124–25, 263
gravediggers, 103, 114, 152, 161, 164, 166, 200, 224–25, 227, 261
grief, 15, 18, 38, 89, 102, 106, 108, 116, 140, 143, 146, 160, 167, 169–70, 203, 245, 259
gumbwa, 9, 87, 95–96, 98, 258

Haar, Gerrie ter, 77
Hakata, 82, 136, 258, 262
healing, 9, 38, 62, 73, 81–84, 98, 139, 141–42, 146
Hiddleston, Jane, 46, 49
Holleman, Johan, 190, 212
Hospital (s), 83–85, 88, 91, 93, 99, 139–50, 153, 156–57, 201, 247, 255
hospitality, 14–15, 26
hut, 2, 67, 96, 98, 117, 124–25, 130, 132, 157, 167–69, 186–87, 190, 226, 230–31, 235, 236, 262

Idowu, Bolaji, 24, 42
Ikenga-Metuh, Emefie, 69

illness, 16, 59, 61, 64–67, 74, 80–81, 84, 91–96, 100, 106, 108, 123, 129, 141, 145–46, 151, 177, 240, 247
indigenous people, 20, 22–23, 41–42, 45–56
industrialization, 98, 144, 200, 209
informants, 33, 36–38, 85, 93–94, 96, 103–4, 116, 132, 145, 152, 162, 166, 178, 187, 205
inheritance, 125, 160, 164, 189–90, 193–94, 196–97, 211–12, 224, 232–33, 235, 237, 263
interviews, 9, 33, 35–36, 38, 209, 241
intravenous feeding, 146

Karanga of Nyajena, ix, 1, 3–5, 8–11, 15, 18–19, 23, 27, 29–30, 36, 39–40, 56–59, 67, 83–85, 87, 91–92, 94–96, 100–2, 106, 117–18, 122, 124–25, 130–31, 137, 153–55, 161–64, 169, 171–72, 174–75, 178, 180, 184–85, 189, 193–95, 198–99, 205, 214, 221, 224–25, 238–39, 240–41, 245–46, 248, 256
Kayode, J. O, 71
kubata mavoko, 115, 127, 166–69, 180, 203, 222, 259
kubata nhumbi, 163, 177–78, 205, 234, 259
Kübler-Ross, Elizabeth, 4, 35
kugara nhaka, 211, 232, 259
kugova nhumbi, 175, 205, 259
kukanda chibwe, 127, 153, 167, 180–81, 204, 259
Kumar, Malreddy van, 54, 56
Kuper, Adam, 26
Kuper, Hilda, 93, 97
kurindira, 9, 87, 260
kurova guva, 182, 207, 228, 260
kusengudza, 9, 87, 96, 98–99, 103, 147, 260
kutanda botso, 67

Law, Eric, 28
Leeuw, Gerardus van der, 27
life cycle rituals, 16

Lynes, David, 46, 50, 53

magadziro, 15, 38, 69, 82, 103, 129, 138, 150, 160–61, 164–66, 172, 174, 177, 182–85, 187–90, 193, 203, 206–10, 213–16, 223–24, 228–29, 232, 235, 245, 247, 258, 260
Magesa, Laurent, 24, 65, 71, 74–75
Mahakurimwi, 169–70, 171, 200–1, 227, 260
Mamhepo, 65, 261
Mashavi, 72, 73–74, 82, 261
Masukafoshoro, 164–66, 199–200, 227, 261
Mbiti, John, 15, 24–26, 68–71, 89–91, 121, 128, 165, 169, 174, 214, 240
Mbugua, Johnson, 211
Mhondoro, 130, 161
Mishra, Vijay, 46, 55
Mlambo, Alois, 20–21, 41
Mortuary, 145, 147
mourning days, 119, 170–71
mourning period, 38, 164, 171
mourning rituals, 15, 127
Muchemwa, Berry, 110–12, 115, 119, 121, 123–24,
Mwandayi, Canisius, 89, 113, 117, 118–19, 166
Mwari, 22, 43, 60, 62, 73, 173, 263

Ndlovu-Gatsheni, Sabelo, 48
Ngozi, 9, 65–68, 72, 113, 174–75, 240, 263
Nyakyusa, 105

old age, 62–63, 96, 173, 175
Olupona, Jacob, 70

palliative care, 145–46, 247
Parrinder, Geoffrey, 64, 70, 75–76, 79
participant observation, 7, 9, 32–33, 36, 38–39, 241
philosophical framework, ix, 10, 31, 40, 57
post-burial rituals, 9–10, 15, 82, 101, 103, 160–61, 166, 171, 199, 214–16, 245

postcolonial theory, ix, 10, 31–32, 40–41, 46–50, 54–57, 205, 239, 241–42, 249
postcolonialism, 41, 46, 48–49
Praagh, James van, 18, 108, 160
Praxis, 2–3, 7–8, 12, 100, 161–62, 185, 188, 209–10, 216–17, 239–40, 246, 248–49, 256
pre-burial rituals, 9, 87, 90, 98, 101–2, 113, 219, 240

qualitative inquiry, 33, 35, 39
Quarcoopome, T. N. O, 25, 42, 70

Rayner, William, 19–20, 74, 77, 105, 115, 126, 165, 172, 185
Reddout, Dona, 217, 218
research methodology, ix, 8, 31–33, 37, 39, 56
resting days, 10, 131, 169–71, 200, 227
rites of passage, 14–17, 88
Rubin, Herbert, 37

sacred bangle, 189–190
sacred days, 131, 161, 170
Said, Edward, 50, 52–53
Sankar, Andre, 17, 102, 140, 146
Schreiter, Robert, 28–29, 250, 254
Shoko, Tabona, 7, 23, 25, 90
Shorter, Aylward, 28–29, 75, 80, 99, 103
Sickness, 9, 27, 58–61, 63, 70, 72–74, 78–86, 89, 95, 100, 110, 174, 182, 202, 240
Snape, Dawn, 34
spirits, alien, 9, 27, 72–73, 82, 84, 129, 174, 175, 261
spirits, avenging, 9
spirits, evil, 9, 26–27, 63–65, 72, 74, 78, 85, 97, 124, 134–35, 162, 169–70, 172, 174, 177, 228, 257, 261–62, 264
Spivak, Gayatri Chakravarty, 50, 53
Strauss, Anselm, 33–34, 37

theoretical framework, 9, 31, 40, 41
Thomas, Douglas, 43, 88
Thomas, Morgan Thomas, 43

INDEX

Tichagwa, Kundai, 22
traditional burial, x, 2–3, 10, 56
traditional medical practitioners, 59, 64–65, 80, 82, 202–3
traditions, xi, 4, 6–7, 12–13, 17, 19, 22, 24–25, 30, 36, 38, 43, 70–71, 73, 84, 89, 112, 171, 200, 241, 246, 256
Turner, Harrold, 203

Undertakers, 10, 88, 123–25, 152, 154, 157, 161–64, 170, 258
urban cemeteries, 144–45, 152, 154, 156–57, 171, 204
urbanization, 88, 98–99, 144
USCCB, viii, 28, 242, 244

Vajena, 5, 22–23, 262, 264
Varoora, 117, 133, 164

Vazukuru, 111, 154, 188, 264

wailing, 9, 93, 101, 105–7, 114
watchperson, 91–92, 99
western medicines, 79, 100, 146, 252
Witch, threatening, 94, 257
witchcraft accusations, 78, 80–81, 83, 99, 105–6
Witchcraft, 9, 39, 43, 73–81, 84–85, 94–96, 98–100, 105–6, 132, 134, 173–74, 177, 202, 240, 258, 262, 264
witches, 9, 27, 62, 64, 72–75, 86–81, 83–85, 94–99, 100, 105, 111, 124, 131–35, 147, 162, 172, 175, 177, 182, 187, 202, 257–58, 262, 264
worldviews, 25, 27, 40, 59, 25

zvidhoma, 9, 27, 64, 174, 264

www.ingramcontent.com/pod-product-compliance
Lightning Source LLC
Chambersburg PA
CBHW050840230426
43667CB00012B/2086